Retiring the Crow Rate

A Narrative of Political Management

Retiring the Crow Rate

A Narrative of Political Management

Arthur Kroeger

THE UNIVERSITY OF ALBERTA PRESS

Published by
The University of Alberta Press
Ring House 2
Edmonton, Alberta, Canada T6G 2E1
Copyright © 2009

Library and Archives Canada Cataloguing in Publication

Kroeger, Arthur
    Retiring the Crow rate : a narrative of political
management / Arthur Kroeger.

Includes bibliographical references and index.
ISBN 978-0-88864-513-5

    1. Crow's Nest Pass Agreement. 2. Grain-Transportation-
Rates-Canada-History. 3. Grain-Transportation-Canada-
Costs-History. 4. Railroads-Freight-Rates-Canada-History.
5. Kroeger, Arthur 6. Pepin, Jean-Luc, 1924-1995. 7. Transportation
and state-Canada-History.

HE2321.G7K76 2009 385/.240971
C2008-908118-8

The University of Alberta Press is committed to protecting our natural
environment. As part of our efforts, this book is printed on Enviro Paper:
it contains 100% post-consumer recycled fibres and is acid- and chlorine-free.

The University of Alberta Press gratefully acknowledges the support
received for its publishing program from The Canada Council for the Arts.
The University of Alberta Press also gratefully acknowledges the financial
support of the Government of Canada through the Book Publishing Industry
Development Program (BPIDP) and from the Alberta Foundation for the Arts
for its publishing activities.

Canada Council   Conseil des Arts
for the Arts   du Canada

Canada

Alberta Foundation
for the Arts

To the memory of The Right Honourable Jean-Luc Pépin:
A minister capable of giving politicians a good name.

*I don't think I altogether understand
a country in which a freight rate could be regarded
as a constitutional right.*

—Carl Snavely, American consultant
on railway costing, 1982

Contents

Preface

THE END OF THE CROW'S NEST PASS rate for the movement of prairie grain is today commonly ascribed to the Canadian federal budget of 1995, which ended the grain subsidy to the railways and required that western grain producers henceforth pay compensatory rates. In fact, however, the first steps toward breaking the mould of the 1897 Crow's Nest Pass Agreement were taken by the federal minister of Transport in 1980 and led to the *Western Grain Transportation Act* of 1983, which was the outcome of more than three years of consultations, studies, debates, and negotiations by the federal government, western stakeholders, and the railways. This prolonged process ended the mystique of the Crow rate in the West and made possible the measures in the 1995 budget.

For most of the twentieth century, the Crow rate was much more than a tariff levied by the railways. For many people in the West, it had a symbolic significance; it was their side of a national bargain. From the late nineteenth century on, there was widespread resentment in the West of the "big interests" in Ontario and Quebec: the banks, the mortgage companies, the railways, and, notably, the manufacturers who were protected by high customs tariffs that raised the prices that consumers in the West had to pay for finished goods, including farm machinery. The Crow—as it was commonly known—was not regarded as an adequate offset for the dominance of these interests, but it was all the West had, and it was fiercely defended in the region.

By the latter part of the late 1970s and early 1980s, however, there was a growing recognition on the prairies that the 1897 freight rate, and the mounting financial losses it was causing the railways, had become unsustainable. The question then became: what system should replace the Crow? This book recounts how the answer to that question was worked out.

I have given the book the subtitle, "A Narrative of Political Management," which may raise questions in the minds of some about the appropriate role for officials in the public service when elected governments are dealing with politically controversial matters.

Political sensitivity is an essential part of the mental equipment of any senior official. Officials have a responsibility to advise governments, not only about *what* needs to be done in a particular area of public policy but also about *how* it might best be done. Those in the Department of Finance who are working on a budget must be able to make good assessments of the likely reaction of stakeholders and the general public to measures that are under consideration. Officials in the Department of Human Resources developing advice about possible amendments to the *Employment Insurance Act* need to be sensitive to views of the EI program that are held in different parts of the country. In the same vein, our responsibility in the Department of Transport was to advise our minister and the Cabinet, not only about the need to deal with the Crow rate because of the effects it was having on the western transportation system but also on measures that would stand the best chance of gaining acceptance in the West. In government, such matters are commonly described as "small p" politics.

Ministers for their part have the prerogative of deciding what advice to accept from officials, both about substantive matters, and about ways of proceeding. In addition, they have to deal with "big P" political issues: how a particular course of action might affect the government's standing in the eyes of the electorate and how to deal with the opposition parties in Parliament. This is territory off-limits to officials.

Given the complexities of government, there is often a grey zone in which the small and large "p" politics of an issue overlap. In such situations, it is part of the professional responsibilities of individual public servants to judge where to draw the line. The good news is that in my observation Canadian ministers have generally been scrupulous about respecting decisions by officials not to be drawn into partisan politics.

For the benefit of those with an interest in how governments function and arrive at decisions, my narrative provides a chronicle of weekly and monthly interactions among ministers, departmental officials, members of Parliament, western agricultural interests, the railways, provincial governments, the media, and many others. The book also seeks to convey a sense of what life can be like in a government department when a major initiative is in train.

It is a minor irony of Canadian history that in the public mind the Crow's Nest Pass is associated with prairie grain. The 1897 agreement for the construction of a railway through the pass actually had nothing to do with grain; its purpose was to provide rail access to the coal fields of the Kootenay region of British Columbia. The main line of the Canadian National Railway over which grain is shipped to the West Coast has always run through the Yellowhead Pass west of Edmonton; that of the Canadian Pacific Railway through the Kicking Horse and Rogers passes. The Crow's Nest Pass is coal mining country and for many years was noted for militant miners' unions and left-wing town councils. It is probable that in the early years of the twentieth century the value of the prairie grain shipped westward through the pass was exceeded by the value of the illicit liquor that moved east into Alberta, which had legislated prohibition, from British Columbia, which had not.

Nevertheless, prairie grain is what the Crow's Nest Pass is associated with, and the politics of prairie grain is what this book is about.

In assembling this narrative, I have drawn upon memoranda, letters, and notes in my personal files, together with declassified Cabinet memoranda and minutes and the texts of many media reports from this period. I have supplemented these with my personal recollections. After the book has been published, the documents in my personal archive that I have drawn upon will be turned over to Library and Archives Canada and so will be available to researchers in the future.

I have benefited from the recollections and advice of present and past members of Parliament and government officials, including Bill McKnight, Jack Murta, Charles Mayer, Nick Mulder, Janet Smith, Jim Roche, and Howard Migie. Others who assisted me included Otto Lang, Dennis Apedaile, Ted Allen, Doug Campbell, and Chris Mills. The former president of the Saskatchewan Wheat Pool, Ted Turner, gave me a valuable account of the perspective of Pool members. As is normal, final judgements are my responsibility.

A final word about the spelling of my late minister's name. Those of us who worked for him were accustomed to seeing it spelled "Jean Luc." However, his widow has pointed out that in formal documents, such as the one he signed upon becoming a member of Parliament, he wrote it with a hyphen, "Jean-Luc." At her request, I have used this spelling throughout.

Arthur Kroeger

Ottawa, March 2008

A New Partnership

ON SUNDAY, MARCH 2, 1980, I was at home preparing lunch for my daughters, aged ten and twelve, and two of their friends. I had been a widower for a year, and it had become a family ritual for me to cook pancakes on Sundays.

The telephone rang. The voice at the other end said, "Mr. Kroeger, this is Jean-Luc Pépin. Unless the prime minister changes his mind between now and tomorrow morning, I am going to be your minister."

I was caught unawares by the call and then realized I had an immediate problem, represented by one frying pan full of pancakes, another full of bacon, and four hungry young people in the dining room. After a moment's hesitation, I said, "Mr. Pépin, I am not in the habit of asking ministers if I can call them back, but in this case I'm afraid I have to," and I then went on to explain the circumstances of the moment. With the good humour and grace that I would come to know well in the future, he readily agreed.

Once lunch was over and my daughters had gone off with their friends, I drove to Mr. Pépin's house, arriving at 2:30. We talked until after 6:00. It was the beginning of a partnership that would

1

last three and a half years. Our backgrounds were very different, but we proved to be a good fit.

###############

I HAD JOINED the government in 1958 as a foreign service officer. My first thirteen years were spent on assignments in Ottawa and abroad. I had then moved to the Treasury Board Secretariat in 1971, and, at the end of 1974, was appointed deputy minister of Indian and Northern Affairs, where I spent the next five years.

On October 1, 1979, I was appointed deputy minister of Transport. The Progressive Conservative government of Joe Clark had taken office the previous June, and my new minister was Don Mazankowski, the mp for Vegreville, Alberta. A good working relationship was developing between us but was cut short when the minority government was defeated on a parliamentary vote of confidence in mid-December. The Clark government lost the election that followed, and the Liberals under Pierre Elliott Trudeau took office at the beginning of March.

I had arrived in the Department of Transport with only a newspaper reader's knowledge of transportation issues. The practice in Ottawa was, and still is, to appoint deputy ministers as general managers rather than as experts in their department's field. You were expected to learn on the job with the support of the permanent staff in your department. The defeat of the Clark government was followed by a two-month lull for officials in Ottawa while the parties fought the election, which gave me an opportunity to concentrate full time on learning about transportation. I was briefed about bilingual air traffic control, the difference between a Port Authority and a Harbour Commission, the organization and financial systems of the department, the under-utilization of Mirabel airport, the outlook for the St. Lawrence Seaway, the requirement of the Coast Guard to replace its aging ice breakers, the work of a commission of inquiry into aviation safety, and the mounting deficits of via Rail, among many subjects.

During this process, one subject stood out. This was the threat to the western railway system posed by the Crow's Nest Pass rate that had governed the shipment of prairie grain since 1897. The situation was summarized for me by John Hartman, the president of a research organization, the Western Transportation Advisory Council (WESTAC), during a dinner I had with him in Vancouver. In response to my query about western transportation issues, Hartman said, "Well, there's the Crow, and then there are all the others put together."

Being from Alberta, I had of course grown up with the Crow's Nest Pass rate. It was not a subject of debate: it was simply a part of our lives, like the prairie sun in summer, going to church on Sunday, the Social Credit Party, and discussions about the iniquities of the Canadian Pacific Railway. Where I grew up, small boys were raised to believe in the imminent second coming of Christ and to hate the CPR. I had, over the years, listened to the locals hold forth in the coffee shop and at the curling rink about how the prairies were discriminated against by the railways, for example by charging more to ship steel from Hamilton to Calgary than from Hamilton to Vancouver. There were some who held that the purpose of such discrimination was not only to enhance the profits of the railways but also to prevent the West from realizing its potential and thereby becoming an effective competitor to Ontario and Quebec—universally referred to as "the East."

Now the Crow, the CPR, and iniquitous railway freight rates were part of my responsibilities.

Jean-Luc Pépin had been born in 1924 in Drummondville, a modest-sized city between Montreal and Quebec City that had at one time been represented in Parliament by Sir Wilfrid Laurier. Pépin's father was a freight clerk for the Canadian National Railway. When young Jean-Luc took a train to begin his university education in Ottawa, he travelled free on one of the passes that railways issued to their employees and their families.

After taking his Bachelor's degree, he went to university in Paris. In 1951 he returned to begin teaching at the University of Ottawa, a bilingual institution that had been founded in 1848 by the Oblate fathers. He was first elected to Parliament as a Liberal from Drum-mondville in 1963 and held several minor ministerial posts under Mr. Pearson in the late 1960s. In 1968 Mr. Trudeau appointed him minister of Industry, Trade, and Commerce. He was the first French Canadian to be appointed to a major economic department in Ottawa; previously such departments had been the preserve of Anglo-Saxon ministers, usually from Ontario. Pépin held the post for over four years, until he was narrowly defeated in his riding when the Trudeau government was reduced to a minority in the 1972 election.

In 1975 in response to strong inflationary pressures, the gov-ernment instituted wage and price controls. The prime minister persuaded Pépin to return from the private sector and assume charge of a federal monitoring and enforcement body known as the Anti-Inflation Board.

His next public service assignment came two years later, after the sovereignist Parti Quebecois won the provincial election of November 1976. In response to this jarring development, Prime Minister Trudeau decided to create a task force on Canadian unity. He appointed as its co-chairs the former premier of Ontario, John Robarts, and Jean-Luc Pépin.

The 1979 report of the task force proved to be a watershed in Pépin's career. It recommended a decentralized approach to the Canadian Confederation, a recognition of Quebec's distinctiveness in Canada, and acknowledgement that the government of Quebec had a unique role in protecting and developing the character of the province. Proposals of this nature were anathema to Prime Minister Trudeau, and the report was abruptly shelved. It also opened a major and lasting gulf between him and Pépin. The two men respected each other, but there was no comfort in the relationship.

Pépin returned to electoral politics immediately after handing in the report. In the election of 1979 he won an Ottawa riding and was re-elected in 1980. However, when the prime minister came to form his government, he did not give Pépin a key post such as Foreign Affairs, to which his seniority might have given him a claim, nor did he make him a member of the Cabinet Committee on Priorities and Planning, which functioned as an inner Cabinet. Instead, he appointed Pépin to the very large, diverse, and unwieldy Department of Transport. Observers in the media correctly drew the conclusion that the objective was to keep him at arm's length from the major constitutional initiative that the prime minister was determined to pursue. Transport would keep Pépin so burdened with work that he would have no time for other matters.

After I had reflected about Pépin's appointment for a time, a European analogy came to mind. In France and in Finland, where prime ministers forming coalition governments during this period had found it necessary to include communists, the post to which the communists were assigned in each case was Transport. Presumably their prime ministers reasoned, as Mr. Trudeau had, that they would be unable to do any serious harm there.

However, in Jean-Luc Pépin's case, his appointment to Transport would have more important consequences than the prime minister could ever have foreseen.

Hallowed Arrangements

WHEN JEAN-LUC PÉPIN BECAME minister of Transport in March 1980, he inherited two daunting problems.

The first was that the railway system in western Canada was being put at risk because of the rapidly mounting financial losses being sustained by the Canadian Pacific and Canadian National railways from hauling prairie grain at an artificially low freight rate that had been set in 1897.

The second problem was an apparently insuperable obstacle to dealing with the first: the powerful attachment of prairie residents to the historic Crow's Nest Pass Agreement, in which the freight rate was enshrined. The agreement, which was older than the provinces of Saskatchewan and Alberta, included the word "forever," and western grain producers were in no doubt that it was meant to be taken at face value. There was long-standing belief, in the West and elsewhere in the country, that the Crow was sacred and that whosoever laid his hands upon the Ark of the Covenant of 1897 would be struck dead politically.

The history of the Crow's Nest Pass Agreement has been written many times. During the 1890s, the province of British Columbia

wanted to bring the coal fields of the Kootenay region into production. In Ottawa, the Dominion government was wary of United
States' designs on the Canadian West and saw a need to assert a
physical presence, especially in regions just above the U.S. border.
For its part, the Canadian Pacific Railway saw opportunities to
develop additional traffic in the Kootenays. The upshot was an agreement whereby the CPR would build a railway line from Lethbridge
in southern Alberta through the Crow's Nest Pass to Nelson in the
Kootenay region of British Columbia. Under the agreement, the Canadian government committed to provide a subsidy of $3.4 million,
representing approximately one-third of the cost of constructing the
line, while the BC government agreed to transfer 3.75 million acres
(15,176 square kilometres) of land that the CPR could use or dispose
of as it saw fit.

Even though the new line would create new infrastructure and
economic activity in the West, many people objected to the CPR being
given responsibility for the project. Their hostility to the railway was
rooted in their experiences with its rate-setting practices.[1]

In eastern Canada during the late nineteenth century, the CPR
had to set rates that were competitive with those of other railways,
but in the West its agreement with the Dominion government, when
it built the railway to the West Coast, had guaranteed it a monopoly
for twenty-five years from the passage of the *Railway Act* in 1881. It
therefore adopted a practice of fixing its rates in the West at a "value
of service" level, which might best be translated as charging whatever the market would bear. Producers in the West were affected by
the CPR's freight rates in two different ways. When they imported
goods from Ontario and Quebec, freight charges were built into the
price, because suppliers, particularly manufacturers, in those provinces were protected from competition by high customs tariffs and
thus had no difficulty in passing on transportation charges to their
customers. On the other hand, for producers the costs of transportation and handling were deducted from the international price of
their grain and thus affected returns at the farm gate. Particularly
when international grain prices were depressed, the large bite taken

out of these returns by the CPR's high freight rates generated strong resentment.

Following the opening of its main line to traffic, the bulk of the CPR's profits came from the West. Hostility to company's rate-setting practices reached a point where in 1888 the government had to buy back the monopoly status it had granted. The objective was to expose the CPR to competition, although it would not be until the twentieth century that the West had more than one transcontinental line.

By the late nineteenth century there were growing demands in the West for government regulation of the CPR's rates. Typical of the times was a resolution passed at a public meeting in Regina on December 15, 1896, which stated that "the rates charged by the Canadian Pacific Railway are excessive and discriminatory and...the development of the North West Territories [i.e., the region that would eventually become Saskatchewan and Alberta] is thereby very seriously retarded."[2] In early 1897 the Winnipeg Board of Trade expressed a similar grievance, including a complaint about discrimination: "the rates of freight charged on the Canadian Pacific Railway from point to point within Manitoba and the North West Territories are very greatly in excess of the rates charged for similar service in the eastern provinces on that road."[3]

The Liberal government of Sir Wilfrid Laurier elected in 1896 adopted a more aggressive approach *vis-à-vis* railways than had its Conservative predecessors. In both Canada and the United States, governments had promoted development and settlement of the hinterlands in the nineteenth century by offering land and cash to railway companies as an inducement for them to build lines. When the Laurier government came to negotiate the Crow's Nest Pass line with the CPR, it put forward an additional stipulation: in return for the government's contribution, the CPR would be required to reduce and then freeze its rates on west-bound shipments of a list of goods from Ontario and Quebec that included agricultural machinery, as well as on grain and flour being shipped from the prairies to Fort William–Port Arthur (now Thunder Bay) on Lake Superior. The CPR agreed, and the condition was duly incorporated into the Act of Parliament giving effect to the agreement. It was a fateful decision, although at the time the commitment looked harmless enough, since there was a general expectation at the time that the long-term trend in freight rates would be downward.[4]

The provisions about freight rates in the 1897 agreement between the government and the CPR were actually not of fundamental importance to either party. The CPR could very probably have built the line out of its own funds, and it sought the subsidy largely because this was the normal practice when governments wanted new lines built. For its part, the Dominion government was to establish the Board of Railway Commissioners in 1904, and would thereby acquire the power to regulate the CPR's rates that it had sought when it negotiated the Crow's Nest Pass Agreement.

Among the "what ifs" of Canadian history is the question of how events might have unfolded on the prairies in the twentieth century if this clause had not been included in the Crow's Nest Pass Agreement.

Transportation has always been a major preoccupation of Canadians. In the words of the MacPherson Royal Commission of the early 1960s, "Transportation is, after all, the very fibre of the Canadian experience."[5] Prime Minister Mackenzie King famously remarked that, "Whereas some countries have too much history, Canada has too much geography." Mr. King was not thinking of the problems of defending Canada's vast territory against foreign invaders; most probably what he had in mind were the problems involved in linking the different parts of the country, politically, as well as physically. And nowhere were people more conscious of geography than in the West. Prairie grain and other products had to travel long distances to reach the Great Lakes and the markets of Ontario and Quebec, while the prices of manufactured goods to prairie consumers were increased by the distances they had to move from these provinces to reach the West. Before the era of civil aviation, a member of Parliament from Alberta had to spend three days on a train to get to Ottawa.

The condition to reduce and then freeze some freight rates under the Crow's Nest Pass Agreement did no more than mitigate the transportation problems that so exercised prairie residents. Among their

179 KOOTENAY CROSSING STA. 12

How it all began: construction of the
CPR line through the Crow's Nest Pass, 1898–1899.
LIBRARY AND ARCHIVES CANADA, PA21848

complaints were what they regarded as the CPR's poor service and its inadequate provision of rolling stock to move their grain. Their concerns figured continuously in Parliamentary debates. On August 5, 1899, a prominent member of Parliament, Leighton McCarthy, wrote as follows to the minister of Railways and Canals:

> *there is great disquiet growing in the Western Country re this freight question, which if not stemmed bids fair to give great trouble politically and will without doubt be a great detriment to the growth of the country…it is so clearly proven by the frequent speeches made upon this question by the Western members of the House.*[6]

Between 1899 and 1976, there were no fewer than twelve successive Royal Commissions or other inquiries into grain handling and transportation, bearing out the comment of one farmer that "wheat is 15 per cent protein and 85 per cent politics."

During the first two decades of the twentieth century there was a surge of populist sentiment in the West. Contributing factors, in addition to the practices of the railways, were the interest rates charged by banks and mortgage companies, and the high customs tariffs that protected central Canadian manufacturers but drove up the cost of farm machinery. The grain companies also contributed: producers felt themselves to be victims of arbitrary practices that gave them unfairly low grades and prices for their grain. They eventually established the first producer-owned company in 1906, which in 1917 became United Grain Growers. It was joined in 1923 and 1924 by the three provincial grain co-operatives that became known as the Wheat Pools.

Following World War I, western populism began to express itself in politics. The United Farmers of Alberta swept to power in that province's election of 1921, while at the federal level the agrarian Progressive Party took sixty-three seats in the election of the same year.

During World War I the Conservative Borden government suspended the Crow's Nest Pass rate because wartime inflation had increased labour and material costs incurred by the railways. After the war there was a protracted controversy, including litigation before the Supreme Court, over whether the rate should be reinstated. The issue was settled in 1925, when Mackenzie King's Liberal government, with the support of the Progressives, legislated the 1897 rate on eastbound grain and flour and made it applicable to all railways and all grain delivery points on the prairies, while dropping the requirement for concessional rates on goods moving from Ontario and Quebec to the West. In the process, the rate acquired the formal title of "the Statutory Rate," but in the West it was simply referred to as "the Crow." In subsequent years the rate was extended to shipments to the West Coast and to Churchill on Hudson Bay.

The end result of this process was to convert a contractual arrangement between the federal government and the CPR covering the shipment of grain to Fort William–Port Arthur from 289 points on the prairies into a legal requirement applicable to both the CPR and the CNR for the movement of grain from some 1,245 points to what eventually became four ports: Thunder Bay, Vancouver, Prince Rupert, and Churchill. The rate was also extended to canola (formerly called rapeseed) when that product became a part of western agriculture.

Over the years prairie residents developed an entrenched belief that the Crow was a fundamental part of "the bargain of Confederation." Prairie spokesmen sometimes referred to it as "the West's Magna Carta." The East (meaning Ontario and Quebec) had the customs tariff, the manufacturers, the banks and mortgage companies, and the rest of the "big interests," but the West at least had the Crow. It was a birthright, and no one was to touch it.

From the 1920s to the late 1940s, the Crow was not much more than an irritant to the railways. During the Depression and prairie drought of the 1930s, it was scarcely mentioned in documents issued by the CNR and CPR. A history of the CPR published in 1935 devoted one paragraph to the freeze on westbound rates and made no mention of grain.[7] The Crow first became a significant financial problem in the late 1940s, when the lifting of wartime controls was followed by a series of wage and price increases across the economy. The MacPherson Royal Commission found in 1961 that the two railways were incurring losses in hauling grain, which it tentatively assessed to have been $22.3 million for the year.[8]

The commission also found that the era of large CPR profits was a thing of the past; the company's rate of return on railway and non-railway holdings combined ranged from a high of 5.35 per cent to a low of 2.77 per cent in the decade of the 1950s. Grain was only part of the explanation. At that time, railway losses from carrying passengers at $78 million exceeded their losses in carrying grain. The railways' costs were also kept high by the refusal of governments to let them abandon uneconomic branch lines. However, the entrenched western view persisted that the CPR was continuing to earn exorbitant profits at the West's expense.

The commission described the effects of the frozen rate as being of "surpassing importance." It recommended that grain transportation under the Crow rate be treated as a public duty imposed on the two railways and that they should accordingly be compensated for their losses. A clause to this effect was included by Lester Pearson's minority Liberal government in the bill that became the *National Transportation Act* of 1967 but had to be deleted in response to a storm of criticism in the West that was taken up by the opposition parties in Parliament. Although there were a number of precedents for the federal government paying subsidies to the railways, the adverse response to the Pearson government's proposal stemmed from a widely held belief in the West that the CPR had been more than adequately compensated by land grants and cash in the nineteenth century and did not deserve anything further. The pervasive view on the prairies was that "the CPR got half the west for the Crow."[9]

That the CNR also stood to benefit from the legislation was not a factor in the debate. Inasmuch as it was a railway, the CNR was never going to be loved on the prairies, but the fact that it was a Crown corporation formed out of bankrupt railway companies after World War I put it in a different category, and it never came in for the same opprobrium that successive generations of prairie farmers directed at the privately owned CPR.

The decision not to compensate the railways for their grain losses brought consequences that some in the West had not foreseen. Because the railways were now losing money with every bushel of grain they carried, they ceased to invest in the grain system. The extensive network of prairie branch lines, used almost exclusively to move grain, was allowed to deteriorate as revenues fell below the costs of maintaining the lines. No move was made to replace obsolete grain boxcars with modern hopper cars, and the boxcars themselves progressively fell into disrepair. The advent of double-digit inflation in the 1970s steeply increased the railways' losses.

In the early 1970s the federal government concluded that it had to intervene but, because of the strong emotional attachment to the Crow rate on the prairies, adopted an *ad hoc* approach. It paid for repairs to grain boxcars and began buying modern hopper cars that had greater capacity and were more efficient than boxcars. These, however, were only stopgap measures.

In the July 1974 election, the Liberal government of Pierre Trudeau was returned with a majority and began to look at more fundamental solutions. In October the minister responsible for the Canadian Wheat Board, Otto Lang of Saskatchewan, made a speech in which he proposed a "bold approach." While promising to preserve the historic benefits of the Crow rate, he called for an examination of new ways in which those benefits might be provided to grain growers. One possibility would be to set up a Crow Rate Fund out of which producers would be compensated for their increased costs in return for the railways being allowed to charge compensatory rates for moving grain. He also raised the possibility of a one-time buy-out of the Crow benefit and for this purpose had obtained the informal approval of key ministers in Ottawa to commit as much as $7 billion.[10]

Although Lang had emphasized his intention to preserve the "hallowed arrangements" that had constituted the Crow, his speech set off a storm of controversy on the prairies. Provincial ministers, the grain co-ops, and various prairie media all sprang to the barricades in defence of the Crow. Assurances from Prime Minister Trudeau that the government had no intention of changing the Crow rate proved unavailing. The Saskatchewan Wheat Pool denounced Lang's proposals as "shocking," and its president declared, "We will not give one damn inch." At its annual meeting in late 1974 the Pool called for Lang's replacement as minister.[11]

It is not hard to understand the concerns of western grain producers. Charges for transportation, storage, and handling of their grain were all deducted from whatever price they got. In 1920 the average price of wheat at Fort William–Port Arthur had been $2.51 per bushel. During the decade of the 1970s, the price fluctuated between $1.60 and $2.00 per bushel.[12] While grain prices were depressed, charges for handling and storage rose from year to year, as did other costs, such as fertilizer and fuel. Only the cost of shipping grain by rail remained constant, thanks to the Crow rate. If ever the Crow were lost, the producers' already difficult situation would become that much worse.

Following his October 1974 speech, Lang continued to advance ideas about future alternatives to the Crow, but the phalanx of opposition against him remained solid. In June 1977 the federal Cabinet took a decision to "defer any action on the statutory rate."[13] From that time on, it limited its efforts to palliatives. In addition to continuing with hopper car purchases, it launched a $700 million program to rehabilitate the deteriorating prairie branch lines. The government also announced the establishment of a "basic network" of branch lines that were guaranteed to remain in service until the year 2000.

Although Otto Lang was thus forced to give up his quest for ways of replacing the Crow, one effect of his initiative was to make it, for the first time, a subject of serious debate in the West. In 1975 he took another step that was to have an important impact in the longer term. He engaged an American expert in railway costing, Carl Snavely, to carry out a detailed examination of the Crow rate's effect on the financial situation of the CPR and CNR. He mandated Snavely to hold public hearings as part of his examination, correctly believing that westerners would be skeptical of any outcome of his study unless they had been given an opportunity to have their say. Snavely's office was located in Washington, DC, where he did work for the American Railway Association and regularly dealt with the U.S. Congress. He had a personable, low-key style, and his expertise on the complex subject of railway costing gave him a credibility that stood him in good stead in the West.

The first of what would be a series of reports by Snavely was issued in late 1976. His key finding was that in 1974 the railways' net revenue shortfall from hauling grain, after receiving the branch line subsidies authorized in the *National Transportation Act* of 1967, had been $103 million. This finding, which Snavely supported with voluminous data, was something of a watershed. Hitherto, the impact of the Crow on the railways' finances had been a matter of conjecture and political debate, in part because of the complexities of railway costing. While calculating the cost of fuel consumed by a train on a particular run might be fairly straightforward, other components of overall railway costs, such as the contribution that freight charges should make to a railway's constant costs and to what was known as "the cost of capital," were highly complex and required exercises of judgement. Consequently, claims by the railways that they were incurring losses hauling grain were rejected out of hand by many western producers as self-interested fabrications. Now, however, Snavely's detailed report had demonstrated that the railways were indeed losing money, and in substantial amounts. From this point on much of the debate shifted and began to focus on possible ways of dealing with the problem. Follow-up studies by Snavely in the next few years documented rapidly mounting railway losses.

There was increasing agreement in the West that the railways had to be compensated for their grain-related losses; the matter of dispute then became how this was to be done and where the money was to come from. A precedent for government intervention had been set in 1976, when the creation of VIA Rail relieved the CNR and the CPR of their money-losing obligation to carry passengers.

In the latter part of the 1970s, a new problem emerged that had a direct impact on grain producers. A series of bumper harvests had put pressure on the transportation system, and the Canadian Wheat Board began to report difficulties in meeting its export commitments because of transportation problems. In June 1978 the advisory committee to the board estimated that it had lost sales at $150 million in the previous crop year. The following year, the board reported that it had had to forego sales of $600 million because of an inability to get grain to export points on time.[14]

The problems in the grain transportation system, and the prospect of large-scale losses of sales, faced grain producers with a new situation, and some of their leaders began to express second thoughts about traditional Crow orthodoxy. Among the first was Jim Deveson, president of the Manitoba Pool. In 1978 he came out with a statement that the time had come when grain producers were going to have to start paying more to ship their product—for which he was hanged in effigy by some of his members.[15] Other leaders, such as Mac Runciman, the president of United Grain Growers, began to express the same view as Deveson. Runciman, however, qualified his comments by adding that the railways should not be allowed to actually make a profit in hauling grain. Another factor in the debate was accumulating evidence that the Crow rate was having some harmful effects on the western economy, for example by subsidizing the shipment of raw grain to the detriment of processing on the prairies.

Among the umbrella agricultural organizations in the three provinces, the first to break ranks was Unifarm, which had been formed in 1969 out of the Alberta Federation of Agriculture and the Farmers' Union of Alberta. In January 1978 it adopted a policy that called for preservation of statutory protection but said that the sharing of future cost increases could be a matter for negotiation with the government and the railways. Following the Unifarm decision, the future of the Crow became a major subject of debate at annual meetings of the Western Agricultural Conference (WAC), a body that had been established to represent the West in the Canadian Federation of Agriculture. Its members were Unifarm, the Saskatchewan Federation of Agriculture, the Manitoba Farm Bureau, United Grain Growers, and the three provincial Wheat Pools.

In the spring of 1979, the Trudeau government was defeated in the general election, and a number of ministers lost their seats. One of them was Otto Lang, partly due to an anti-government sweep, and partly because of controversies that had arisen during his tenure as minister responsible for the Wheat Board.

When the Progressive Conservative Clark government took office, its western members were well aware of the growing debate in their region. Some of its MPs, such as Jack Murta of Manitoba, urged that the Crow issue be addressed, but the most that the government was able to do during its short life was to put out some exploratory feelers and to appoint a task force of MPs led by Murta, which produced a set of recommendations on ways to improve the functioning of the grain transportation system.

In addition, Transport Minister Don Mazankowski successfully pressured the provincial governments on the prairies and the Canadian Wheat Board to supply additional hopper cars to the grain fleet. The central problems of what to do about the Crow, and how to respond to the stirrings in the West, were, however, left untouched.

Those problems, and the emerging threat to the future of the western railway system, were inherited in 1980 by the re-elected Trudeau government and its new minister of Transport, Jean-Luc Pépin.

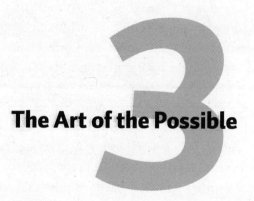

The Art of the Possible

FOLLOWING THE SWEARING in of Mr. Trudeau's Cabinet on March 3, 1980, Jean-Luc Pépin began learning about his new department. Briefings by departmental officials extended over the next few weeks, interspersed with his attendance at meetings of Cabinet, Cabinet committees, and the Liberal Party caucus.

At the beginning of the 1980s, Transport was one of the largest departments in the government, comprising over 20,000 employees. It operated the major airports and the air navigation system, oversaw the railways, subsidized the ferry service on the east coast, provided maritime navigation aids, operated the Coast Guard, regulated the transportation of dangerous goods, and much more. In addition, there were a number of Crown corporations that reported to the minister, including Air Canada, Canadian National Railway, the St. Lawrence Seaway, and VIA Rail, plus various port authorities, harbour commissions, and four pilotage corporations.

The potential claims on a minister's time were almost limitless. They were also exceptionally diverse. A random sample of subjects on any given day might include damage to a railway bridge in the port of Vancouver, complaints from bus companies about the government's subsidy to VIA Rail, possible de-regulation of trucking, the CNR's debt-equity ratio, and bilingual advertising in airports.

Pépin immediately immersed himself in his new responsibilities, to such a degree that he left himself no time to find staff for his office. To help him with the transition, I lent him my own very capable executive assistant, Margaret Amoroso. I little realized at the time that I would not get her back until some six months later, when Jim Roche was finally engaged as Pépin's executive assistant and then set about recruiting staff for a normal ministerial office.

Pépin found his first months in Transport difficult. He was by nature a policy-oriented minister, while Transport is a department in which there are always an endless number of operational issues, often suffused with local politics, that the minister has to deal with.

During my service in the department, I came to the view at a fairly early stage that the public in Canada held three fundamental beliefs about transportation services and facilities:

1. *They were inadequate;*
2. *Those that did exist cost too much; and*
3. *Whatever the costs, they should be borne by someone else, preferably in another part of the country.*

The validity of this assessment was demonstrated by the political pressures that the minister had to cope with every day. Pépin used to remark that he could not walk across the government lobby in the House of Commons without being button-holed about transportation projects by at least four members of his caucus, and that on the current subject of establishing direct air connections between Ottawa and New York, even the dogs on the street barked at him. He did not have a "feel" for such issues and would spend hours studying them, with the result that he was often criticized for failing to make decisions. His office staff at times found him dispirited and frustrated. Former Minister of Transport Don Mazankowski was somewhat harsh, but not entirely inaccurate, when he said in

December 1980, "Mr. Pépin is a professor. He lacks an inherent understanding of the technical aspects of the job."[1]

Part of the appeal that the Crow had for Pépin was that it was a major policy issue, in contrast with the "nitty gritty" matters that he was continually pressed to deal with. Our initial briefings on the subject immediately caught his attention. What also contributed to his interest was that the issue primarily involved the West, a part of the country for which he had always felt an affinity, perhaps reinforced by his experiences when Prime Minister Pearson had given him responsibility for the Canadian Wheat Board for a time in the late 1960s. He sometimes remarked that he would have liked an opportunity to run in a western constituency.

Central to the issue of western grain transportation was the finding of the Snavely Commission that the two railways' net revenue shortfall from moving grain, after federal branch line subsidies, had been $103 million in 1974, and that in the ensuring years the shortfall had grown at a rate of 15.5 per cent per year, reaching $174 million in 1977 and $244 million in 1980. Fuel costs alone increased by 45 per cent between 1979 and 1981. Snavely had forecast that if past trends were to continue, the annual shortfall in railway revenues could reach $1 billion by 1990. It was not a tenable situation.[2]

In parallel with rapidly mounting financial losses by the railways, the federal government during the 1970s had spent a total of $1.3 billion on the grain transportation system, including the rehabilitation of deteriorating branch lines and the purchase of hopper cars for use by the railways. Projections by the Department of Transport indicated that government expenditures on grain transportation could amount to a further $1.8 billion in the first five years of the 1980s.

The strong economic growth of Canadian exports to Asia, which was forecast to continue and perhaps accelerate in the 1980s, had important implications for the railway system. The Coal Association of Canada predicted that its exports through the port of Vancouver would quadruple by 1990. Other predictions were for a 300 per cent increase in potash shipments, and 25 per cent in the case of sulphur.

In addition, the Canadian Wheat Board had set a target of increasing its grain exports by 50 per cent by 1985. Whether these very large increases would materialize could only be known in the future, but the responsibilities of the minister of Transport dictated that he take them seriously.

Traffic growth of such magnitudes would severely tax the two railways, particularly on their main lines through the mountains to the West Coast. Unless major investments were made, the railways would hit the limits of their capacity by the mid-1980s and would then have to begin rationing traffic. In such an eventuality, the losses to the Canadian economy would soon mount into hundreds of millions of dollars. Capacity limitations on the western railway system were thus not merely a problem for grain producers, or for the West, but rather for the entire country.

Moreover, there was little time for delay. Given the lead times involved in bringing major capacity expansion projects into operation, work would have to begin in the early 1980s if traffic rationing by mid-decade were to be avoided.

How was it all to be paid for? The CNR's estimate was that double-tracking and other major projects would require some $3 billion, while the CPR's projects, including a tunnel in the Selkirk Mountains, were expected to require $2.2 billion. It was out of the question that the two railways could finance investment on this scale if their losses on carrying grain continued to escalate at double-digit rates. The financial hemorrhage had to be dealt with.[3]

The federal government was running large budgetary deficits and could not continue to increase without limit its expenditures on western grain transportation. The only alternative was to seek an increased contribution by grain producers, who by 1980 were bearing only 20 per cent of the actual cost of shipping their product. The point had been reached where the cost of mailing a letter from Calgary to Vancouver was greater than the cost of shipping a bushel of grain.

It was the possibility of increasing charges to producers that we had to test. With the initial round of departmental briefings behind us by mid-March 1980, the minister and I set out for our first exploration of the western political landscape to assess what might constitute the art of the possible in grain transportation.

Of the three prairie provinces, the hard core of opposition to changing the Crow rate was in Saskatchewan. Manitoba had a diversified economy in which agriculture was a substantial but not dominant component. Its farmers also produced a number of specialty crops that did not benefit from the Crow rate. In Alberta, opinion was divided. The province was more free market–oriented than its two neighbours, and while many of its grain producers were committed to the Crow rate, its large cattle industry was an advocate of change. In Saskatchewan, on the other hand, grain production was dominant; for years, Saskatchewan's licence plates carried the slogan, "Wheat Province." And the province's geographic location meant that it stood to be the most affected by increases in transportation charges because its grain had to travel the farthest to reach either Vancouver or Thunder Bay.

More fundamentally, Saskatchewan had particularly strong co-operative traditions and had been governed for most of the period after World War II by the New Democratic Party and its socialist predecessor, the Canadian Co-operative Federation (CCF) that had been founded in the Depression of the 1930s. These governments reflected popular sentiment in their strong commitment to the Crow rate, which was widely regarded as the underpinning of social structure of rural Saskatchewan. Although the Wheat Pool was nominally non-partisan, its members tended to be on the political left; a 1946 survey found that 85 per cent of its delegates were supporters of the CCF that had been founded in the drought and depression of the 1930s.[4]

Reflective of the prairie co-operative ethos was a poll that found that, while 60 per cent of grain producers wanted an efficient system, some 35 per cent said they wanted an equitable system that treated everyone the same way. This poll was taken in 1999. The latter figure would almost certainly have been a good deal higher in the early 1980s.[5]

In each of the three provinces the various agricultural organizations were grouped together under an umbrella body: the

Saskatchewan Federation of Agriculture, the Manitoba Farm Bureau, and Unifarm in Alberta. Each was a fairly loose federation, and the interests of the members often diverged.

The largest members by far were the three Wheat Pools and the United Grain Growers (UGG). Among the Pools, the Saskatchewan Wheat Pool was dominant, with 70,000 members as compared with 56,000 members in the Alberta Wheat Pool and 18,000 in Manitoba Pool Elevators. Among them the three Pools handled the bulk of the grain produced on the prairies. UGG, which unlike the Pools was not a co-op but a producer-owned company, had a membership of about 60,000, some of whom were also members of the Pools. SaskPool (as it was commonly called) not only dominated the grain industry in the province but as time went on became increasingly diversified, with some twenty highly successful subsidiaries in fields such a fertilizer and flour milling.

Time magazine once observed that "there is no organization in the world quite like the Saskatchewan Wheat Pool."[6] No co-op had a stronger grassroots network. In its heyday it had a corps of "field men" who criss-crossed the province holding meetings of members, making speeches and helping local producers with problems. It also had 632 local committees. The Wheat Pool's president, Ted Turner, made thirty to fifty visits to Pool districts every year. The Pool's delegates were elected in 144 districts spanning the province, and from their number were elected the directors who governed the co-op. Many of the directors were leading farmers in their districts. Debates during delegates' meetings were highly participatory and often animated.

In the early 1980s the Pool had a staff of over 4,000 across the province, and handled 40 per cent of all Canadian grain. During the late 1970s and early 1980s, the prominent role that the Pool derived from its size was reinforced by Ted Turner's exceptional leadership. Ted had deep roots in the Pool. His father had been on the provisional committee that established it in the 1920s. Ted was elected a delegate in 1957, became a director in 1960, and then, in 1966, first vice-president. He was elected president in 1969 and served in that capacity for seventeen years. Ted and his members would be key to any action the government might attempt in relate to the Crow rate.

The Saskatchewan Wheat Pool was a major political force. Radio stations across the province carried Pool broadcasts twice a week. If on average the 70,000 members of the Pool each had a spouse and three children, this meant that something like one third of the population of Saskatchewan had an affiliation with the Pool. The Pool's president and directors never had any difficulty in having access to Saskatchewan ministers. Premier Allan Blakeney once wryly said of the Pool that, "Like Harvard University, they were a little aware of their own importance."[7]

Not everyone in the province was an admirer of the Pool's political dominance. A free market–oriented farmer once growled in conversation with me that, "This is the only province in the country that has a premier *and* a president."

Considerably to the ideological left of the Pools was the National Farmers' Union (NFU). Its members numbered only about 8,000 and were primarily the smaller, more marginal grain producers. However, this figure understated the NFU's influence because many other grain producers felt an affinity for the views that it expressed, notably including its hostility to the railways. The NFU was highly activist. It held frequent public meetings and regularly put in briefs whenever a commission or legislative body of some kind was conducting hearings about grain, which on the prairies was quite often. The conservative *Alberta Report* magazine once remarked that the NFU was the last organization in Canada to regard agriculture as an expression of the class struggle rather than simply as a business. In the same vein, a Saskatchewan Wheat Pool delegate once remarked that, "The NFU would always sooner fight than talk."[8]

In the early 1970s, the first cracks began to appear in what had been solidly co-op sentiment about the prairie grain handling and transportation system. Some free market–oriented producers came together and established what they called the Palliser Wheat Growers, which began to advocate changes to the system. In the next few years, they were joined by groups such as flaxseed, barley, and canola growers. Their natural ally was the livestock industry, which had always been free market–oriented. The combined body was given the name of the Prairie Farm Commodity Coalition (PFCC). The NFU viewed the emergence of pro-free market groups as a threat to western society, and its members would sometimes hold demonstrations outside places where PFCC meetings were taking place.

They key group in the West for purposes of dealing with the Crow issue was the Western Agricultural Conference (WAC), which comprised the three provincial umbrella organizations and—because of their importance in western agriculture—the three Pools and the United Grain Growers. Although considerably more hesitant about change than the PFCC, the WAC had become concerned about the growing problems in the grain transportation system, and in 1979 its members for the first time adopted a position that future increases in the cost of moving grain could be shared among the government, the railways, and grain producers. This was an historic shift on the part of the prairie agricultural organizations, which only five years before had vehemently and unanimously denounced Otto Lang for proposing that the Crow system be modernized. While the WAC took this step rather tentatively and over the objections of the Saskatchewan Wheat Pool, it was still a milestone because in substance it signalled a willingness to depart from the historic Crow rate. The WAC reaffirmed this position in January 1980, a few months before Jean-Luc Pépin became minister of Transport.[9]

||||||||||||||||||||||

ON MARCH 24, 1980, the minister and I began our exploration of the western political landscape with a three-day trip that took us first to Vancouver, then to Prince Rupert where a consortium wished to build a large grain terminal with federal assistance, then to Edmonton for meetings with Alberta ministers, and on to Winnipeg where we had dinner with Otto Lang. The following day we had meetings

The minister and his deputy:
Jean-Luc Pépin (right) and Arthur Kroeger, December 1983.

with the Canadian Wheat Board and several other organizations in the industry, such as the Canada Grains Council. The various meetings dealt with a wide range of subjects and overall gave us an initial sense of the state of mind of major players in the West, including their views about the Crow issue. On the last day Pépin held a press conference during the course of which he said explicitly—some thought fearlessly—that the Crow had to be dealt with.

Upon returning from this trip, I sent a memo to the department's Surface Administration, which was responsible for railway matters, advising them that the minister wanted us to start developing ideas on how to deal with the Crow issue.

The following week Pépin and I continued our soundings. We went to Regina for a meeting with the Prince Rupert Grain Consortium, after which we had a working dinner with Saskatchewan ministers. In early May we attended a meeting in Victoria of federal and provincial ministers with responsibility for transportation. At about the same time I began discussions with the president of the Western Transportation Advisory Council (WESTAC) about the possibility of his organizing a private, high-level discussion of possible ways of dealing with the Crow issue—an idea that we eventually had to drop because of opposition from the Canadian Wheat Board and the Saskatchewan minister of Agriculture, Gordon MacMurchy, who regarded *any* discussion of the Crow as dangerous.

In all, during the minister's first four months, he and I made six trips to the West, as well as holding frequent meetings with ministers and officials in Ottawa. Although he and I also had to deal with the numerous other subjects that were a part of life in the Department of Transport, western grain transportation was the dominant subject for us during this period. Pépin was seized of the subject, recognized its importance, and was determined to push ahead. Officials in the department fully shared his mindset. In response to the minister's decision to pursue Crow reform, officials began producing a series of analyses of the issue, together with some ideas about how the government might proceed.

By early June our discussions with agricultural leaders in the West had led us to conclude that it was not only necessary but actually possible to tackle the issue of the Crow rate. Those we spoke to did not cheer at the prospect of paying more to move their grain, but they were realists and recognized that the existing situation could not go on indefinitely.

There were also encouraging signs from the provincial governments. At a meeting Pépin had with western agricultural ministers in early June, Manitoba and BC declared themselves in favour of change, Alberta was cautious, but only Gordon MacMurchy of Saskatchewan was strongly opposed.[10]

On June 18 the minister and I again set out for the West. Our purpose this time was to test specific approaches to dealing with the Crow, including the possibility of involving western stakeholders in the development of measures. We began in Winnipeg, went on to Regina, then Calgary and Edmonton and back to Calgary. In all, we held meetings with twelve major agricultural organizations, including the three Wheat Pools and the three provincial federations of agriculture. The meetings confirmed that the major agricultural organizations on the prairies, with the single exception of the NFU, were ready to enter into discussions about modernizing the Crow regime and were looking to the federal government to take the lead.

Upon returning to Ottawa the minister and I had a meeting with the chairman of the Cabinet Committee on Economic Development, Senator Olson of Alberta, through whose committee any proposals to Cabinet about the Crow would have to be routed. We also spoke to the two railways, which understandably reacted with relief and enthusiasm at the prospect that something might finally be done about their losses from moving grain. In parallel, I held meetings with deputy ministers in departments such as Finance, Agriculture, Industry, and the Ministry of State for Economic Development, as well as with officials from the Privy Council and the Prime Minister's Office, to brief them on our findings in the West and to give them advance notice of our intention to submit proposals to Cabinet for dealing with the Crow.

We had consulted widely in the West and had obtained a clear picture of agricultural leaders' views. When I left for Alberta at the beginning of July to visit family with my two daughters, I was in no doubt that the West was ready for change.

Ottawa, however, would prove to be another matter.

The Shoals of History

When Pierre Trudeau returned to office as prime minister following the election of February 23, 1980, the furthest thing from his mind would have been that his government would launch a major initiative in the field of transportation.

After losing the election in the spring of 1979, Trudeau had in December announced his intention to resign as leader of the Liberal Party. However, following the Clark government's defeat on a vote of confidence in Parliament, he had been persuaded to continue as leader, and his party went on to win the ensuing election. Having regained office, Trudeau adopted a single-minded approach. He was above all determined to effect the changes to the Canadian Constitution that had eluded him during his 1974–1979 ministry.

In the lead-up to the May 1980 referendum on Quebec sovereignty, which the federal side had won, he explicitly promised constitutional change. In addition, he and his government believed it essential to legislate a National Energy Program in response to the instability in oil prices and supplies that had characterized the 1970s. To free himself up to concentrate on these two subjects, the prime minister delegated most other matters to various Cabinet committees.

Constitutional change and the National Energy Program were bound to be highly controversial in the West. The last thing the government needed, therefore, was for Jean-Luc Pépin to come along with a proposal that it should also deal with the historic Crow's Nest Pass rate on western grain shipments.

The outcome of the 1980 election had left the Liberal government with serious problems of legitimacy in the West. The party had taken just two of the seventy-seven seats west of Ontario, both of them in metro Winnipeg. Entirely in the hands of opposition parties were Saskatchewan, Alberta, and British Columbia. Insofar as the possibility of dealing with the Crow was concerned, the Liberals had no elected representatives from rural constituencies anywhere on the prairies. Compounding the Liberals' problem was the fact that the western provinces, after decades of being treated as something like a colony by governments in Ottawa, had become markedly more assertive during the 1970s and were less disposed than in the past to acquiesce in decisions by the federal government.

His dearth of western MPs caused the prime minister great concern, particularly because of his plans for a major constitutional initiative. In quest of a solution, he proposed to Ed Broadbent, the leader of the New Democratic Party, that members of his party should join the government in a coalition with the Liberals. Broadbent refused, on the NDP's traditional grounds that it differed from the Liberals in a number of fundamental respects and that it should continue to offer a distinct alternative to the electorate.

Lacking any elected representatives from the three westernmost provinces, the prime minister had to appoint Liberal senators to represent them in his Cabinet. They were Ray Perrault from BC, who became leader for the government in the Senate; Bud Olson from Alberta, minister of State for Economic Development; and Hazen Argue from Saskatchewan, who was given responsibility for the Canadian Wheat Board. These appointments were the only course open to the prime minister, but they did not materially increase the legitimacy of his government in the eyes of westerners.

THE GOVERNMENT WAS in principle committed to investing in railway infrastructure in the West. During the 1980 election campaign the Liberals included in their platform a promise to have CN double-track its entire line from Winnipeg to Vancouver. However, the question of whether additional capacity was actually needed on every part of the line was not addressed. In addition, the platform gave no indication of how CN was to come up with the billions of dollars required to finance such an undertaking. The insouciance of this promise bespoke a lack of serious thought about railway issues on the part of the Liberal Party, as indeed would be confirmed in the months after it returned to office.

In the West, and particularly in Saskatchewan, the party was strongly populist in philosophy. Its hostility to the CPR fully matched that of the New Democratic Party and the National Farmers' Union. In particular, the western Liberals subscribed to the widespread view that the CPR had been excessively compensated by governments for the construction of its lines, and that its offshoot, Canadian Pacific Investments, had been created in the 1950s to enable the company to spin off its lucrative holdings into a safe haven, while leaving the railway as a poor relation that needed government assistance.

Those in the West who held such views—and they were many— believed that the best way of exposing the CPR's machinations was for the government to establish a judicial inquiry into the company. On more than one occasion, Liberal governments considered taking such a step. On December 12, 1974, after Otto Lang had publicly advanced proposals to modernize the Crow regime, the Cabinet decided to establish a Royal Commission to investigate the CPR. This decision reappeared in a Cabinet record of February 10, 1975, but was never implemented. However, this was not the last time that the subject would be heard of.[1]

In July 1980 the Liberal Party held a national convention in Winnipeg. A resolution proposed by the Saskatchewan delegation was passed with near-unanimous support. It called for "a special Judicial Inquiry to examine the current structure of CP Limited, the historical development of that structure from its original railway roots in the last century, the advantages obtained by the CPR and its corporate successors beginning with its land grants and mineral holdings, and CP's current obligations to the people of Canada, and particularly to farmers in the West."[2]

An examination of these subjects had actually been carried out by the MacPherson Royal Commission, as part of its inquiry into transportation in the late 1950s and early 1960s. In its 1961 report, the commission pointed out that the CPR's returns from the railway *and* its other holdings combined had been in single digits through most of the 1950s. It also pointed out a number of legal and other difficulties about trying to force CP to use the profits from its non-rail holdings to subsidize grain transportation. On the question of whether, in accepting grants of land, the CPR had incurred an obligation to provide such subsidization, the commission flatly stated, "We find no evidence that the donor or the receiver contemplated such action. Grants were made to get the railway built."[3]

Succinct as the commission's conclusions were, they had no discernible effect on the durable and widespread prairie view that an investigation of the CPR was required. Illustrative of the suspicions prevalent on the prairies was a particular theory that held that, in seeking to abandon rural branch lines, the CPR was trying to promote the movement of people from farms to the cities in order to increase the profitability of its urban real estate subsidiary, Marathon Realty.

Another proposal related to the CPR that came up frequently through much of the twentieth century was that the government should nationalize the roadbeds of the railway and combine them with those of CN into a single system. The railways would then operate their trains on any part of the system that they saw fit. The objective was to increase competition between CN and CP and thereby drive down their charges. In 1974 the federal government and the western provinces commissioned a consultant to look into this possibility. The consultant's report in 1975 found that there would be a number of complexities to taking such action, and the matter was dropped—for the time being.

Pépin's prospects for getting the government's agreement to deal with the Crow were also affected by the Liberal Party's long-standing strategy of trying to appeal to voters on the left in the West. Party strategists believed that trying to induce western conservatives to vote Liberal was hopeless and that the best prospects for gaining electoral support lay in outflanking the NDP on the left. One practical expression of this strategy was the government's sudden decision in 1979 to appoint former NDP premier Ed Schreyer as Governor General, after the position had been offered to and accepted by diplomat George Ignatieff. The following year, when Trudeau came to form his government after the election, he accepted the advice of his advisors to select as Saskatchewan's representative in the Cabinet a left-wing populist, Senator Hazen Argue, who became a minister of state in the Department of Transport with responsibility for the Canadian Wheat Board. The prime minister also put Argue in charge of the government's efforts to strengthen its relations with western co-ops, for which purpose it allocated $100 million to match investments by the co-ops in the energy sector.

During Jean-Luc Pépin's first months as minister of Transport, no one at a political level took much notice of his discussions of the Crow issue with westerners. Those who did were apt to attribute what he was doing to inexperience and assumed that prairie opposition would bring the whole business to a halt before it could do any real political damage. Some in the Prime Minister's Office also thought that letting Pépin get bogged down in the Crow was one way of keeping him away from the Constitution.

In the late spring of 1980, the Ministry of State for Economic Development (MSED), which served as the government's co-ordinating agency in the field of economic policy, was given the task of assembling, with contributions from line departments, a list of initiatives that the government could take in the West. In parallel, the prime minister authorized the creation of the Consultative Cabinet Committee on Western Affairs, to be chaired by Lloyd Axworthy of

Winnipeg. The committee was not given decision-making powers but was tasked with providing advice on matters affecting the West.[4] These and other steps were taken with a view to remedying the Liberal Party's lack of elected westerners in future elections.

For planning purposes, the government adopted the figure of $5 billion (later reduced to $4 billion) as its target for expenditures in the West over the first half of the 1980s. This amount, to be known as the Western Development Fund, would be set aside from the revenues that would accrue to the government under the National Energy Program. In addition, the government intended to pursue a number of non-expenditure measures in the West.

As the MSED document took shape in June, it came to include initiatives in fields such as industrial development, transportation, research and development, and water management.[5] The final version proposed that nearly half of the notional $5 billion should be allocated to transportation projects, on grounds that transportation problems were the greatest impediment to western growth. Specific initiatives included upgrading the Yellowhead Highway, rail access to coal fields in northeastern British Columbia, and grain transportation.

At the invitation of the MSED, the Department of Transport supplied an extensive section of the Cabinet document. Reflecting the discussions that the minister and his officials had had in the West during the spring, the department's contribution stated that, because of problems that had developed in the grain transportation system, "many Westerners are prepared to alter the Crow arrangement; to renegotiate the historic charter so long as it is replaced by an equally meaningful and beneficial charter for Western producers...There is an opportunity, indeed an obligation, to accommodate and encourage that desire for change..."[6]

The Department of Transport's contribution to the document therefore proposed that the government:

1. should announce that it would put an end to railway losses by providing an annual subsidy to close the "Crow gap," i.e.

the difference between railway revenues from hauling grain
and the actual costs incurred;
2. publish a "Crow Charter" in which it would set out the
means by it would preserve the benefits of the Crow rate in
contemporary conditions; and
3. establish a task force of westerners to work out with the
government the specifics of the new approach, including a
formula for sharing future cost increases between the
government and grain producers.

Recognizing that someone was bound to raise the question of nationalizing the CPR's roadbed to create a single system on which the two railways would run trains in competition with each other, the document recounted the results of the study that had been carried out in 1974–1975, but held out the possibility of seeking a re-examination of the costs and benefits of such an initiative.

Although these proposals figured in the draft western strategy document, they were preliminary and were not intended to result in decisions at the time. Pépin's intention was that they should be fully discussed in the fall.

The assessment of the West provided by the department was borne out on June 19, when the Western Agricultural Conference issued a statement urging the government to take the first step toward Crow modernization, after which negotiations about the sharing of future cost increases could follow. They subsequently followed up with a stronger message that "change is not only necessary, but imminent." They also said that there was a "consensus on the nature and magnitude of the problem."[7]

When the Cabinet met on July 24 it dealt, not with the representations from WAC, but with the resolution passed by the Liberal Party earlier that month concerning the inquiry into the CPR. The minutes of this discussion read as follows:

The Minister of State for Economic Development (Senator
Olson) suggested that the Senate be recalled in August to allow a

committee to be set up to inquire into the Crow rate and into the CPR, in accordance with resolutions of the Liberal Party's recent national convention.

The Minister of Employment and Immigration (Lloyd Axworthy) indicated that the Committee of Ministers on Western Affairs had the issue well in hand and a report would be ready in September.

The Minister of Transport (Mr. Pépin) agreed, but noted that he doubted the wisdom of an inquiry into the CPR and hoped that no action would be taken on the Crow rate that would prejudice consideration of a paper he was preparing for Cabinet in September.

The following other points were raised in discussion:

1. Opening up the Crow rate was dangerous. If it were solved, it would provide further public funds to CPR, when the public believed that the flow of funds should be the other way;
2. The resolution on CPR made the company nervous and more flexible, and this was a good thing;
3. It was important politically for ministers to focus on the constituency in the West [i.e., the left] to which the government wished to appeal.[8]

With this discussion, ministers dispersed to their constituencies for the summer break.

╫╫╫╫╫╫╫╫╫╫╫╫╫╫╫

JEAN-LUC PÉPIN WAS not deterred by the July 24 discussion, if only because he knew that retaining the status quo was not an option. Through the summer, the minister and departmental officials continued holding meetings with agricultural representatives and the railways, making trips to the West, analyzing options, and pursuing discussions with other departments within the government.

By late August we had a near-final draft of a Cabinet memo-randum. It assessed the Crow problem, set out the positions of the various stakeholders, and stated that a "climate favourable for change exists." It proposed that the federal government should adopt the WAC position, on grounds that it had the broadest support. To this end, the government should issue a "Crow Charter" setting out its intention to take action and the objectives it would seek to achieve. Implementation would then be assigned to a "negotiating task force" reporting to the minister that would seek to work out the elements of a Crow settlement with parties in the West.

In the third week of August, the CNR and CPR invited ministers and officials to go on a tour of their mountain main lines. In addi-tion to Jean-Luc Pépin, those who joined the tour included Senators Olson and Argue and Eugene Whelan, the minister of Agriculture, together with ministers from the Manitoba and Alberta govern-ments. The railways' briefings on the need for double-tracking and other capacity expanding projects along their routes were impres-sive, and we were left in no doubt that large-scale expenditures would be required to meet the increased traffic that was forecast for the 1980s.

At the end of the summer I sent Pépin a memo that listed twenty-three issues that would have to be dealt with in the coming year. The Crow headed the list.

On September 9, the Cabinet Committee on Western Affairs had its first discussion of the Cabinet document we had been working on through the summer. Given the political context of the times, we fared reasonably well. The committee reacted very warily to our proposal to seek modernization of the Crow regime, but the min-ister managed to obtain approval to develop a further paper on the subject, which was to be considered together with proposals for additional branch line rehabilitation and hopper car purchases. The question of an inquiry into the CPR figured in the discussion, as did the possible nationalization of the CPR's roadbeds, but without a clear conclusion in either case.[9]

A basic element of our approach was to keep stakeholders in the West abreast of what we were doing. During the fall of 1980 Pépin was quite explicit in his speeches and in private discussions about the need to modernize the Crow and his desire to have westerners play a major role in decisions about ways of proceeding. On October 1, 1980, the Canadian Federation of Agriculture wrote to the minister endorsing WAC proposal that the federal government should provide a subsidy to cover the railways' current losses and that the sharing of future increases in costs should be a matter of negotiation between the government, grain producers, and the railways.

In early October I made a trip to Regina and Edmonton to alert stakeholders that work was getting underway on modernizing the Crow.

I decided that while in Regina I should make contact with a new and fairly small free market–oriented group called the Palliser Wheat Growers. When I left the hotel in a taxi I found myself being taken far south to a shopping centre on the edge of the city, where I eventually managed to locate Palliser on the second floor. Its small office was sparsely furnished, with a plywood table on which stood a coffee pot and some styrofoam cups. I had a sense of dealing with a subversive group of revolutionaries in a co-op dominated universe. In our discussion I explored with them the prospects for bridging the differences between the various groups in the West and thereby strengthening the consensus that had emerged about the need to modernize the Crow.

Following my discussion with Palliser, I went back into town to see the Saskatchewan Wheat Pool. Their offices were in a large former department store in the heart of downtown Regina. The floors were carpeted, and the furniture was comfortable. Whatever the populist origins of the Pool, its present status as a pillar of the Establishment was unmistakable. Executives of the Pool reacted coolly to my suggestion that it would be helpful if they would enter into discussions with groups such as Palliser with a view to arriving at an agreed position.

Pursuing our "no surprises" approach, my next stop was a lunch with the deputy minister of Agriculture, Gerry Gartner, and the associate deputy who was also head of the Transportation Agency, Marj Benson. When I briefed them on our current activities concerning the Crow, they reacted with consternation. I was somewhat taken aback, although perhaps I should not have been, since both were NDP political appointees, and Marj Benson had reportedly worked in the election campaigns of her minister, Gordon Mac-Murchy. They warned that any attempts by the federal government to change the Crow would "mean war with Saskatchewan." When I pointed out that we were following proposals that had emanated from the Western Agricultural Conference, they said that the provincial government did not accept and was opposed to the WAC position. Marj went on to express doubt that they could treat as confidential what I had outlined to them, on grounds that not using what they had learned would be to "betray our people." The discussion left no room for doubt that in Saskatchewan the Crow was still a lot more than a freight rate.

I went on to Edmonton, where I briefed the chairman of WAC, Howard Falkenberg, whose organization's proposals were central to what we were working on. When I returned to Ottawa I was relieved to find that the Saskatchewan government had not gone to the media with what I had told the two officials.

From early October on, our activities were no longer below the radar screen in Ottawa. The subject was addressed at a series of meetings of the Cabinet Committee on Economic Development and the Committee on Western Affairs.

Following are excerpts from the minutes of a four-hour meeting on October 7 of the Committee on Western Affairs:

> As the Crow rate was a very sensitive topic in the West, the government should proceed with extreme caution...In terms of political support, Saskatchewan was the key province...it would be highly desirable to have the backing of the Saskatchewan Wheat Pool...The Committee considered that it would be essential that a government initiative on the Crow rate be accompanied by a high profile, public inquiry into the role of Canadian Pacific...

to determine the relevant benefits and costs...before asking either producers or Canadian taxpayers to pay more.... the approach to the resolution of the Crow rate problem...modeled after Western Agricultural Conference proposal did not appear promising....the financial implications were unacceptable and would need funding... greater than the total amount envisaged for all Western Initiatives.... the central issue with respect to Western Initiatives was... the modernization of the transportation system in the West.[10]

It was a less than satisfactory discussion. In effect, ministers had found that the costs to the government of what we were proposing were excessive, that it would be dangerous to seek a financial contribution by grain producers, but that the railway system had to be modernized—by unspecified means. Nevertheless, it was the best we could have looked for in the circumstances.

During this period Pépin displayed increasing mastery of transport issues; after six months as minister, he was beginning to find his feet. When we went to Cabinet committees together, I found him articulate and able to hold the attention of his colleagues when he spoke.

Activity by the department and the minister continued unabated in the autumn months. I spent the three days of the Thanksgiving weekend editing and rewriting parts of our Crow paper. The Cabinet Committee on Economic Development met again two days later. On October 31, Pépin signed and sent into circulation a twenty-nine-page Cabinet memorandum with eight appendices setting out his fully developed proposals for dealing with the Crow issue.[11]

The key recommendation was that the government should take action to modernize the Crow, "within the limits of what may be acceptable to producers and farm organizations on the prairies." More specifically, the document expressed a disposition to adopt the fairly conservative set of measures that the WAC had endorsed, on grounds that they stood a better chance of gaining broad acceptance, as opposed to the more aggressive, free market–oriented measures favoured by groups such as Palliser and the cattle industry. In proposing a conservative approach, we were in part influenced by a very tough letter from Ted Turner, president of the Saskatchewan Wheat Pool, to the effect that if we departed in any way from the strict WAC position, the Pool would go into total opposition. While taking his representations seriously, we did provide in our document that alternative measures could be explored during the consultations with interested parties in the West.

With regard to process, our Cabinet document said that the government should issue a policy statement responding to the proposals that had been put forward in the West. In its statement the government would set out its position on the Crow issue and would propose the creation of a consultative task force of westerners that would seek to enlarge the areas of agreement between the government and representatives of agriculture in the West.

The document cautioned that there would be producer opposition to change despite the policies endorsed by the organizations.

Pépin's document included a recommendation for a commission of inquiry into Canadian Pacific, not because the minister favoured such a course but because he regarded it as the price of being allowed to move ahead with the rest of his measures. Even this concession did not mollify some of the ministers who were opposed to what Pépin was proposing. Over the ensuing weeks, the Western Affairs and Economic Development committees met frequently but were unable to arrive at a definitive outcome on the subject of grain transportation. Equally inconclusive were the recurring discussions among ministers about a western strategy that the government could pursue to improve its electoral fortunes. Until these discussions yielded some kind of conclusion, Pépin's proposals could not go on to the full Cabinet.

The principal difficulty that we faced during these meetings was getting people to believe us when we argued that the West was ready for change. While senior officials in other departments recognized the importance of what we were attempting and gave us their full support, the reaction at political level was uncertain and in some cases hostile. Ministers from Ontario, Quebec, and Atlantic Canada had some sense of what Pépin was proposing but had difficulty grasping the specifically western complexities. The chairman of the Committee on Western Affairs, Lloyd Axworthy, represented an urban riding and had little knowledge of agriculture. He also had his eye on the future leadership of the Liberal Party and wanted to use the Western Development Fund for politically attractive projects that would strengthen the party's—and his—position in the West. In the 1980 meetings of his committee he did not support Pépin.

The other two key ministers were the prairie senators, Olson and Argue. Senator Argue was a former member of the socialist CCF who had left the party when he failed to gain the leadership of its successor, the New Democratic Party. He was elected as a Liberal in 1962 but was defeated in 1963 and was subsequently appointed to the Senate. A burly figure in his sixties with a strong voice, he embodied all the beliefs of a prairie populist and was highly emotional in his defence of the Crow regime. Senator Olson was more moderate in his outlook. On most subjects he was a model of balance and thoughtfulness, and he was greatly respected by his officials. However, whenever the subject of the CPR was raised, his prairie origins as a former member of the populist Social Credit Party came to the fore. Neither senator had assimilated the new thinking that had developed on the prairies; both were convinced that the Crow was as sacred as ever.

In the face of opposition from Axworthy, Olson, and Argue, other ministers were uncertain of what to make of Pépin's claim that the West had changed and that it would accept modernization of the Crow. After all, Otto Lang, a native of Saskatchewan, had as Transport minister tried to deal with the Crow a few years before and had been beaten back by opposition on the prairies. Were ministers seriously supposed to believe that a French Canadian former professor from the University of Ottawa, a native of Drummondville, Quebec, who represented a riding in Ottawa, could succeed in taking away what the West regarded as its birthright? The notion was rather as if Alberta MP Don Mazankowski had come to Cabinet with proposals for a federal initiative to deal with the future of the French language in Quebec.

The hesitation felt by Pépin's colleagues was reinforced by events outside the field of transport in the autumn of 1980. The prime minister was single-mindedly intent on constitutional change, and for this purpose convened a meeting of the provincial premiers in early September. The meeting ended in failure, and the federal government determined that it would push ahead unilaterally, which provoked an angry reaction from a number of provinces, particularly those in the West.

The issue of the Constitution completely overshadowed what Pépin was trying to do. A particular factor was that the prime minister was trying to persuade Premier Blakeney of Saskatchewan to come onside for constitutional reform, which meant that any action by other federal ministers that might offend the premier would be very unwelcome.

Another major development in the fall of 1980 was the federal government's launch of its National Energy Program. It had been developed in maximum secrecy by a small group of ministers and officials in Ottawa and was unveiled in the budget of October 28. Its provisions constituted a major incursion by the federal government into provincial jurisdiction over resources, and it generated intense acrimony in the West, particularly in Alberta. Premier Lougheed became so incensed that for a time he forbade his ministers to have any contact with the federal government, to the point that on one occasion when Pépin and I went to Edmonton, the Alberta ministers of Agriculture and Economic Development arranged for us to meet in a motel well away from the downtown area, whether with the premier's consent or not we did not ask. On another of our visits, an Alberta journalist, Don Braid, despairingly predicted to us that what the federal government was doing was inflicting scars that would not heal for a generation. His assessment would prove to be prescient.

In this climate, Pépin's proposals to open up a third front with the West were troublesome and unwelcome to the prime minister and key members of his Cabinet, the more so because they regarded transportation as of secondary importance. At the level of officials, the secretary to the Cabinet, Michael Pitfield, was less than pleased with my involvement in Pépin's doings. The prime minister's principal secretary, Jim Coutts, went to see Pépin and urged him to give up the whole business. Pépin declined. Even if his colleagues had failed to grasp what was at stake, he for his part knew that prolonging the status quo was no longer an option.

However, there was one development during this period that gave us grounds for optimism about our prospects. At its annual meeting in the third week of November, the Saskatchewan Wheat Pool was to vote on a motion endorsing the Western Agricultural Conference's policy of being willing to negotiate the sharing of future cost increases in grain transportation between producers, the government, and the railways—a policy that amounted to a decision to end the fixed 1897 Crow rate. When the WAC policy was adopted in January 1980, SaskPool had acquiesced but had not formally endorsed it. Now, at the annual meeting in November, the subject was up for decision. The Pool's president, Ted Turner, made the case that change was coming and that the Pool had to be at the table when negotiations got underway, in order to keep damage to its interests to a minimum. It was said in some quarters that SaskPool faced a risk that, if it did not join the WAC consensus, the Alberta and Manitoba Pools, together with UGG, would go it alone with the government. Among the delegates, recognition of the need for change was uneven, and in advancing his proposal Turner was displaying considerable leadership, not without some political risk to himself.

Pépin was due to speak at the Pool's meeting, and the night before we left I worked until nearly 3:00 AM, editing and rewriting in longhand the text that had been prepared by the department. In the morning I sent it for typing, and we used the trip on the government plane to Regina to discuss the text and the outlook for the meeting. When we arrived, a worried Mike Farquhar, our director general of Grain Transportation, reported that Saskatchewan Agriculture Minister Gordon MacMurchy that afternoon had delivered a barn-burner of a speech opposing federal action to change the Crow.

Adding to our problems was that Senator Argue had also given a strong "keep the Crow" speech earlier in the conference.

A two-thirds majority was required for the WAC policy to be approved, and the floor debate among the delegates had featured strong expressions of views on both sides. Pépin spoke the next day and was reasonably well received. Following his speech we had lunch with the directors of the Pool, and Pépin then spent an hour responding to questions from the floor. He made a useful contribution to the debate, but in the end it was Turner's leadership that determined the outcome. The delegates voted 122 to 22 in favour of adopting the WAC position.

It was a major breakthrough. The Saskatchewan Wheat Pool represented approximately half the grain producers on the prairies, and its strong opposition to any modification in the Crow had been the rock on which Otto Lang's initiative had foundered in the 1970s. With its vote in November 1980 the Pool had recognized, however reluctantly, that the 1897 freight rate could not be preserved forever.

We returned to Ottawa with a restrained sense of triumph, more convinced than ever that we were on the right track. Now that the Saskatchewan Wheat Pool had come onside, surely ministers would have to believe us and endorse what we were proposing.

But they did not, despite more discussions, some of them quite diffuse, in Cabinet committees. At its meeting on December 3, the Committee on Western Affairs, led by Lloyd Axworthy, had objected to putting the bulk of the Western Development Fund into transportation. They proposed an allocation of only $850 million over three years, with the rest being spent on a variety of politically appealing projects—what one official called a "spend it on everything" approach.

On December 18 Senator Olson wrote to the prime minister expressing the view that tackling the Crow issue was "unsound" because the government had not developed the necessary political support. In addition, the prospective financial requirements were too large to be accommodated by the Western Development Fund, and only a limited amount from it should be allocated to transportation.

Senator Olson went on to urge that any initiative related to the Crow rate should be accompanied by an inquiry into Canadian Pacific and either a nationalization of the railway's roadbeds or the purchase by the government of a controlling interest in the company.[12]

In the New Year, Senator Argue continued his public campaign against what Pépin was proposing. At the Western Agricultural Conference annual meeting in January he delivered a "keep the Crow" speech so strident that members of the WAC executive remonstrated with him afterward, telling him, "We don't need any more speeches like that." Their concern was that the senator's activities would stir up producers to the point that their leaders would be unable to proceed with what they knew needed to be done. Undeterred, Argue went on to deliver much the same speech to a meeting of the Canadian Federation of Agriculture and then reiterated his views in a series of press statements during the ensuing days.

The Western Affairs and Economic Development committees were unable to come to a consensus on Pépin's proposals, so the Privy Council Office decided to break the impasse by placing his memorandum on the agenda of the Committee on Priorities and Planning, which was chaired by the prime minister and served as a *de facto* inner Cabinet.[13] The minister and the Department of Transport went to great lengths in preparing for the meeting. I spent an entire weekend drafting and redrafting a letter that Pépin would send to the prime minister in advance of the meeting, with copies to all members of the committee. It documented the railways' growing losses from moving grain and strongly warned that capacity problems on the western system lay in the near future. The letter was distributed to ministers on January 13, and I had copies delivered to their deputies at the same time. I also drafted a set of talking points for my minister to draw upon during the discussion.

On the morning of January 20, prior to the meeting of Priorities and Planning, I went to see Pépin. Being confident that we had an irresistible case, I cheerfully greeted him with the query, "Wellington on the eve of Waterloo?"

He shook his head, and replied, "Remember that it was Napoleon who thought he was going to win."

He was more prescient than I. He did not prevail in the three-hour discussion, particularly because of opposition from the three prairie ministers: Olson, Argue, and Axworthy.

Following this meeting, we learned that the executive of the Western Agricultural Conference were to be in Ottawa in early February for the annual meeting of the Canadian Federation of Agriculture. We saw this as an opportunity to have the leaders of western agricultural organizations set out their thinking for ministers at first hand. Pépin made this proposal in a telephone call to the WAC executive, and they agreed. He later recounted to me that, "I told them to swallow their 'buts.' If Hazen [Argue] asks you if we should move, you have to say, 'Yes!,' not 'yes, but.' When he asks you whether the consultative task force is a good idea, you say, 'Yes!,' not 'yes, but.'" Pépin had been quite explicit about the situation in Cabinet, and told the WAC executive that it was "now or never."

On February 9 and 10 the WAC executive held meetings with a succession of ministers in which they set out their position on the Crow. At one meeting Senator Argue launched on one of his vintage performances: opposition to change in the West was strong and growing, SaskPool were in trouble over their pro-WAC vote in November, the government should just leave things alone, and so on. Members of the WAC executive began to shift uncomfortably in their chairs, and as soon as Argue was done, they jostled with one another in rebutting his statements. It was exactly what we had hoped for: contemporary Westerners expressing a contemporary position.

We next learned that the WAC executive had been given an appointment with the prime minister. Having observed that some of the executive's meetings with ministers had strayed off to peripheral issues, I decided to draft a list of six key questions that should be addressed during the meeting with the prime minister. I sent them to Janet Smith in Privy Council Office, who incorporated them into the prime minister's briefing note. I then passed the same set of questions to the WAC executive, as a means of ensuring that both sides would use their limited time together to discuss the things that really mattered. When I subsequently told Pépin what I had done, he fully concurred.

On the day following their meeting with the prime minister, the farm leaders sent a letter to him, with copies to thirteen other ministers in which they reaffirmed their desire for a government initiative and their willingness to negotiate an increase in grain producers' share of transportation costs.

Their representations proved to have no effect.

At a meeting of the Cabinet on February 12, the following discussion was recorded in the minutes:

> *The Prime Minister indicated that the government's strategy toward the Crow was to react to proposals advanced by interested groups rather than take the initiative of advancing its own proposals. He said the interested groups should state their policies publicly and generate support before the government should react.*
>
> *In the general discussion that followed Ministers expressed their agreement with the reactive strategy outlined by the Prime Minister.*[14]

Following the Cabinet discussion, the prime minister held a press conference at which he said, "I would not have the folly to say that I am going to tamper with the Crow." When a prairie journalist pointed out that the position of WAC was endorsed by every major agricultural organization in the West with the exception of the National Farmers' Union and asked whether this did not represent a sufficient consensus, Trudeau simply replied, "No."[15]

In a further statement the following day he rejected the proposals presented to him by the farm leaders and did so in terms that verged on trivializing the issues they had raised. He referred to the fact that he had had a meeting with farm leaders and "some of them [sic] advocated reopening the Crow rate...I told them—and yesterday

I said it publicly—that we do not want to fiddle with the Crow rate unless there is some very strong feeling throughout the West..."[16]

Pépin was alone. It was clear that his warnings about the impending threat to the western railway system had simply made no impression on Trudeau and his advisors.

In the aftermath of the prime minister's statement, there were press reports, attributed to anonymous sources in his office, that Pépin was to be dropped from the Cabinet and perhaps made ambassador to France.[17]

Trudeau often acknowledged to his staff that he had difficulty understanding the West. He was particularly puzzled at how nothing that he tried in relation to the West ever elicited a positive response. Lacking confidence in his own judgement, he made it a practice to rely on his western ministers—of whom only Axworthy was elected—and on advisors such as his principal secretary, Jim Coutts, who was originally from Alberta, and on Lloyd Axworthy's brother, Tom, who came from Manitoba. In 1980 all members of this group were either hesitant, or openly opposed, to what Pépin proposed. During the weeks leading up to the Cabinet's decision, Trudeau had at times expressed interest in bilateral discussions with Pépin about what Pépin was trying to do, but in the end he had allowed himself to be warned off the subject by his western advisors.

On February 24 the Cabinet returned to the Crow one more time. The tone of the discussion was negative. All that Pépin was able to come away with was a concluding comment from the prime minister to the effect that he could pursue the subject with people in the West but should not do anything that would embarrass the government.

In the days that followed there was some to-ing and fro-ing about what the prime minister had meant. The uncertainty was dispelled at a meeting I had on March 11 with Michael Pitfield, the secretary to the Cabinet, two senior officials of the Privy Council Office, and Ian Stewart, the deputy minister of Finance. The message from Pitfield was very explicit. It was essential for future national unity that the government be able to win some representation in the West. The agricultural organizations could not be relied upon, and their views were given no weight whatever. The western provincial governments were key, and Saskatchewan (which in fact was the only one of the four opposed to Crow change at the time) was of particular importance. No action would be taken on the Crow until Saskatchewan's Blakeney government not only agreed, but asked for it.

Finally, with regard to the question of the prime minister's concluding statement at the February 24 meeting, Pitfield confirmed that he was in effect giving Pépin a polite brush-off. We were not to make any further sallies to round up support in the West for changing the Crow. The subject was too politically sensitive.

The Crow was still sacred. We had run aground on the shoals of history.

On Hold

ALTHOUGH PRIME MINISTER TRUDEAU, in February 1981, justified his refusal to deal with the Crow issue by saying that there was insufficient consensus in the West, the reaction to his decision suggested a different assessment in that part of the country.

The leaders of western agricultural organizations in particular felt with some reason that the government had hung them out to dry. Having come to recognize over a period of several years that the status quo had become untenable, they had risked the anger of their members by offering to negotiate changes to the Crow regime. Now the federal government had rejected their offer and had done so in a fairly cavalier fashion. Transport officials did not find it easy to respond to queries from western agricultural leaders asking, in effect, "What the hell do we do now?"

Particularly exposed were the president and directors of the Saskatchewan Wheat Pool. At a social evening with several officials of the Privy Council Office they expressed worries that pressure from their members could now force them to rescind their support of a pro-negotiation position. They urged that the government act quickly to accept the compromise position of the Western Agricultural Conference and open discussions on implementing it.[1]

They were not alone in their concern about the government's decision. On February 23 the Council of the Canada West Foundation, the premier research organization in the West, sent a telex urging the prime minister to open negotiations. On the same day, the president of the Alberta Wheat Pool wrote expressing the growing concern of grain producers about the ability of the western railway system to handle the traffic that was in prospect and urging the federal government to open negotiations with producers. On March 4, the Saskatchewan Federation of Agriculture, in a letter to the prime minister, called upon the federal government to come forward with a railway policy and to enter into negotiations with producers. On April 30, the Alberta Wheat Pool renewed its representations, stressing the urgency of the situation and advancing a new offer: the federal government should agree to cover the railways' financial losses but could make its financial support conditional on the success of negotiations with producer organizations about future cost sharing.

Among provincial governments, Alberta had for some time been particularly concerned about the future of the railway system and had made an extraordinary offer to provide $2 billion of its increased oil revenues to finance an expansion of the system. Immediately following the Cabinet's negative decision in February, the Alberta minister of Economic Development, Hugh Planche, wrote to Pépin renewing this offer and providing a list of suggested projects to which these funds could be applied. During the same period, we also began hearing from several sources that the province of Saskatchewan was considering purchases of locomotives and other rolling stock. The difficulty was that railways were a federal responsibility, and if provincial governments entered the field there could be complications later on.

Further indications of provincial concern came in mid-May, when the Western Transportation Advisory Council (WESTAC), whose membership included ministers from all four western provinces, reviewed projections of railway traffic and expressed concern at the prospect of capacity problems.

None of these representations from the West had any effect. The prime minister was heavily engaged with his constitutional initiative, and on April 16 chaired a meeting of First Ministers in Ottawa to deal with the subject. The meeting went badly and ended with eight provinces, including all four of the western provinces, issuing an angry communiqué in which they stated:

> the federal constitutional proposal is the most visible example of this new federal government's attitude and is the most flagrant denial of the spirit of Canadian federalism....
>
> Ottawa has adopted an approach of division and confrontation in its dealing with provincial governments.[2]

The reaction of many in the West when the federal Cabinet decided to turn its back on the Crow problem was captured by a *Financial Post* editorial of February 16, 1981:

> Governments have a duty to govern, and if Mr. Trudeau cannot find a Western consensus on the Crow at the moment he should at least be prepared to help find one, or create one. His Transport Minister, Jean-Luc Pépin, has suggested a task force to study the issue under orders to make its report without undue delay. That at least would get the issue off dead centre.

Referring to the National Energy Program, the editorial went on to say:

> Mr. Trudeau's attitude that, because the West is suffering from his government's impetuousness in one area, it should suffer from his timidity in another, is just not good enough.[3]

In the aftermath of the Cabinet's decision to leave the Crow untouched, the anti-change forces celebrated their victory. On February 26 Senator Argue made a gratuitous public statement that Pépin's idea of a task force made little sense and had no support.

The following week a large group from the National Farmers' Union made a "trek to Ottawa" by train, where it held a demonstration in support of the Crow. During their visit Pépin and I had an unproductive ninety-minute meeting with their leaders. Hazen Argue for his part arranged for them to see the prime minister.[4]

Despite the satisfaction and relief felt by the anti-change forces, the core problem remained. An announcement by the government that it had concluded an agreement to sell 25 million tonnes of wheat to the Soviet Union elicited a public statement from the president of CN on June 3 that, because the Crow rate covered only a fraction of the actual cost of moving grain, this sale would cause the two railways to lose $375 million over the next five years.

Within the Department of Transport, Crow-related activity tapered off and eventually stabilized at a fairly low level during the spring and summer. Officials continued to have periodic discussions with agricultural organizations and the railways, as well as with officials in other departments, but the path to any substantive outcome was blocked by Cabinet's February decision. We therefore turned our attention to other matters: ports policy, a possible transfer of traffic from Mirabel to Dorval airport in Montreal, future policy on transportation of the handicapped, the deficits of VIA Rail, and ways of increasing diversity in the department's human resources.

The most important matter we had to deal with in the spring of 1981 was a review of VIA Rail, which was growing during a period when the government's fiscal position was becoming increasingly difficult. Pépin and the department therefore concluded that action to contain the cost of VIA was essential, and we developed proposals to effect a 20 per cent cut in VIA's services, primarily on routes with very low ridership, and to reallocate the savings to purchasing new rolling stock for VIA. These proposals were well received by the Cabinet and readily gained approval.

The decision was announced in July and set off a huge reaction. Although VIA was actually used by a relatively small minority of the travelling public, the emotional attachment of Canadians to the idea of railway travel, including the historic transcontinental service, meant that the controversy went on for months. It was yet another cross for Pépin to bear and did further damage to his reputation with the public; what was not known at the time was that some of his colleagues had wanted to make much deeper cuts than those Pépin had proposed.

Western demands for the government to take action on grain transportation continued during the summer. On July 30 a delegation from the three Wheat Pools came to Ottawa and renewed their requests for the government to take the initiative. Some of the Pools' leaders were concerned that if there was no response from the government before their annual meetings in November, their members could repudiate the pro-negotiation policy that they had endorsed, with some hesitation, in the past.

Continuing pressure to address the Crow issue left little room for doubt that some kind of action would eventually have to be taken; the question was what. I decided to detach our long-standing assistant deputy minister for Strategic Planning, Nick Mulder (who in later life would become deputy minister of the department) and assigned him full time to the Crow file with the title, "Coordinator, Crow Task Force." Reporting to him henceforth would be the Grain Transportation Division headed by Mike Farquhar. Mulder had been in the Strategic Planning position for six years and was very knowledgeable about a range of transportation issues; Farquhar was younger and a more recent appointee but was rapidly mastering the field of grain transportation.

An important development in the spring and summer of 1981 was that non-agricultural bulk shippers for the first time began to focus collectively on the implications for them if congestion were to develop on the western railway system. In mid-April, a vice-president of BC Resources, Gary Duke, came to see me on this subject. In early May he returned to Ottawa with the president of the Coal Association of Canada, Walter Riva. At the beginning of June, Riva saw the minister and then held a press conference in which he expressed concern about the prospect of congestion developing on the western railway system. Others who began to speak up during this period were the Canadian Exporters' Association and the Canadian Manufacturers' Association.

Out of this and other activity came an announcement on August 6 about the creation of a private sector "Task Force on Canada's Crisis in Railway Transportation." The stated objective of the task force was to persuade the government to take action to ensure adequate rail capacity, and it warned about the risk of traffic rationing by 1985. To broaden its membership, it deliberately did not take a position on the Crow rate *per se*, although the implications of its policy stance were fairly clear.

The chairman of the task force was Garnet Page of the Coal Association. He was succeeded in January 1982 by the president of the Canadian Exporters' Association, Tom Burns. The two vice-chairmen were the president of the Western Agricultural Conference, Howard Falkenberg, and the president of the Prairie Farm Commodity Coalition, Ivan McMillan. The member organizations included the Council of Forest Industries, the Coal Association, Sultran and Canpotex (respectively the export organizations of the sulphur and potash producers), the Chemical Producers, the Canadian Manufacturers' Association, and an organization of some 450 shippers known as the Canadian Industrial Traffic League. The combination of agricultural and industrial members on the task force was unusual and underlined the concern about the transportation problem felt by many in the West.

In all, some fifty organizations signed on as members of the task force. An exception was the Saskatchewan Wheat Pool, which was uneasy about where this initiative might lead. In a letter to the chairman, Ted Turner firmly told him that the task force was not authorized to speak on behalf of the Pool. He maintained that, because the Crow rate was central to the debate, leadership on the capacity issue should remain with agricultural organizations.

In the meantime, the guardians of the status quo remained in control. In mid-July 1981 Senator Olson, the chairman of the Cabinet Committee on Economic Development, proposed that $1 billion from the Western Development Fund be allocated to projects such

Jean-Luc Pépin and Nick Mulder, head of the Crow Task Force,
October 1982.

as branch line rehabilitation and purchases of additional hopper cars, with an additional $500 million being provided to the railways as subsidies over the next three years—in effect, a continuation of the *ad hoc* project approach of the 1970s, plus a new subsidy for the railways that fell far short of covering their losses.[5]

A further expression of the government's adherence to the *ad hoc* approach came in August. Following a meeting of the prime minister with the chairman of Canadian Pacific, Michael Pitfield telephoned me and asked that the department explore with the CPR possible interim steps for railway improvements.

I remained pessimistic about the outlook. In a list of impending Cabinet submissions that I sent to the minister on August 31, there was nothing about grain transportation. The subject was as pressing as ever, but we saw no prospect that going back to Cabinet would get us anywhere.

On September 9 and 10 the Cabinet Committee on Priorities and Planning met at Keltic Lodge in Cape Breton to plan the government's work program for the coming months.

One of the key documents before the committee was an analysis of the government's fiscal situation by the Department of Finance. We in Transport had worked extensively with Finance on parts of the document during the early summer and had contributed financial and other data about the needs of the railway system. However, we did not entertain expectations that Finance's document would result in any material change to the government's stance in relation to the Crow.

As matters turned out, we were mistaken. While we knew that none of our arguments in favour of change had had any effect on the government, there was one additional factor that we had not taken sufficiently into account. What ultimately determined the decisions of Priorities and Planning, and subsequently of the Cabinet, was not the representations of the western agricultural groups, nor of the shippers in other industries, nor the views of the provincial governments in the West; neither was it the eloquence of our minister, nor what we regarded as the incisive analyses with which we regularly provided him. As happens so often in government, what finally determined the Cabinet's course of action was not what ministers would have liked to do, but what they could afford.

The Western Development Fund that had been announced in the October 1980 budget provided for the expenditure of $4 billion up to the end of 1986–1987. In February 1981 Priorities and Planning had decided that the fund should be used primarily for transportation, Aboriginal programs, and economic diversification in the West. In his presentation at the Keltic Lodge meeting in September, the minister of Finance, Allan MacEachen, stated that transportation capacity was of strategic importance and that modernization of the western transportation system should be given priority. Our many months of meetings with officials in the Department of Finance had not been wasted.

The financial analysis prepared by the departments of Finance and Transport showed that the federal government was forecast to spend $2.2 billion over five years on branch line subsidies and *ad hoc* projects such as hopper car purchases and branch line rehabilitation. If the Crow rate were left untouched, the government would also have to cover CN and CP financial shortfalls amounting to $3.2 billion if the two railways were to carry out the investment programs that would be required to meet future traffic growth. However, even after the government had made these very large expenditures, the basic problem would remain and the financial requirements of the railways would be still higher in future years.[6]

MacEachen pointed out that if, instead, the government adopted the proposals put forward in the past by the minister of Transport, the financial impact would be considerably reduced. He therefore proposed an initial allocation of $1.35 billion to Grain Transportation from the Western Development Fund. This amount, taken together with the branch line subsidies that had already been provided for, would enable the minister of Transport to cover the railways' deficits as they stood and on this basis to open negotiations with grain producers about the sharing of future cost increases, as WAC had proposed.

In the area of finances, Pépin was an indirect beneficiary of the National Energy Program. The very large revenues raised by the NEP were primarily to be used for energy projects such as exploration in the North and offshore on the east coast, but the expenditures on transport could be met out of the $4 billion in NEP revenues that the government had set aside for the Western Development Program. In the absence of the NEP, it would have been very difficult for the government, which was already running a large deficit, to find the funds that Pépin needed for his Crow initiative.

Faced with these financial alternatives, ministers at Keltic Lodge for the first time began to display an interest in Pépin's option. To ensure there was no misunderstanding of what would be involved, the deputy minister of Finance at one point said to the prime minister, "You realize that this will involve an increased producer contribution to grain transportation costs?" With the same calm detachment that had characterized his rejection of Pépin's proposals seven months before, the prime minister confirmed that he accepted this consequence.

The outcome of the Keltic Lodge meeting rather caught us by surprise in the department. Pépin was not a member of Priorities and Planning, and he learned of the decision to revisit the Crow issue only when his colleagues returned to Ottawa. During the ensuing days I had a series of meetings with senior officials from Finance and the Privy Council Office to get a picture of what Cabinet had actually decided.

Priorities and Planning's conclusions about finances were placed before the full Cabinet in Ottawa in mid-September and were discussed at length. A factor that figured in the discussion was that the government would be running a deficit of some $20 billion, and the current inflation rate of 13 per cent was driving up the cost of programs, such as pensions that had been indexed to annual price increases. The minister of Finance wished to reduce the deficit, but to do so would require cuts in a number of fields, such as social policy. The pressure on the government's resources and program budgets would be still greater in future years if expenditures on grain transportation were allowed to increase indefinitely and without limit. The Cabinet therefore agreed to make a major allocation of funds to a "comprehensive transport initiative" and called for the minister of Transport to bring forward specific proposals.[7]

The record of the Cabinet's decision as drafted by the Privy Council Office was a model of circumspection when it came to the subject of transportation. The word "Crow" never appeared. Instead, the decision listed among the government's highest priorities, "expansion and modernization of the transportation system through a five year plan of investment in necessary rail transportation *and/or reform* [emphasis added] of the freight rate structure."[8] Nevertheless, the record said all that was needed. The door to action on the Crow was now half open. On September 30 I made an entry in my schedule for that day: "departmental staff—launch of Round 2 on Crow."

The September meetings bore out an observation that we often heard from Pépin. He used to say that in government it was the small decisions that caused all the trouble. When it came to the big decisions, it usually became clear in the end that the government had no real choice. This had proven to be the case in respect of the decision to seek an increased contribution from producers toward the costs of transporting their grain.

In response to the Cabinet's decisions, we began work on a document that would respond to the request for specific proposals from the minister of Transport for implementation of the decisions taken in September. For his part, the minister reopened his public campaign about the Crow with a series of speeches in the fall of 1981, including one to the Empire Club in Toronto on October 1, and then by more speeches and press conferences in the West. Officials in the department worked at assembling data, and in the third week of October the two railways came to the department with the updated traffic forecasts that we had asked for.

In parallel, Garnet Page's private-sector task force on future rail capacity began making the rounds in Ottawa. Reports reaching us indicated that they had had some success in making an impression on members of the Cabinet.

During the years that we worked for Pépin, and particularly during periods of high activity such as the fall of 1980, Sunday-night meetings in his basement study at home were a weekly feature of our lives. His wife, who had long since become accustomed to his work habits, would welcome us and then occupy herself in another part of the house.

In the West, the WAC executive were pressing for a government decision before the annual meetings that various agricultural organizations held late in the year. Ted Turner was reported to be particularly worried that the annual meeting of SaskPool might reverse the endorsement of the WAC approach of the previous year. On the other side, former Supreme Court Justice Emmett Hall, who after retiring from the court had become something of an icon to the pro-Crow forces, affirmed, "there is no position to take except to adhere through thick and thin that the Crow rate is not bargainable."[9]

In late October, the chairman of the Committee on Western Affairs, Lloyd Axworthy, circulated a draft document entitled "A Strategy for the West." The contents of the document demonstrated that the tide that had run so strongly against Pépin a year before had turned. The section on transport concluded with a recommendation that:

> *The Cabinet accept that the current level of consensus is adequate, in the present circumstances, to warrant immediate action on revitalization of the transport system and the resolution of the related question of freight rate structures.*[10]

The chairman of the committee was now fully onside. Axworthy saw the major investments to be made by the railways as a major contribution to western development, and he spoke enthusiastically of them as the equivalent of building a third transcontinental railway—which was indeed quite accurate, given the $13 billion in expenditures by the railways and the government that would be involved.

In his November budget, the minister of Finance announced the additional $1.35 billion allocation to transportation that had been agreed by the Cabinet in September. The leaders of the Liberal parties in the four western provinces and Yukon passed a resolution calling for these funds to be spent on branch line rehabilitation, double-tracking, and similar projects.[11]

In November the Conservative government of Sterling Lyon in Manitoba was defeated by the NDP, led by Howard Pawley. This shifted the balance in the West, as Manitoba would now join Saskatchewan in the "keep the Crow" camp. In Alberta, ministers strongly favoured change but could give us only muted support because of Premier Lougheed's very cautious approach to the subject. British Columbia had always been enthusiastic about change, but its support was taken for granted. For purposes of political assessment, what counted were the grain-producing regions of the prairies, and two of the three provincial governments were now against us.

In the third week of November, the Saskatchewan Wheat Pool held its annual meeting. I spent the weekend before the meeting drafting and redrafting the minister's speech. By most standards of executive practice, this should have been left to departmental staff, with my role being limited to reviewing and editing. However, our Crow undertaking was a very high-stakes affair, and I quite often chose to personally draft memoranda and correspondence, as well as the minister's speeches on this subject. Fortunately, I was able to free up time by delegating a good deal of the management of the department to my very able senior assistant deputy minister, Jaffray Wilkins.

Writing speeches for any minister is usually a demanding under-taking, but in Pépin's case it was especially so. He would take a double-spaced draft text and write between the lines, then in the margins and then at the top and bottom of the page. When he ran out of blank space, he would take out one of the straight pins that he always carried on the reverse side of his lapels and use them to affix scraps of paper on which he would write further interpolations. When he sent a draft text back to his office, his staff would have to remove the pins and incorporate his changes. Some of them remarked that at times this literally left them with blood on their hands.

Pépin's delivery of speeches was similar to his approach to written texts. It was not a matter of making an orderly progression in sentences and paragraphs from page one to page two to page three. Instead, he would frequently interpolate digressions and the oratorical equivalent of cadenzas into his texts. But the overall result was impressive to his audiences.

At the opening of the annual meeting of the Saskatchewan Wheat Pool, the federal minister of Agriculture, Eugene Whelan, called on the delegates to support modernization of the Crow. Four days later, his colleague Hazen Argue, in an impassioned speech, urged the delegates to do nothing of the kind. Brushing aside data on the subject of the railways' large financial losses and the risk of traffic rationing in the future, he said, "I just don't believe it." He also contradicted the analyses done by the Department of Agriculture and asserted that ending the Crow would not help the livestock and processing industries. A few days later he delivered a similar speech to the Alberta Wheat Pool's annual meeting, exhorting them: "Come to the defence of the Crow! Don't let anyone take it from you."[12]

Viewed against the normal standards of Cabinet solidarity, Senator Argue's actions were unconscionable. He and his office periodically gave us a good deal of trouble, and at times westerners were understandably left confused about the federal government's actual policy in regard to grain transportation, since ministers were contradicting one another in public. On the other hand, there could be no doubt about the sincerity, as well as the strength of the senator's convictions, and his presence at the Cabinet table served to give ministers a first-hand exposure to views that were held by a substantial number of grain producers in the West.

In his address the day after Argue's, Pépin pursued the themes he had used the year before, warning of the dangers that the status quo posed for the railway system and, by extension, for grain producers. The title of his speech was "Shared Problems and Shared Solutions." His core message was, "If you and other westerners are really determined to do it, you might be able to scare off a minister trying to modernize the Crow regime. But if you do so and succeed, be prepared to miss opportunities and take the consequences." Pépin received a respectful hearing, as he had at the 1980 meeting. The delegates were realists and recognized the validity of what he was saying, even though some of them were in a difficult political position.

The vote by the delegates to support the WAC position at the 1980 meeting had generated considerable controversy among Pool members. At a number of meetings across the province the leadership were accused of being out of touch with their members and of having "sold out." Nevertheless, thanks primarily to Ted Turner's leadership, the delegates in 1981 did not rescind their 1980 decision, but the vote after a four-hour debate was closer—99 to 45, representing a shift of twenty-three ballots to the "No" column.

The erosion of support was in part a consequence of the Cabinet's refusal the previous February to accept Pépin's proposals. During the intervening months there had been a loss of the momentum that had built up among western agricultural organizations in 1979–1980, and, on the part of some, second thoughts had set in. Although the document submitted to Western Affairs by Axworthy called for a recognition that the level of consensus in the West was adequate "in present circumstances," in fact the consensus had been considerably stronger the year before.[13] In the fall of 1981, for example, dissidents in the Manitoba Pool forced a vote on the Pool's participation in negotiations about the Crow.[14] The Alberta Pool also came under pressure and hardened its position.

At the end of November, our document with proposals for the implementation of what Cabinet had decided after Keltic Lodge went into circulation. It was placed on the agenda, first of the Committee on Western Affairs and then of the Cabinet Committee on Economic Development. Once again Pépin had his colleague Senator Argue to contend with. On November 27, Argue circulated to ministers a lengthy "Commentary" on our Cabinet memorandum. Officials in Transport were considerably annoyed that there had been no advance discussion with us, but one benefit was that many of the statements in Argue's document were ill-informed and did not stand up to scrutiny. I sent Pépin a copy on which I had entered a series of terse marginal notes rebutting the main points. In the end, neither committee spent much time on the Senator's document.[15]

Our paper was thirty-nine pages long and provided a comprehensive discussion of the subject. One of the principal purposes of preparing Cabinet memoranda is to enable officials in the proponent department and others with an interest in the subject to work through the various considerations, to test possible approaches on each other, to make the presentation as factually accurate and complete as possible—in brief, to ensure that what is eventually presented to ministers provides a comprehensive and reliable picture of the principal considerations involved. However, experienced officials also know that ministers do not generally read thirty-nine-

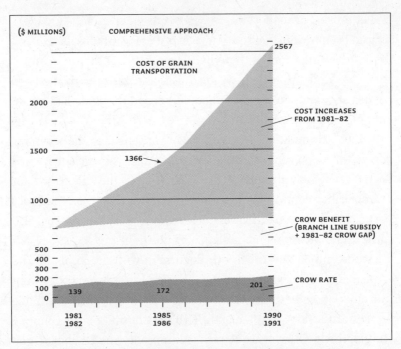

Figure 1: Chart used to brief Cabinet committees, November 1981.

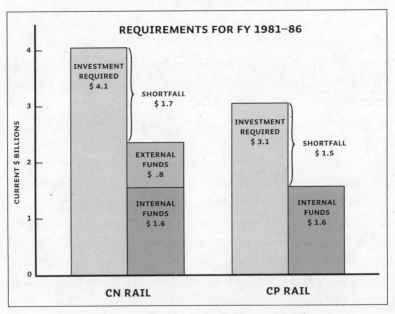

Figure 2: Chart used to brief Cabinet committees, November 1981.

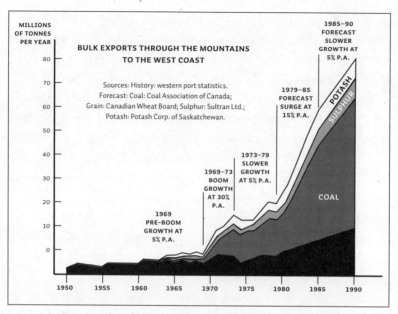

Figure 3: Chart forecasting the growth in traffic on the railways'
mountain main lines, published by the Western Transportation
Advisory Council, October 1981.

page documents. Politicians tend to function orally rather than on the basis of written texts—something that was confirmed for me when I had done an oral presentation to the Economic Development committee on the subject of the VIA rail cuts the previous summer. When we were given leave to resume work on the Crow in the fall, I put this lesson to good use.

In the days prior to the meetings of the two Cabinet committees on November 24, my staff and I spent many hours designing a set of charts on cardboard that would display in summary form the main messages in our document. Included on them were descriptions of the western economy, graphs showing the forecasts of traffic growth on the western rail lines, summary tables of the financial factors in play, a map showing the major rail lines in the West, and much else. Among the charts was one that reproduced WESTAC's forecast of traffic growth on the railways' main lines in the West. Another provided evidence that traffic congestion was already developing; in 1978 the average speed of a CNR train had been 24 miles per hour (38.6 km/hr); by 1980, as trains had to spend more time in sidings when meeting other trains, the speed had fallen to 21.5 miles per hour (34.6 km/hr) and, in 1981, to 19.5 miles per hour (31.4 km/hr).

At each meeting I spent perhaps thirty minutes on my feet taking the committee through each chart, dealing with subjects such as future traffic forecasts and financial issues, following which I would sit down beside my minister for the ensuing discussion. The process was a success in the sense that by the end of each meeting ministers had a fairly clear picture of the issues before them and apparently found the picture of looming problems to be fairly daunting.

The central question placed before the committees was whether the government should continue with its "project approach" of past years or whether it should opt for a "systems approach."

The project approach that had been pursued since the early 1970s amounted to a series of *ad hoc* measures to meet the needs of the grain transportation system: rehabilitation of boxcars, purchases of hopper cars, rehabilitation of branch lines, and so on. Such measures were decided upon year over year by the federal government and paid for with federal funds; charges to producers by the railways for the transportation of prairie grain by rail remained at the level fixed in 1897.

Under a systems approach, however, the railways would be allowed to charge compensatory rates for moving grain and, as a concomitant, would assume responsibility for modernizing and maintaining the grain transportation system. They would receive federal subsidies to cover most of the "Crow gap" (i.e., the difference between their actual costs and the amount they were able to charge shippers), but for the first time producers would also be required to contribute to closing the Crow gap. The amount of the producers' contribution would be a matter for negotiation.

Up to a point, the question of whether to move to a systems approach had been settled by Priorities and Planning at Keltic Lodge in September, and by the minister of Finance's announcement of the funds for grain transportation, but there was still a need to spell out for ministers in some detail what was entailed by each of the two alternatives. After fairly lengthy discussions, the two committees agreed with Pépin's recommendation that a systems approach be adopted and that a consultative process giving a major role to western farm leaders be established. In its main elements, what ministers approved was what Pépin had proposed over a year before.

The one important change was that the inquiry into the CPR had been dropped. Ministers had come to realize the seriousness of the transportation problem they faced, and it was no longer necessary to offer up the CPR inquiry in order to obtain their assent to dealing with the problem.

We were not out of the woods yet, however. Following the first set of committee meetings in late November, Nick Mulder and his staff had to prepare and circulate a lengthy document responding to questions that had been raised by ministers. The subjects addressed in this document included CN's capital budget, the reliability of traffic forecasts, the scope for increasing capacity on the main lines without major investments, and why the railways could not simply increase their charges for moving other products to offset their losses in moving grain. Following a discussion of these subjects, we were next required to produce another document describing how the "systems approach" would actually work.

Predictably enough, given the participation of senators Olson and Argue in the discussions, there were also questions about the railways' rate of return on investment. In response, the department, using methodology developed by the Canadian Transport Commission, reported that in the three years 1978–1980, CN's return on investment had ranged from 4.7 per cent to 6.1 per cent, while Canadian Pacific's, including CP Investments, had been 7.6 per cent to 9.3 per cent. For purposes of comparison, Bell Canada's rate of return had been 10.8 per cent, Canadian General Electric's had been 15.6 per cent, while in the United States, according to Carl Snavely, the Interstate Commerce Commission had estimated that an adequate rate of return for railways was 19 per cent before taxes. During this period, the rate of return on Government of Canada long term bonds was 12.3 per cent. These data satisfied most members of the committees and cleared the way for us to get on with the work that lay ahead.

Some sense of our high level of activity during this period may be gleaned from the following excerpts from my daily schedule for the first part of December:

December 1: Western Affairs, "Round 2." Two hours. Evening: minister sees PM.

December 2: departmental staff outline of next Crow paper

Friday, December 4: staff. Evening meeting with Howard Falkenberg and others.

Saturday evening: Howard Falkenberg.

Sunday: draft Cabinet document for Western Affairs—preliminary version of government's negotiating position on Crow.

Monday, December 7: Minister and Senator Olson, then minister and Senator Austin (BC and the Crow). Evening meeting with the minister.

December 8: Breakfast with Manitoba Pool; then Western Affairs Committee—elements of a "system approach" to western grain transportation. Post-mortem with the minister. Dinner with Howard Falkenberg and Lorne Parker, Manitoba Farm Bureau.

December 9: meetings: Gary Duke, Ivan McMillan and Ken Stickland of PFCC, minister. Evening meeting of Cabinet Committee on Economic Development. Post-mortem with minister.

The above entries illustrate, among other things, our "no surprises" approach in dealing with agricultural organizations and other interested parties in the West. We made a point of keeping them fully abreast of the main developments as we went along, and they always respected the confidences that we imparted to them.

All of this activity came to a head in mid-December. Because a good deal of the discussions in the Cabinet committees had been

Bottle of Old Crow whisky presented to Pépin after Cabinet's decision to
proceed with Crow reform. On the left, Lloyd Axworthy.
COLLECTION OF THE AUTHOR

disorganized and fairly confused, I spent the weekend of December
12–13 drafting a document setting out the specific elements of the
decision that we wished to obtain. The subject was complex, and we
could not afford to leave anything to chance. On the Sunday night we
took the proposed text to Pépin at his house to ensure he was comfortable with it and to prepare for when he would need to take the
committee through it. The following day, December 14, we had the
text distributed to members of the committees.

The Cabinet committee discussions of the next few days were the
culmination of our months of work. The outcome was summarized
by Pépin as, "We didn't get a No, so it's a Yes." The committees also
agreed that the minister of Transport should come forward in January
with detailed proposals for the implementation of his proposals.

Notwithstanding the progress made by the two committees, nervousness persisted among the prime minister's advisors. On December 7, Pépin received a letter from Trudeau that first expressed great wariness and then went on to say, "the issue necessitates the most delicate handling, not just of the substance of the problem, but also the process of its resolution."[16] This enjoinder was not well received in the department. Given how the minister and we had managed matters in the preceding year or so, we did not feel that we had any lessons to learn from the Prime Minister's Office when it came to dealing with the West.

Indicative of what we had been up against was a speech by Jim Coutts, who by this time had left the Prime Minister's Office. At a Liberal Party convention in December he emotionally called for the West "to be given some economic justice..."[17] What he had in mind did not include raising the Crow rate.

Despite such expressions of unease, by mid-December the way had effectively been cleared for us to proceed with our proposed Crow initiative. Although Priorities and Planning would have to give its formal blessing in the New Year, the outcome was not in doubt, since the prime minister had already been briefed about the state of play.

We were no longer "on hold." The question now was whether we would be able to deliver a politically tolerable solution to the Crow problem.

At Centre Ice

THE MANDATE THAT JEAN-LUC PÉPIN had obtained from the long series of Cabinet committee meetings in the fall of 1981 was provisional at best, particularly insofar as Prime Minister Trudeau and his advisors were concerned. Pépin had been given leave to try what he had been advocating, but there was no strong commitment by the government to see it through if he ran into trouble. Partly for this reason—but also because the minister and the department were convinced that trying to force change on the West would be the wrong approach—the manner in which we operated from the outset was open, transparent, collaborative, and flexible. We maintained a dialogue throughout with the prairie agricultural leaders, the provincial governments in the West, the railways, and other interested parties including the major users of the railway system.

Our central objective was to have the solution to the Crow issue designed in the West, by westerners. Instead of developing a comprehensive and detailed set of measures in Ottawa, as the government had done with the National Energy Program, we had decided to begin by issuing a policy statement setting out the main elements of the government's approach, including explicitly the need for change to the Crow. The principal western stakeholders would then be invited to collectively develop ways of modernizing the Crow within the framework of the government's stated policy.

Our first task, therefore, was to draft the policy statement that would set the framework for the consultations on modernizing the Crow. In parallel, officials in the department also had to begin work on a document for Cabinet to review in January that would pull together the decisions taken during the long series of meetings in the fall. Work began on both documents in the week of December 21 and continued through most of the Christmas–New Year's period. We also alerted various interested parties in the West that we wanted to have meetings with them in the first few days of January 1982.

On the morning of January 5, 1982, the minister's executive assistant, Jim Roche, and I boarded a flight to the West. Our purpose was to begin testing the specifics of the government's approach by showing western stakeholders the draft text of the government's policy statement. In Winnipeg our first meeting was with the president of UGG, Mac Runciman, to whom we outlined what the government proposed to do. His response was positive. In the afternoon we consulted former Minister Otto Lang, to draw upon his experience in trying to deal with the Crow in the 1970s. We then flew to Calgary, where the presidents of the three Wheat Pools had assembled at our request.

As we had foreseen, this was our most difficult meeting. The Pool presidents were critical of a number of points in our draft statement, and Ted Turner at one juncture indicated that he would prefer a continuation of the government's "project approach" of the 1970s to what was in our paper. Wallace Fraser of Manitoba and Allan Mac-Pherson of Alberta also expressed a number of strong concerns, but all three remained at the table and pursued the discussion with us to its conclusion.

Late that evening we boarded a plane that had been chartered to enable us to get from Calgary to Regina that night. We arrived at 2:00 AM At 7:00 AM we sat down to a breakfast meeting with the presidents of the three prairie farm federations—Unifarm, the Saskatchewan Federation of Agriculture, and the Manitoba Farm Bureau, together with a representative of UGG. In the afternoon we were back in Winnipeg, where we saw the president of the Canadian Chamber of Commerce, had dinner with the Prairie Farm Commodity Coalition, and then went to a meeting with the Canadian Cattlemen's Association. Our objective was to test the proposed measures as widely as possible before trying to produce a final version.

At each of the meetings with agricultural organizations, I would distribute copies of our draft policy statement and then take people through it, section by section, inviting comments as I went along. At the end of the meeting I would ask that all copies of our document be handed back, in order to ensure that this preliminary draft did not find its way to the media. I would then repeat the process with the next group, and the next, and so on. During the discussions, Jim and I mostly listened, provided explanations at times, and took notes.

The morning after our Winnipeg meetings, Jim and I returned to Ottawa. A three-hour debriefing with the minister and departmental staff followed, and that evening we began redrafting the policy statement to take account of what we had heard in the West. Many of our changes were editorial, but we also made several that were fairly substantial: for example, we added a provision making it explicit that the government's financial commitment would be statutory and would continue year after year.

Activity continued at a high level through the week: meetings with officials from other departments, the assembly of financial data for inclusion in our Cabinet document, and apparently endless editorial changes to our policy statement. Our document was due in the Privy Council Office on January 12. On the night of January 10, Mike Farquhar and I had a meeting with the minister and then worked on the Cabinet document until 1:00 AM. The next day the minister and I had a meeting with the Pool presidents, whom we had invited to Ottawa to bring them up to date on developments, including the changes we had made to the policy statement. This was followed in the afternoon by a discussion with Senator Olson, and then another with Senator Argue. Neither was particularly happy with Cabinet's decision to seek changes to the Crow, and Pépin wanted to ensure they were informed.

The following morning, January 12, we made the final changes to our Cabinet document, got the minister's signature, and forwarded it to the Privy Council Office for distribution to the Cabinet. The final stage was at hand.

During the series of autumn meetings of ministers, the practice had been for our documents to go before the Committee on Western Affairs first and then on to the Committee on Economic Development for decisions. In practice, the value added by Western Affairs was generally fairly limited—not surprisingly, given that the committee had only one elected member from the West. Nevertheless, the fact that Western Affairs had reviewed a document served to increase the comfort of the ministers on the Economic Development committee, most of whom had only limited familiarity with western matters.

This sequence was used again for the meetings on January 14. Once again, I had designed a set of charts on cardboard that I used to take ministers through the substance of our document. We gained the approval of each committee.

Our document then went to the Priorities and Planning committee, which was chaired by the prime minister, where it received final approval.

Our thinking on the kind of consultative process that we should establish had gone through a number of iterations. Several times we considered a task force comprising perhaps three westerners with good agricultural credentials who would work with the various stakeholders in devising ways of dealing with the Crow issue. At another point I had thought that I might participate directly in the process, only to be told firmly—and correctly—by the secretary to the Cabinet, Michael Pitfield, that I was to stay in Ottawa and manage my department. We eventually concluded that the ideal choice would be to engage the services of the widely respected Mac

Runciman, who had recently retired as the president of UGG. When the minister and I sounded him out, he expressed a willingness to consider taking on the task. The executive of the Western Agricultural Conference reacted favourably when we consulted them about this possibility, but when we tested his name with the Pools we encountered opposition, possibly because they thought he might be too free market–oriented in his approach. So we were back to square one.

After we had canvassed a number of other possibilities, Doug Campbell, a former assistant to a Conservative minister of Agriculture, suggested the name of Clay Gilson. This turned out to be an inspired choice.

Dr. Gilson was a professor of agricultural economics at the University of Manitoba. He had previously been Vice-President (Academic) at the university, Dean of Graduate Studies, and a vice-chairman of the Canada West Foundation. In 1982 he was the president of the Agricultural Institute of Canada. The Toronto *Globe and Mail* described him as one of the most respected agricultural economists in Canada. The question was, would he agree to do it? And time was running out.

On Thursday, February 4, I had a meeting with the minister and then phoned Gilson in Winnipeg. I explained the proposed assignment, and we agreed to speak again the next day. During our second discussion he agreed in principle to take on the task, subject to a face-to-face discussion when I got to Winnipeg on Sunday.

Another piece had been put in place.

In parallel with my activies, Jean-Luc Pépin saw the prime minister to keep him abreast of developments. The announcement of the government's decisions, including the initiation of Gilson's consultative process, was set for Monday, February 8, in Winnipeg, the historic headquarters of the prairie grain industry.

At the end of the day, the department's Crow staff, Jim Roche, and I opened a bottle of champagne. We had finally rolled the rock to the top of the hill. It had been twenty-three months since Pépin's and my first trip to the West.

THE MONTHS OF consultations we had had with western interests, and the generally open style in which we had operated, meant that residents of the prairies were fully aware by early 1982 that a federal initiative to modernize the Crow was imminent.

The prospect of such a change had implications for the West that extended well beyond whatever charges would be levied in future for transporting grain. In social terms, rural residents of the prairies regarded the Crow as important to the survival of their communities.

When the prairies were settled in the late nineteenth and early twentieth centuries, the landscape came to be covered with a network of branch lines that were usually about twenty miles (32 km) apart and ran parallel in an east–west direction. On each railway line the Pools and other grain companies erected wooden grain elevators at eight-mile (13 km) intervals. The objective of this configuration was to enable any farmer in the area to load a horse-drawn wagon with wheat, deliver it to an elevator, and return home in time to milk his cows that night.

The elevators usually had around them a small town comprising a cluster of grocery stores, gas stations, garages, a post office, and sometimes a hospital or a municipal office. The main streets ran down to the railway station and the loading platform by the tracks. The station agent was an important member of the community. Some of the prairie settlements developed into good-sized towns, while others never attained populations of more than sixty or seventy. Regardless of the size of these communities, their residents and those who lived in the surrounding areas developed strong attachments to them. They were also convinced that the local railway line was the lifeline of the community, and that if the branch line were ever abandoned the town would die.

Consequently, when a railway proposed to abandon an unprofitable line, local residents would rise in united opposition, the more readily because, under the Crow rate, the amount that railways could

Farmers delivering grain with horses and wagons, Vulcan, Alberta, 1928.
CANADIAN PACIFIC RAILWAY ARCHIVES, IMAGE W.71

charge for hauling grain on a particular line was fixed and bore no particular relationship to the actual cost. There was thus no economic incentive for producers and community residents to accept changes that would reduce costs. In response to community pressures, members of Parliament from across the prairies, regardless of party, were a powerful lobby in support of branch line retention, and governments reacted by regularly prohibiting the railways from abandoning branch lines that had become uneconomic.

In 1933 the network reached its peak at a level of 19,200 miles (30,900 km) of line. In 1980–1981, despite the development of an extensive road system and a substantial reduction in the rural population, only 2,500 miles (4,023 km) of line had been abandoned, and some 15,980 miles (25,720 km) had been placed in a "basic network" to be kept in service until the year 2000. By way of comparison, in the United States, where there was no Crow rate, some 33,000 miles (53,110 km) of line had been abandoned by the early 1980s. In addition, nearly 3,000 wooden country elevators remained in operation on the Canadian prairies, slightly over half of the 5,700 that had been established under very different conditions during the 1920s and 1930s.[1] Any traveller approaching a prairie town could get a sense of its size from a distance by counting its elevators.

Despite the Crow and the protected branch lines, a good deal of change necessarily took place on the prairies as the rural population continued to shrink. Many one-room country schools were closed, hospitals and municipal services were consolidated, grain companies closed some local elevators, and the sites of what had once been small communities came to be marked by commemorative cairns. When the federal government concluded in late 1981 that it had to deal with the distortions being caused by the 1897 Crow regime, many prairie residents feared that this would accelerate a rationalization process that had already caused them considerable concern. This is what Premier Blakeney was referring to when he said that the federal initiative would destroy the "social structure of Saskatchewan."[2]

▓▓▓▓▓▓▓▓▓▓▓

ON THE MORNING OF Sunday, February 7, the minister and some of his political staff flew to Regina, where the provincial Liberal Party and its young leader, Ralph Goodale, were in a state of acute distress at what the Liberal government in Ottawa was about to do. The minister described for them the statement he would be issuing the next morning, gave them what comfort he could, and then flew back to Winnipeg in the evening.

That same day I had flown directly to Winnipeg from Ottawa, where I spent nearly four hours with Clay Gilson discussing the task that he was about to undertake. We had no difficulty in reaching a meeting of minds. He fully understood the Crow issue and the importance of finding ways of dealing with it that western stakeholders could live with. The rest of the day I spent in preparation for the launch of the federal initiative the next morning, including briefings for federal officials based in Winnipeg. That evening I had dinner with the leaders of the western agricultural organizations who had been invited to Winnipeg for the event. When the minister returned to Winnipeg late that evening, he and Gilson met for the first time and established a comfortable working relationship.

The next morning the full program got underway. The minister had a meeting with the agricultural organizations at the beginning of the day. He then made the formal announcememt, after which I did an extensive media briefing, using the charts that I had previously used with the Cabinet committees. The event was heavily attended, with over fifty media representatives present. The *Manitoba Co-operator* described the announcement as "a policy decision of massive proportion."[3]

What followed was a media blitz that had been thoroughly planned in the weeks leading up to the launch. The minister had a press conference, followed by lunch with the editorial board of the *Winnipeg Free Press,* followed by radio and television tapings and meetings with reporters from the farm weeklies. We then flew to Regina for what amounted to a repeat performance, including dinner with representatives of the two major Saskatchewan dailies, the *Regina Leader-Post* and the *Saskatoon StarPhoenix.* The following morning we went to Calgary and then on to Edmonton; the day after that to Saskatoon. I left the minister there and flew to Regina for a meeting with Marj Benson, Saskatchewan's associate deputy minister of Agriculture, as part of our approach of giving special attention to the Saskatchewan government.

The reaction of the media and the agricultural organizations to the federal announcement was as good or better than we could have looked for. Following were some of the headlines that appeared the next day:

"Good for Ottawa"—*Edmonton Journal*[4]

"Most farm groups laud Crow move"—*Winnipeg Free Press*[5]

"Pépin's grain rate stance furthers his gutsy image"
—*Vancouver Province*[6]

"West farm leaders happy with Gilson"—*Calgary Herald*[7]

In Saskatchewan, the *Saskatoon StarPhoenix* was critical of some of the specifics but termed the initiative "a reasonable first step."[8] In smaller centres, the *Swift Current Sun* called it "another kick in the pants for the West"[9] but the *Melfort Journal* described it as "a beginning."[10] Of the two major agricultural weeklies on the prairies, *The Western Producer*, owned by the Saskatchewan Wheat Pool, was cautious, but next door the *Manitoba Co-operator* said, "It is time to get on with the responsibilities that others have long evaded."[11] *Alberta Report* described Pépin as, "A very good Minister in a very bad government."[12]

During the weeks following our launch, I took some satisfaction in remarking to some in Ottawa that it was not easy to think of any other recent federal initiative that had elicited eight favourable editorials in the West during the first week.

The *Montreal Gazette* captured the reaction of many in a February 11 editorial:

> At least so far, it looks as if federal Transport Minister Jean-Luc Pépin may be about to pull off on of the greatest coups of Canadian history: abolition of the Crow's Nest Pass freight rates for grain...Mr. Pépin has started reasonably well and he is on the right track.[13]

It would however be a long time—longer than any of us foresaw—before what had started so promisingly would reach its conclusion.

Senator Argue continued to be a disruptive factor in our lives. Notwithstanding the clear assertion in the government's policy statement that, "an increased contribution by grain producers will be required," he assured the Canadian Federation of Agriculture a few days after the launch that the government would not force an increase in the freight rate on producers.

Cartoon by Roy Peterson that appeared in
The Vancouver Sun, February 10, 1982.

Following the initial announcement in Winnipeg and the ensuing media blitz, the government embarked on a wide-ranging communications effort intended to maximize support. A "Crow Work Program" that was circulated in the Department of Transport on March 15 listed twenty-six activities, including:

- *press releases and letters to editors;*
- *brochure;*

- *minister's trips to West and interviews;*
- *[activities by] other ministers and MPS;*
- *meetings with provinces; and*
- *meetings with truckers, railway unions.*

The communications battle was joined. The Saskatchewan Wheat Pool distributed a pamphlet criticizing the federal announcement to 120,000 residents of the province, while Pépin sent a letter to all grain producers in the West setting out his case.

While I kept an eye on this program, I saw no need to become actively involved. We had a communications unit in the department and had also contracted for consultants' services. In addition, staffs in the offices of various ministers were eager to bring their political talents to bear on communication needs. I did not feel that I had much to add to their efforts.

One unorthodox step the department took with my approval was to designate one of our officials who was particularly familiar with the West, Henry Ropertz, to undertake speaking engagements in small centres on the prairies. He had a plain style and established easy communications with farmers. There proved to be no shortage of invitations, and for a good deal of the next twelve months Henry was to be found in Weyburn, Altona, Tisdale, Brandon, and many other prairie centres. He was careful throughout to respect the limitations of his role as an official and to concentrate on providing a factual picture of what the government was and, more particularly, was *not*, proposing to do.

Even so, there were some who were not pleased by his activities. A vice-president of the Saskatchewan Wheat Pool, Garf Stevenson, who was perhaps not accustomed to being contradicted on his home territory, complained to the media that, "this guy has been a problem since Day One."[14] In any case, Nick Mulder and I thought that what Henry was doing was important and should continue, particularly since some of our critics on the prairies were not allowing themselves to be constrained by a passion for accuracy. An erroneous claim that Henry often had to deal with, for example, was that freight rates would increase five-fold immediately if the government's proposals were implemented.

During the late winter and spring of 1982, Pépin tirelessly criss-crossed the West, making speeches, meeting groups, and holding media interviews. The essence of his message was that modernizing the Crow could no longer be avoided, that the end result would be a better transportation system for the West, and that the financial impact on grain producers would be limited.

An event that still stands out in the memories of those involved was what came to be known as the "Delisle Meeting." The minister and the department had decided that he should go to a rural centre in Saskatchewan and meet producers on their own ground.

Arrangements were made for him to do so in late February. The site chosen was the town of Delisle in the west-central part of the province. It proved to be a less than ideal choice, because that area was a stronghold of the National Farmers' Union. When the NFU heard that the minister was coming, they were not slow to respond. Because of the numbers who sent word that they were going to attend, the organizers moved the site from a hall to the local hockey arena.

When Pépin arrived in the arena he was greeted by a chorus of boos and yells from the 1,200 farmers who had assembled. Undaunted, he walked alone out to a microphone at centre ice, where he spent more than an hour delivering his speech and then answering questions. Given the circumstances, he received a reasonable hearing, although at one point an angry denunciation of the government's action by Ted Strain, the president of the NFU, brought thunderous applause. When the meeting was over, Pépin spent another hour in face-to-face dialogue with a number of individual farmers.

Because the television cameras focussed on the tumult, the principal impression conveyed to the public was one of farmers' anger, which was obviously not what we had sought when we decided to hold the meeting. There was, however, a degree of solace in the fact that some also came away crediting Pépin with having had the courage to come to rural Saskatchewan. They also observed that he had shown grace under pressure. It was not the last time that he would do so.

One of Pépin's major assets was that people found it impossible to dislike him. He was endowed with a good measure of natural charm and was very articulate in discussion. More fundamentally, his manner was free of the artifice and theatrics that the public often associate with politicians. Even his vehement adversaries would sometimes preface their criticisms with, "I wouldn't question his integrity, but..." Among those farmers who supported what he was doing, the sentiment tended to be, "Hey, that Pépin is all right."[15]

Departmental officials and Pépin's office staff found his work habits to be something of a challenge. He was less than discriminating in deciding what subjects he should spend time on, and he would often keep material in his study at home for long periods until he could "find time to revisit them." As a result, documents requiring early decisions would often get stuck in his study, so his office staff adopted a practice of putting urgent material in a special red folder when filling his briefcase for his evening reading. The success rate of this tactic was about 50 per cent.

Pépin also had little appetite for the more crass side of politics. At one point, he learned that the Prime Minister's Office was planning to appoint a prominent Liberal as chairman of one his Crown corporations. Pépin mounted a prolonged effort to prevent this appointment, wanting instead to appoint someone with a knowledge of the work the Crown corporation did. He urged that if the Prime Minister's Office wished to reward the individual they favoured, they should appoint him to the Senate, to which the response was that there were no vacancies among the Senate seats for the province from which the individual came.

Then one morning Pépin opened his newspaper and saw that a senator from the province had died. He arrived at his office with a look of triumph. To his staff he explained, "It is not permitted to ignore a sign from Providence." Unfortunately, Prime Minister Trudeau, himself the product of a Catholic upbringing and education, chose to place a different interpretation on the senator's demise, and proceeded with the appointment of the chairman as he and his political advisors had desired.

In dealing with some other proposals for political appointments, Pépin fared better, but his general approach led some of the more hard-edged partisans in the government to be dismissive of his political instincts.

┼┼┼┼┼┼┼┼┼┼┼┼┼┼┼

Two weeks after the announcement in Winnipeg, radio station CFQC in Saskatoon announced that it had obtained copies of three of our Cabinet memoranda, including the one of January 12 that presented a comprehensive picture of our proposed "systems solution" and how we intended to proceed. In the ensuing weeks other documents became public; on March 11 the *Manitoba Co-operator* reported that it was receiving various "brown envelopes" containing government papers.[16] However, when we went back over the documents involved we found nothing that could be construed as a "hidden agenda," or that contradicted what the minister and officials had been saying in public for months.

These were not the only leaks we had to contend with. The briefing book prepared for the prime minister's trip to Saskatchewan in March 1982 also found its way to station CFQC, as did a public opinion poll we had commissioned some months before.

In government, the rule of thumb when a leak occurs is to think of who would stand to benefit from it and/or who was opposed to what was going on. The immediate assumption of officials in Transport was therefore that the source was Senator Argue's office. It was a plausible assumption, although no conclusive evidence ever came to light. In any case, the leaks did us no harm, and on reflection I derived from them a lesson in public administration: just because people find out what you intend to do does not mean they can stop you.

While the reaction of the media and the agricultural organizations to the government's initiative was fairly favourable, the political reaction was another matter. The New Democratic Party denounced it as "a destructive plan, not only for the prairie provinces, but for all of Canada," and, ignoring Snavely's series of studies on railway costs over the past eight years, went on to declare that the railways' claim that they needed more money to improve the system was "a complete and deliberate fabrication."[17] The Saskatchewan legislature, including the Liberal members, passed a resolution denouncing the federal initiative, and the provincial minister of Agriculture, Gordon MacMurchy, launched a series of community meetings to stir up opposition to the proposed changes.[18] In company with Ed Broadbent, the leader of the federal NDP, he also attacked Dr. Gilson and called for his removal, as did the Liberal leader in Saskatchewan, Ralph Goodale.[19]

In Manitoba, the legislature in which the NDP had a majority passed a resolution condemning the federal proposals. The opposite reaction might have been looked for from Alberta, but there the provincial government largely remained on the sidelines, to the frustration of Unifarm and other agricultural organizations in the province. The provincial ministers of Agriculture and of Economic Development in Alberta were strongly in favour of Pépin's actions but were constrained from expressing their support in public by Premier Lougheed's very cautious approach. Among federal officials, we conjectured that the explanation lay in the provincial government's very strained relations with Ottawa over energy matters. Another possible explanation was that a western separatist movement had emerged in the province, and a separatist candidate had recently won a provincial by-election. A plausible inference was that the premier did not want to risk angering pro-Crow grain producers in the province and drive them into the separatist camp.

At the federal level, the Progressive Conservatives were deeply divided at the time of Pépin's announcement and remained so to the end. Some of their MPs, such as Bert Hargrave of Alberta, and Jack Murta and Charles Mayer of Manitoba, openly supported Pépin's initiative, while Saskatchewan members, such as Alvin Hamilton and Bill McKnight, were opposed. Notwithstanding their divisions, the party used an opposition day on February 26 to put forward a motion that the House "condemns the government for abandoning the historic and statutory rights of Western grain producers." Ignoring the initiation of the Gilson consultations and the months of meetings that had preceded them, the party's motion went on to attack the government for proceeding "without producer participation."[20]

In a perverse way, the fact that the federal Liberal caucus west of Ontario included only two elected MPs from Winnipeg—Lloyd Axworthy and Robert Bockstael—proved to be an advantage. If Pépin had had to cope with the electoral fears of, say, eight members from rural Saskatchewan plus perhaps a few others from Alberta, he might have had even greater difficulty than he did in securing Cabinet approval for what he considered had to be done. As matters stood, the Liberals had virtually nothing to lose in the West and perhaps even stood to gain if in the longer term their reforms of the western grain system were to yield positive results. And by early 1982 a number of ministers and Liberal MPs had come to think that Pépin's initiative, rather than being politically dangerous, might in fact become a political plus. Lloyd Axworthy arranged for his Committee on Western Affairs to meet in Winnipeg in connection with the February announcement, and the attendees included a number of ministers in addition to the regular members.

In mid-March Prime Minister Trudeau spent several days in Saskatchewan, during the course of which he addressed the provincial Liberal Party and held several public meetings. As matters turned out, the prime minister's visit was less than helpful to our cause. In his statements and speeches he continued to say, as he had in previous years, that the government would act on the Crow only in response to a western consensus and that any specific actions would be governed entirely by what westerners wanted. He thus took no cognizance of the policy statement that his Cabinet had approved. The implication of his public comments was that the government still had no assessment of the future needs of the western railway system, that it had no objectives of its own, and that it would limit its actions to those things that the West (undefined) asked it to do.

His personal lack of interest in the whole Crow issue could not have been more clear.

In addition, judging by media reports of his speeches, the prime minister did not at any time refer to his minister of Transport or express support for him.

The Pools were not slow to see the opportunity that the prime minister's statements had presented to them. On April 2 Ted Turner sent him a letter expressing great satisfaction with the public position that the prime minister had taken. He then went on:

> You said that if grain producers indicated to Professor
> Gilson that they do not want variable rates, there will be
> no variable rates. You also said that if there is consensus
> of who should get federal payments, it will be heeded...
>   ...your position on the variable rates and payments question
> is so positive and the consensus so clear, you should be able to
> accept these as settled, removing them from the discussions
> with Dr. Gilson.[21]

In effect, the entire Gilson process, and the policy framework that was to guide it, were now in question.

When the letter arrived in Ottawa, officials of the Privy Council Office and the Department of Transport met to discuss what kind of reply could be made. Our eventual conclusion, in which the prime minister apparently concurred, was that his statements to the audience in Regina had been off-the-cuff and did not take precedence over the collective decisions of the Cabinet that had led to the policy statement and the terms of reference for the Gilson consultations. The consultations therefore remained on track. But it was an episode that we could have done without.

Cobbling Together a Consensus

THE CONSULTATIONS LED BY Clay Gilson in the spring of 1982 were a watershed in our efforts to modernize the Crow system. All our activities for nearly two years had been directed to establishing the kind of consultative process that he was to lead. The report that he produced in June 1982 affected in one way or another everything that happened afterwards.

The government's policy statement of February 8 constituted the framework within which the consultations were to be carried out. The statement began by describing the strong economic growth in the West and the resultant pressures on the railway system. It went on to observe that matters had reached the point where the charges to producers under the 1897 freight rate now covered only 20 per cent of the costs of moving grain by rail with the result that, if no action was taken, cumulative railway losses could come to $2.4 billion over the next four years. Unless the railways had sufficient revenues to expand their system to handle the increased traffic that was widely foreseen, the consequences for the West could be very serious.

Under the heading, "The Government's Approach," the statement set out the following seven principles that the government believed should guide remedial action:

1. *A statutory framework should be created by Parliament to to the new arrangements...[for providing] compensation to the railways for moving grain.*
2. *In accordance with proposals made to it by the major producer organizations...the Government of Canada is prepared:*
   a. to commit itself by statute to the payment on an annual basis of an amount equivalent to the 1981–82 shortfall in railway compensation; and
   b. to enter into discussions with the producer organizations and the railways concerning ways of meeting cost increases incurred in the fiscal years beyond 1981–82.
3. *While the government is prepared to bear a substantial part of the cost of grain transportation in future years, its resources are limited. An increased contribution by grain producers will be required.*
4. *In return for being compensated, the railways will be required to take action on several fronts...*
5. *The economic distortions within the agricultural sector stemming from the Statutory rate should be reduced...*
6. *The new framework to be developed should promote increased efficiency and economy in the operation of the grain transportation system...*
7. *Nothing in the new arrangements shall affect the existing Government's financial commitment for branch line rehabilitation [and the purchase of]...an additional 1280 hopper cars in 1982.*[1]

The statement committed the government to spend $1.85 billion under existing programs and to allocate an additional $1.35 billion, for a total of $3.2 billion, over the next four years. It also announced the appointment of Dr. Gilson and provided an illustrative list of the subjects that could be dealt with in the consultations that he would be leading. Following the statement's release in Winnipeg, it was widely publicized across the West.

It was clear from the outset that the issue of increased charges to producers would play a major part in the consultations. There were, however, two other issues that were at of at least equal and perhaps even greater importance in relation to the future of the grain transportation system and for agriculture in western Canada. One was captured in principle five, which spoke of the need to reduce the economic distortions stemming from the Crow rate. The other was in principle six, which called for increases in the efficiency of the grain transportation system.

These two sensitive issues also figured in the list of subjects that the policy statement suggested should be dealt with in the consultations. Using wording that we had chosen with exquisite care, the list spoke firstly of examining "possible suggestions from Western agricultural associations concerning variable rates consistent, however, with the principle that such rates should not work to the detriment of the individual producer."[2] Secondly, the list of subjects to be discussed included "the manner in which the Government will expend its contributions"—a reference to the question of whether the government's subsidy should be paid entirely to the railways, or whether it should, in whole or in part, be distributed among grain producers, who would then use the subsidy to meet the compensatory freight rates that the railways would be allowed to charge under this system. These two subjects were connected, and their inclusion in the policy statement was bound to make the consultations more difficult and complex.

The problem was that in 1982 western Canada had an inefficient and costly system for handling and transporting grain, comprised of some 3,000 country elevators at 1,295 railway loading points that were served by a large number of high-cost branch lines. For decades, prairie communities had been typically served by "mixed freights" comprised of grain cars, cattle cars, boxcars for general freight and mail bags, and a passenger car. Such a train would take an entire day to cover a railway division of some ninety miles (135 km), with stops at some twelve to fourteen communities along the route at which some cars would be dropped off and others picked up. In the 1960s a process of rationalization got underway, with the movement of much general freight being progressively taken over by trucks, and the movement of passengers by buses. As a result, the railway branch lines were increasingly used only for grain, but they nevertheless had to be kept open due to political interventions by governments. The railways therefore had to continue collecting grain at a large number of small delivery points—a typical country elevator such as the one at Carstairs could load only ten cars per week.[3]

A study done by railway costing expert Carl Snavely at the request of the Department of Transport in 1982 found that the variable costs of moving grain on the Canadian railway system were 40 to 60 per cent higher than on railways in the United States.[4] In another study, Snavely reported that the cost of moving grain on branch lines was 30 cents per ton-mile, compared to 21 cents on the more efficient Canadian lines. These figures represented averages. There was anecdotal evidence that on some inefficient lines the cost of handling and moving grain exceeded the value of the grain being moved.

Attempts to increase the efficiency of the system often met with resistance. The construction of a large new terminal with the capacity to handle high volumes of grain efficiently at Weyburn, Saskatchewan, in the 1970s had been greeted with alarm and hostility by many, who regarded it as a threat to the rural way of life, notwithstanding the finding in the 1977 report of the commission led by Emmett Hall that consolidation of the system into a network of such terminals could substantially reduce grain handling costs.[5] In the same vein, the Canadian Wheat Board, which controlled grain car allocations, resisted the assembly of grain cars into what were known as solid trains (trains made up entirely of grain cars). Although this was an efficient way of moving grain to the terminal elevators at export points, the board aligned itself with those who opposed a rapid rationalization of the system. In one year in the early 1980s the Burlington Northern Railroad just across the border in the United States operated over 1,200 solid trains while the Canadian Wheat Board allowed just three.[6]

In a speech at a conference in Edmonton in September 1982, I remarked that matters had apparently reached the point where Canada had a grain handling and transportation system that no one could afford: not the railways, not the producers, not even the government. My speech earned me a reproving letter from the Alberta Wheat Pool, but Snavely's figures spoke for themselves.

Officials in the Department of Transport had no view about the amount of financial support the government should provide to the grains and oilseeds industry on the prairies. Our only pre-occupation was that any system of support should not jeopardize the western railway system, as the Crow was doing.

How the proposed government subsidy would be delivered—the "method of payment," as the issue was commonly called—was relevant both to the future efficiency of the system and the eco-nomic distortions caused by the Crow rate. The essence of the Crow system was that it subsidized the shipment of raw grain from the prairies. In doing so, it had detrimental effects on other components of the western economy.

A long-standing grievance of agricultural processors, such as oilseed crushers and the livestock industry in the West, was that the Crow rate had the effect of increasing the cost of the grains they had to buy. This was because the cost of grain on the prairies was the international price less the cost of transportation, and since the Crow rate kept the cost of transportation artificially low, the cost of grain on the prairies was commensurately higher than it other-wise would have been. To illustrate, using over-simplified figures, if the price of barley at the port of Vancouver were $100.00 per ton, and the cost of transporting it under the Crow rate was only $5.00, then the cost of barley to a livestock producer in Alberta would be $95.00, whereas if the railways were allowed to charge the full cost, say, $25.00, then the cost to the livestock producer would be $75.00.

In 1978 the Alberta Cattle Commission calculated that the Crow rate increased costs to livestock producers in the province by $85 million per year. For the same reason, agricultural processors on the prairies, such as those crushing raw canola to produce oil and meal, faced artificially high costs.

A further distortion resulting from the Crow rate was that it worked against agricultural diversification in the West. Anyone wishing to produce a crop like peas or lentils had to be prepared to pay a much higher freight rate than producers growing the six grains covered by the Crow. Despite this constraint, crop diversification on the prairies began to take place in the 1950s but at a pace slower than would have been the case under a normal freight rate structure.

Studies by the federal Department of Agriculture found that if the distortions caused by the Crow rate could be eliminated, the net benefit to the prairie agricultural economy, even after absorbing increased transportation costs, could be as high as $170 million per year.[7] Politically, of course, there could be no question of eliminating the distortions by simply abolishing the Crow rate. Another way of getting this result, however, would be to allow the railways to charge fully compensatory rates for moving grain and to offset the increased costs to producers by distributing the government's subsidy to them rather than paying it to the railways. Under such a system, producers could ship their grain to export points by rail, but they would also be free to use it for other purposes if they saw fit, such as feeding it to their cattle, or trucking it to a processing plant in their region. In one way or another, a system of payments to producers would introduce market forces to a degree that had previously been excluded in the prairie grain economy.

Such a system could, however, have important consequences for the Pools' system of country elevators.

Because the Pools were co-ops and subject to direction by their producer members, they regularly came under pressure from their members to make uneconomic decisions. Thus, in November 1981 the chief executive of the Saskatchewan Wheat Pool announced at the annual meeting that the Pool would construct six new elevators and eight new annexes to existing elevators and would refurbish twenty-two others—even though, as he acknowledged in his statement, the elevators in question would be marginally economic at best.[8] By this date there had been a good deal of downsizing of the elevator system, and the leaders of the Pools knew that more had to come, but they wanted it to take place in ways and at a pace that would protect the large investments they had made on behalf of their members. What greatly concerned the Pools was that a system of payments to producers could result in rationalization proceeding at a pace that they would be unable to control. Ted Turner warned that a system of payments to producers would force "a massive consolidation in the grain handling system."[9] The risk would be even greater if at the same time the railways were given freedom to vary their charges on the basis of the actual cost of moving grain on any particular line. And in the eyes of the Pools the one would inevitably lead to the other. If the producers had the government's subsidy in their pockets, they would wish to put it to the best use, which would lead them to seek cheaper rates on the more efficient railway lines. The effects on large numbers of small country elevators located on inefficient branch lines could be devastating.

Warnings about the degree of rationalization that could be unleashed by changes to the existing system had considerable resonance with residents of prairie communities, who were alarmed at the prospect of losing their local elevators and branch lines. It was from this concern that the Pools drew much of their political power.

Contributing to the mindset of community residents was the fact that for much of the twentieth century grain producers had largely been insulated from market signals. Because of the Crow rate, they were able to ship grain without regard to the actual cost of using inefficient branch lines. Similarly, the Saskatchewan Wheat Pool, for example, equalized its charges for handling grain so that producers all paid at the same rate regardless of whether they used old inefficient elevators or modern high-capacity structures. In the same vein, the Hall Commission had observed in 1977 that "marketing costs are masked and accrue to the system rather than the individual."[10] Because of such arrangements, the actual costs of preserving the status quo were largely invisible to prairie residents.

An adverse factor in the winter of 1982 was that there had been some erosion of the support for change in the months leading up to the release of the government's policy statement. The leaders of the major agricultural organizations were agreed that the climate had been better the year before and that there had been a significant loss of momentum following the refusal of the government in February 1981 to respond to the proposals that had been advanced by the prairie leadership.[11]

In a telephone conversation with me in the weeks following the minister's February 8 announcement, Ted Turner remarked, "Saskatchewan is exploding a little bit right now." He had been receiving a good deal of mail and phone calls that were often abusive. Before joining others at Gilson's table, he took the precaution of calling an extraordinary meeting of Pool delegates on March 11. While he obtained the mandate he sought, some five hundred angry Pool members held a separate meeting at which they denounced the action their delegates were taking.[12] At one point Turner left his meeting to speak to the dissidents and managed to lower the temperature somewhat. Nevertheless, in the Pool's election that spring, nine delegates were defeated.[13]

Grain producers were deeply divided on the subject of the Crow. A poll in February 1982 found that 48 per cent of producers believed that grain freight rates should rise, an approximately equal number believed they should not, and 77 per cent expected that they would.[14] However, it was those opposed to change who were the most vociferous and exerted the greatest pressure on their leaders. Indicative of the provincial split of opinion was a poll conducted by the Saskatchewan Wheat Pool in 1981 on whether the railways should be allowed to charge more than the Crow rate. In Alberta, 51 per cent of producers agreed, in Manitoba 55 per cent, but in Saskatchewan the figure was only 29 per cent.[15] The strength of anti-change sentiment in Saskatchewan was a major constraint on the leadership of the Pool.

Following the release of the government's policy statement in February, we received a report in the department that Turner and his executive had had a meeting with Premier Allan Blakeney and his minister of Agriculture, Gordon MacMurchy, concerning the high-decibel public campaign the provincial government was engaged in. Their message was, "cool it." They feared the provincial government might stir up their members to such a degree that the Pool's leadership would be forced into a position of all-out opposition to the federal initiative. The end result could be the federal government taking unilateral action that would be worse for the Pool's members than the controlled process represented by Gilson.

Turner was not alone in having to cope with dissent. At the beginning of April signs of a spreading revolt among Alberta Wheat Pool members led the leadership to convene a special meeting about the Gilson process. Here, too, the Pool did obtain a mandate to join the Gilson process, but only after a turbulent discussion.[16]

Something that none of us in the department had foreseen was that the cuts to VIA Rail made by the Cabinet the previous July would have an impact on the thinking of prairie farm leaders. Both Howard Falkenberg, the president of the Western Agricultural Conference, and Ivan MacMillan, the president of the Prairie Farm Commodity Coalition, warned that the federal government might take comparable action in relation to grain transportation unless the western stakeholders could come together and work out future arrangements.

They were not necessarily wrong. By the winter of 1982, Pépin's message was beginning to sink in with his colleagues. A number of ministers had come to realize that doing nothing, and leaving the western railway system to seize up a few years hence, was not an option and that if consultation failed to produce results then the government might well have to take action on its own.

It was the sense that change was bound to come that led even those grain producers who were opposed to the federal government's initiative to join in the Gilson consultations. Their leaders also recognized that if the point were reached where the railways had to begin rationing traffic because of congestion on their lines, grain would inevitably be accorded a lower priority than other commodities.

╫╫╫╫╫╫╫╫╫╫╫╫╫

THE TIMETABLE THAT we had agreed upon with Clay Gilson was that he should try to produce a report on his consultations by late spring.
His terms of reference required him to:

> *Identify and enhance the consensus among agricultural*
> *organizations:...and to propose to the government specific*
> *measures which in his judgement will most effectively achieve*
> *the objectives contained in the Government of Canada's*
> *Policy Statement on Western Rail Transportation...*
> *In developing the consensus, the Federal Representative must*
> *have due regard for the financial limits contained in the*
> *government's statement, especially the $ 3.2 billion the*
> *government is prepared to commit...*[17]

Although not explicitly stated, the message of the policy statement was that if the agricultural organizations, the railways, and other stakeholders in the West could come to an agreement that respected the seven principles, and did not cost more than the $3.2 billion, the government would implement it. Gilson began by extending invitations to participate in his consultations to nine major farm organizations, the two national railways, and an association representing a group of agricultural processing companies. Of those invited, only the militant National Farmers' Union rejected the invitation and instead submitted a written brief. All of those who participated chose to be represented at very senior levels, including the presidents of Western Agricultural Conference and Prairie Farm Commodity Coalition, the presidents of the three Pools, the president of the CNR, and an executive vice-president of the CPR.

During March Gilson held only one meeting that brought together all the participants in his process. The rest of the month he spent in bilateral discussions with them. The formal consultations began on April 1, and meetings were then held at intervals over the next six weeks. Advice was periodically sought from Carl Snavely and other experts.

An important feature of the consultations was that, as a result of a conscious decision by the minister and the department, there was no government representative at the table. Nick Mulder and Mike Farquhar from Transport, together with Howard Migie from Agriculture, attended the meetings as observers. They participated in informal conversations with Gilson and the participants during breaks, but they played no part in the discussions *per se*. On three occasions during the course of the consultations Gilson came to Ottawa for discussions with the minister and me, but these meetings took place at his initiative rather than ours.

The discussions led by Gilson were dominated by three issues:

1. *The amount of compensation to be paid to the railways.*
The producer groups sought to keep the figure as low as
possible, since producers would in future be paying a
percentage of this figure when cost increases occurred in
future years, while the railways, for their part, sought to
maximize their revenues.
2. *The share of future cost increases that should be borne*
by producers.
3. *The "method of payment"—whether the entire government*
subsidy should be paid to the railways or whether some
part of it should be distributed to producers.

It did not prove possible to arrive at a consensus on the first two of these issues, while on the third the Pools agreed only to consult their members about Gilson's recommendations.

On non-monetary issues the results were considerably better. Consensus was reached on a wide range of subjects, such as the nature of the guarantees to be given by the railways in return for being compensated, the statutory framework that should govern grain shipments in the future, and the need to establish a Central Coordinating Agency to oversee the workings of the system.

All participants found Clay Gilson to be an excellent chairman and credited him with holding the discussions together despite the sharply divergent positions of the various participants. He was personable, calm, and had the indefinable quality known as "presence." When difficult junctures were reached, he would call a recess and have private conversations with the co-ordinator he had engaged, Professor Ed Tyrchniewicz of the University of Manitoba, or with his executive assistant, Don Leitch, or with Nick and Mike, or with one or other of the participants. All of Gilson's meetings were held with no media present, and the participants without exception treated as private whatever went on at them.

Among the participants, Chris Mills of the Alberta Cattle Commission came to play a major role as an advocate of the government's subsidy being paid to producers rather than the railways. He was joined by other members of PFCC and UGG. At the other end of the spectrum were the three Pools, for whom Ted Turner became the principal spokesman. Not surprisingly, considering his constituency, he generally took a hard line. He recognized the need for change, but there were severe limits on how far it was politically possible for him to go. The railway representatives proved to be accommodating and constructive throughout, and they often helped the discussions along by producing factual information at short notice.

In a news release on April 16, Gilson reported that "the meetings have so far been strenuous as we have dealt with a large number of details in a candid and constructive way." He went on to say that "the participants are really committed to making it work."[18]

He was putting a positive face on what was proving to be an extremely difficult series of meetings. The discussions frequently became emotional, and at one point Gilson had to call a one-week recess because the Pools appeared to be on the point of walking out. As he searched for ways of keeping the discussions alive during his informal discussions with various participants and the federal observers, he acknowledged the stress he was feeling.

During the last half of May Gilson circulated a draft of his report and then convened a final two-day meeting to discuss it. In mid-June we received the final version in Ottawa.

In his report, Gilson stated at the outset that the CNR and CPR faced "a crisis in financing and rail capacity."[19] During the discussions considerable time was spent on the question of how large the railways' financial losses were and what level of compensation they should receive. Among the issues in play were what contribution grain should make to their "constant costs," and the highly technical issue of the railways' cost of capital. The Pools believed that the total

Dr. J. Clay Gilson.
DEPT. OF AGRIBUSINESS
AND AGRICULTURAL
ECONOMICS, UNIVERSITY
OF MANITOBA

level of compensation should be approximately $600 million, while the railways put the figure at $770 million. The participants were unable to arrive at agreement about this issue, and Gilson eventually settled on a figure of approximately $650 million.

Gilson went on to recommend that:

a) for the period 1983–84 to 1985–86, cost increases beyond the $650 million be shared equally between the federal government and the producers up to a maximum of 3 per cent annual increases for the producers; b) for the period after 1985–86, the shippers would pay the first 3 percentage points of cost increases and share equally with the federal government the next 3 percentage points of cost increases, with an aggregate maximum increase of 4.5 per cent

for the producers; c) any remaining cost increases be borne by the
federal government.[20]

Thus, if costs in a particular year were to increase by 5 per cent on the base of $650 million, charges to producers would increase by 3 per cent or $19.5 million, while the government would be responsible for the remaining $13 million. If after 1985–1986 costs increased by 10 per cent, producers would pay 3 per cent, amounting to $19.5 million plus a further 1.5 per cent or $9.75 million, while the federal government would pay $35.75 million.

On the controversial issue of how the government's subsidy was to be paid, Gilson recommended what he termed a "hybrid system," in which the railway revenue shortfall would be paid entirely to the railways in 1982–1983, after which an increasing percentage would be directed to producers each year until it reached 81 per cent in 1989–1990.[21]

An important and innovative recommendation made by Gilson was that the participatory process he had begun should be carried forward into the next phase, when the details of the new system would have to be worked out. For this purpose, he called for the creation of four joint task forces that would respectively deal with:

1. *The detailed freight rate structure that was to govern future shipments of grain;*[22]
2. *The functions of the Central Coordinating Agency that participants had agreed should be established to oversee the workings of the new system, including the performance of the railways;*[23]
3. *The specific elements of the system for paying part of the government's subsidy to producers;*[24] *and*
4. *The legislation that would be presented to Parliament to implement the new system.*[25]

A potentially troublesome component of Gilson's report was that it breached the $3.2 billion limit that the government had set on its contribution and called for the allocation of an additional $400 million, *inter alia*, for a fund to assist producers in making the transition to the system of payments that Gilson had recommended.

Viewed overall, Gilson's report represented a major achievement. Some observers in fact expressed surprise at the number of subjects on which he had been able to get the habitually fractious western participants to agree. Reduced to its essence, his process had gained the acquiescence of every major agricultural organization in the West, with the exception of the NFU, in the termination of the Crow's Nest Pass rate.

Especially remarkable was his achievement in keeping everyone at the table while the sensitive question of payments to producers was discussed. In his report he duly recorded that, "some organizations clearly indicated that 'pay the railway' was the only official position they could adopt."[26] This was unmistakably a reference to the Pools, but the presidents nevertheless agreed to take Gilson's report in its entirety for discussion with their members at special meetings.

Gilson's process had proved a success, one in which rhetoric gave way to a sharing of problems. Gilson's report gave us what had been our objective from the outset: a "made in western Canada" solution to the Crow issue. Even though the rather precarious consensus he had forged on a few key questions would fall apart later, his report provided a reference point for all our future actions.

My advice to the minister was therefore quite straightforward: "Nail your colours to Gilson's mast and sail him through the House of Commons." Pépin needed no persuading; his assessment was identical to mine. Accordingly, I moved to establish a "Gilson implementation committee" of officials from Transport and Agriculture, with Nick Mulder in charge.

The minister made Gilson's report public on June 28. Predictably enough, the release was immediately followed by an emergency debate in the Saskatchewan Legislature. The Blakeney government had been defeated at the end of April, and the minister of Agriculture, Gordon MacMurchy, had lost his seat, but the change was not for the better. Regardless of how we might have felt about the NDP government's all-out opposition to Crow change, its approach was consistent and clearly was driven by intense conviction. The Grant Devine Conservative government's expressions of opposition were no less strident, but its specific actions tended to be erratic and difficult to gauge. From our point of view, much of what it did appeared to derive mainly from political expediency, particularly since Premier Devine, as an academic economist a few years before, had been an open exponent of changing the Crow and of paying the subsidy to producers.

In Ottawa, the weeks following the receipt of Gilson's report were dominated by interdepartmental meetings of officials, discussions with the minister, meetings with the railways and the private sector task force on rail capacity, and trips to the West for discussions with agricultural organizations and provincial ministers. The resulting Cabinet document was classified as "ministers' eyes only," in the hope of reducing the risk of leaks.[27]

In preparation for the Cabinet committee meetings in July, at which our memorandum would be debated, I again had the department's graphics unit prepare a set of large charts, ignoring some mild jokes that had developed among staff about "Arthur's charts." From my point of view, they worked, which was what mattered.

In late July the minister and I flew to Edmonton for a meeting with the three Pools. As agreed at the end of the Gilson consultations, the presidents had taken the report back to special meetings with their members. On the question of increased freight rates on grain shipments, the response had been fairly realistic. The government's policy statement had been explicit that such increases were essential, and many members—albeit far from all of them— were resigned to the prospect.[28] They did, however, express criticisms of some of the specifics in Gilson's proposals.

The impact that Gilson's financial recommendations stood to have on producers was actually fairly modest. In his report he recorded that in 1981 farm cash receipts on the prairies had totalled

$9.5 billion, while farm costs had been $5.6 billion. Of the latter figure, only $150 million, or about 2 per cent, represented the cost of shipping grain under the Crow rate. Thus, an individual producer with 1,000 acres (405 hectares) under cultivation who was paying $1,500 to ship his grain in 1982–1983 would under Gilson's formula be paying $2,175, or $675 more three years later, as compared with a forecast increase of $8,000–10,000 in his other costs during the same period.

What had generated the strongest opposition at the Pools' meetings had been the proposal for payments to producers. As Pépin and I were preparing to file into the meeting in Edmonton, I had a brief, private conversation with Ted Turner. He simply shook his head and said quietly, "I couldn't sell it." In their presentation to Pépin, the presidents of the Pools described producer payments as "absolutely unacceptable." In addition, although Gilson had not in fact raised the question of variable rates in his report, the Pools went beyond the careful wording of the Western Agricultural Conference position on this subject and called for an outright prohibition on variable rates.

Among producers, views about a system of payments to producers were more divided than the Pools' demands might have suggested. A survey taken by the Alberta Wheat Pool found that 57 per cent of its members favoured payments to the railways, while 43 per cent favoured payments to producers.[29]

The reaction of the Prairie Farm Commodity Coalition was the opposite to that of the Pools. They gave wholehearted support to the proposal for payments to producers on grounds that this would stimulate an overdue rationalization of the grain handling and transportation system. We welcomed the Coalition's support, but we were also conscious of the reality that when it came to political power the big battalions were the Pools.

The railways' response to the report was negative on the subject of Gilson's financial conclusions. The figure of $650 million that he had settled on was close to that advocated by the producers but far below the $770 million that the railways regarded as their requirements. Both the CNR and the CPR issued statements expressing disappointment in Gilson's financial recommendations. A vice-president of the CNR described Gilson's recommendations as "enlightened but parsimonious."[30]

One of the problems experienced by the railways during this period was that the economy had gone into recession, resulting in a sharp drop in their revenues from all sources, and they had had to cut back on their investment programs. Both the CNR and the CPR were therefore anxious to see the federal subsidy begin flowing in the latter part of 1982. The CPR in particular wanted to start work on their major tunnel project through the Selkirk Mountains, which would take up to five years to complete, but they were not prepared to do so until the Crow issue had been definitively dealt with. From the government's point of view, there was a silver lining of sorts to the recession: the decline in railway traffic pushed further into the future the day when CP and CN would hit their capacity limits. As a result, the one year delay produced by the Cabinet's insouciant decision in February 1981 to do nothing about the Crow problem did not have the consequences that it otherwise might have.

By July 9 our Cabinet document had been signed by the minister and sent to the Privy Council Office for distribution. The Committee on Western Affairs spent two meetings on it. Then it went before the Committee on Economic Development, which approved it and sent its decision on to the Cabinet for ratification. On August 4 the minister announced the government's decision.

Pépin's key recommendation to the Cabinet had been that it adopt Gilson's report as the basis for future action. However, he proposed that the government defer its decisions about the share of future cost increases to be borne by grain producers, and Gilson's recommendation that the government provide an additional $400 million for agricultural adjustments, until the Department of Finance's annual fiscal forecast in September.

In recommending adoption of Gilson's report, Pépin and his officials were fully conscious of the fact this approach would bring us into conflict with the Pools. A safer course would have been to accept the Pools' demand that the government subsidy be paid to the railways—and indeed, in our initial thinking during 1980, we had concluded that such an approach, which was part of the proposals advanced by the Western Agricultural Conference that year, offered the best prospects of success. By the summer of 1982, however, none of us was attracted to this very conservative option. We found persuasive an analysis by the Department of Agriculture that the western economy would become more diversified and stronger if the distortions produced by the Crow rate were eliminated, and Gilson's proposals for payments to producers pointed the way to this result. In addition, his system, if combined with variable rates, held out the prospect of bringing about badly needed cost reductions in the grain handling and transportation system.

We knew that this approach entailed risks. Governments trying to deal with major issues of public policy quite often find it necessary to back off somewhat from their initial proposals because of opposition they encounter from one quarter or another. In the case of the Crow, we did the opposite. In obtaining Cabinet's approval to implement Gilson's recommendations, we were in effect raising the stakes halfway through the game. Whether this ambitious approach would succeed remained to be seen.

The Centre Cannot Hold

THE FALL OF 1982 WAS A PERIOD of hard slogging for the minister and the department, as we set about preparing to implement the government's decision to accept the Gilson report. The political climate in the West was more adverse than the one that had prevailed six months before. An October article in *The Western Producer* spoke of "the alliance between competing farm groups falling apart, the pools threatening to withdraw support for the package if they do not get their way, and some eastern farm groups and politicians trying to add an east-west dimension to the tension."[1] It was an accurate diagnosis. In particular, while there was agreement in the West that the Crow had to be dealt with, there was no agreement on what a post-Crow world should look like.

Our first task, and the one that proved the least difficult, was to obtain the additional funds that Gilson had recommended. The government's policy statement of February 8, 1982, had specified $3.2 billion as the amount that it was prepared to make available over a four-year period to establish the post-Crow system. However, the outcome of the Gilson consultations had resulted in a requirement for an additional $400 million, mainly to facilitate the transition to the system of payments to producers that he had designed. In late September I wrote to the deputy minister of Finance about this requirement.

As the government department responsible for the functioning of the economy, Finance fully recognized the importance for the Canadian economy of bringing the Crow issue to a resolution and had given us strong support from the outset. Their minister, Marc Lalonde, was easily the second-most powerful minister in the Cabinet after the prime minister, not only because of the traditional pre-eminence of the Finance department but also because of a personal relationship between Lalonde and Trudeau that went back to the 1960s. At a meeting with Pépin at the end of September, Lalonde agreed to provide the additional $400 million.

His willingness to provide additional funds on this scale is evidence of the importance the Crow issue had acquired. During the same period that Lalonde took this step, the Cabinet was engaged in difficult discussions about how to cut expenditures in a number of other areas, partly because of the need to reduce the prospective deficit and partly because the government's fiscal situation had deteriorated as a result of the severe economic recession that had set in earlier in the year.[2]

Outside the government, however, the clouds were gathering. In the West, general opposition to changing the Crow was beginning to emerge. While it might have been expected that the months of public discussion and the Gilson process would result in producers getting used to the prospect of change and eventually accepting the need for it, in fact the opposite happened. A poll taken in the fall of 1982 registered a sharp increase in producer frustration.[3] Grain prices had fallen by 15 per cent, farm costs were continuing to rise, and interest rates were in double digits. Hard-pressed grain producers saw the prospect of increased freight rates for grain as yet another burden.

In effect, the passage of time had worked against us. However, it was impossible to see how we could have short-circuited the process. In the field of public policy the shortest distance between two points is often not a straight line. Had the government simply moved to legislate a solution to the Crow in 1981, it would have run into the same wall of opposition that Otto Lang did in the 1970s and that the National Energy Program did in 1980. The extensive consultations with farm groups in the West, the release of the policy statement inviting western participation in devising ways of dealing with the Crow issue, the public debate about optional ways of implementing change, and the Gilson process were all necessary if we were to avoid inflicting the kinds of scars caused by the National Energy Program.

During the autumn months of 1982, there were meetings of officials with agricultural organizations and the railways, discussions within departments about how to cope with the emerging opposition in Quebec, and consultations between Pépin and his colleagues, all with the objective of presenting the Cabinet with a comprehensive plan to implement the decisions taken the previous July. Gilson's report had provided us with a set of measures devised in the West, and our strategy was to implement his report as a package.

However, there was one area in which the government had to depart from Gilson's recommendations. This was his formula for sharing future increases in grain transportation costs, which called for producers to bear only the first three percentage points of cost increases in each of the first three years. Thereafter producers would share equally with the government the next three points, to a maximum of 4.5 per cent. In addition, producers would be required to pay all costs resulting from any increases in grain shipments above the 30.4 million tonnes forecast for 1982–1983, on grounds that larger grain sales would provide producers with additional income and thus enable them to meet higher transportation costs.

While Gilson's proposals for grain producers to pay a share of future cost increases elicited a good deal of opposition and were regarded as excessive by many in the West, the government's reaction was the opposite. Gilson's formula to limit the producer share of future cost increases would saddle the federal treasury with an open-ended commitment. Depending upon inflation and future volumes of shipments, the cost to the government could rise from the starting

"Crow benefit" of approximately $650 million to $1 billion per year by 1991–1992. The federal government was already running budgetary deficits of $20 billion, and such cost increases stood to make matters worse. Moreover, western grain would become the most heavily subsidized industry in the country once the payment of the "Crow benefit" got under way. The government was faced with the issue of what share of national resources should be allocated to this industry as compared with other potential claimants on the federal treasury.

After a series of Cabinet committee discussions in the fall of 1982, ministers settled on a formula whereby instead of Gilson's proposed schedule of 3–3–3 per cent for the first three years, and then a maximum of 4.5 per cent in each year after 1985–1986, producers after that year would pay the first six percentage points of annual cost increases, plus half of any increases above 6 per cent. In adopting this formula ministers knew they were courting trouble, but they felt they had no choice, given their fiscal situation.

This was a fateful decision in two respects. First, unlike all previous steps by the government in relation to Crow reform, this one was taken without any consultation with western stakeholders. Second, it tipped large numbers of producers and their leaders into a position of strong opposition to the government's initiative and thus greatly strengthened the resistance that we faced. From this point on, the gap between what the government thought it could afford and what producers were willing to pay became unbridgeable and, if anything, progressively widened.

The other major flashpoint for opposition in the West was Gilson's proposal for paying much of the government's subsidy to producers, rather than simply subsidizing the two railways. Although this proposal had been strongly rejected by the Pools' members at their July meetings, it was one of the central features of Gilson's report, and the federal government therefore endorsed it in its statement of August 4. These two developments—the shift of the financial burden to producers and the approval of Gilson's proposed system of payments to producers—marked the beginning of the end for the precarious consensus Gilson had put together. At the end of September, the three Pool presidents came to Ottawa for a meeting with Pépin. They urged him to reverse his position on producer payments and warned that he would encounter strong opposition from them if he persisted. Pépin affirmed the government's commitment to Gilson's "made in western Canada" solution to the Crow. He also argued that a system of payments to producers would do much more to stimulate the development of the prairie economy than simply subsidizing the export of raw grain by rail. In effect, both sides held to their established positions.

In contrast with the opposition of the Pools, Gilson's proposal was strongly supported by the Prairie Farm Commodity Coalition, which grouped some twenty organizations, such as the barley, flax, and canola growers, as well as the producers of non-Crow crops and the livestock industry. The latter were particularly agitated about the high feed grain prices that were one of the effects of the Crow rate, which they said had virtually destroyed the pork industry on the prairies and threatened to do the same to the beef industry if no action was taken.[4]

The issue became increasingly divisive, and western agricultural organizations began to tear themselves apart as time went on. The Alberta Cattle Commission withdrew from Unifarm, while next door the Saskatchewan Association of Rural Municipalities, which feared the impact of producer payments on prairie communities, withdrew from the Saskatchewan Federation of Agriculture, which favoured Gilson's report. A proposal by United Grain Growers to give Gilson's system a three-year trial went nowhere. In Manitoba the Pool withdrew from the Manitoba Farm Bureau, and the other two Pools were disposed to take similar action in their provinces if their position was not accepted. Howard Falkenberg, the president of Unifarm in Alberta was defeated in a January 1983 election, as was the president of the Saskatchewan Federation of Agriculture. The process of fragmentation continued into 1983 and beyond. In 1984 the Western Agricultural Conference was dissolved.

TROUBLESOME AS DEVELOPMENTS in the West were, a much more serious problem emerged in the East during the fall of 1982.

Our Cabinet document that had set the stage for the launch of the Crow reform process in January 1982 included a passing observation that, "Quebec has voiced concern about the potential impact that a change in the statutory rate may have on its livestock sector."[5] This was the biblical "cloud no bigger than a man's hand" that would grow into a tempest.

The two principal organizations representing agricultural interests in Quebec were the *Union des producteurs agricoles* (UPA) and the *Coopératives fédérées* (Co-ops). They had for some years kept a close eye on federal efforts to deal with the growing issue of the Crow's Nest Pass rates, and their attention increased sharply when the federal government announced its intention to modernize the Crow. In May the two groups presented a written brief to Gilson. The core of the concern in Quebec was that remedial action on the Crow could eliminate the economic distortion that kept feed grain prices artificially high on the prairies. The organizations claimed that if this were to happen, the Quebec livestock industry would lose a competitive advantage that it had enjoyed for many years.[6] The government's announcement on August 4 that it had accepted Gilson's report, including his system of payments to producers, set off alarm bells in the Quebec agricultural community, as it did—for quite different reasons—with the Pools in the West.

The two Quebec organizations accurately described the situation in a brief that they presented to the federal Department of Agriculture in August 1982, immediately after the government's announcement that it had accepted the Gilson report. Summarized, the brief stated: If the price of a tonne of barley at Thunder Bay were $150.00 and the cost of shipping it from a prairie point was only $5.00 because of the Crow rate, then the cost of barley to a livestock producer on the prairies would be $145.00. If on the other hand the grain producer in the West was required to pay the full cost of shipping grain to Thunder Bay, say $25.00, then the cost of barley to prairie livestock producers would fall to $125.00. The brief went on to analyze the effects of such a change on pork producers: production costs would shift in the West's favour by $5.81 per hog—a change that the two organizations said could "completely destroy the Quebec hog industry."

It is worth noting in passing that the arithmetic in this brief about the way the Crow kept feed grain prices artificially high on the prairies was precisely what so agitated the livestock industry in the West.

The UPA and Co-ops' arithmetic was incontestable, but the brief did not take into account the way in which North American livestock markets worked in practice. Contrary to the claims of the two organizations, the West was not in fact a competitor to Quebec in livestock production. Most agricultural economists regarded it as virtually certain that whatever increase in western production took place because of Crow reform would go south to nearby markets in the United States rather than travel across Canada to compete with Quebec pork. Moreover, since the West accounted for only 5 per cent of North American pork production, any increase in the West would have virtually no effect on continental prices. Insofar as beef was concerned, Quebec was a net importer, and if additional western supplies were to make their way to the province they would simply displace imports from the U.S.

A fear also expressed in Quebec by some, including Jean Garon, the minister of Agriculture, was that increased freight rates would raise the price of western feed grain in Quebec.[7] It was another piece of bad economics. The price of feed grain was set by international markets, and the cost of getting feed grains from the prairies to Thunder Bay was irrelevant. The price to Quebec producers was simply the international price at Thunder Bay plus the cost of getting the grain from there to Quebec.

An additional factor in the public debate was Gilson's recommendation that 81 per cent of the Crow benefit of $650 million plus the government's share of future cost increases should be paid to producers. Thus, not only would Quebec farmers lose their competitive advantage deriving from artificially high grain prices in the West, but, in the future, farmers in the West would be receiving a subsidy that Quebec producers would not. The fact that this subsidy was primarily to offset the loss of the Crow and the imposition of compensatory railway freight rates was not relevant in the eyes of the Quebec organizations.

Following the federal government's August announcement, serious opposition began to emerge in Quebec. The UPA and Co-ops launched a publicity campaign, and media commentary became apocalyptic; Gilson's recommendations were described in major daily papers as *un coup mortel* (a fatal blow) to Quebec agriculture.[8] The minister of Agriculture said that these measures were the greatest threat to agriculture that Quebec had faced in many years and announced that he would organize a major conference to assess ways of defending Quebec's interests. At the end of September representatives of Quebec agriculture had a meeting with federal MPs from the province and got a good hearing. The UPA and Co-ops had thousands of buttons printed bearing the slogan, *Sauvons notre industrie agro-alimentaire* (Save Our Agri-food Industry) and distributed them in rural areas. There were alarmist speeches about "a drain of all agricultural activity out of the East to the West."

Matters were sometimes not helped by inaccurate media reports. At one point the French language service of the CBC carried a report that each grain producer in the West would receive a subsidy of $23,000.[9] In fact, the correct figure would have been in the order of $4,500, depending upon what was counted as a subsidy. In terms of interregional equity, a member of the minister's staff pointed out that this figure was well below the $6,300 subsidy received by the average Quebec dairy farmer that year.

Pépin and I were fully aware that, despite the misconceptions and badly flawed economics on which the opposition in Quebec was based, we faced a real threat. In early October I sent a lengthy letter to alert the secretary of the Cabinet, Michael Pitfield, to the controversy that was developing. I warned that "this threat to our flank [is] so serious that it could cost us the battle." I also expressed the view that Pépin's chances of persuading his Cabinet colleagues to support him were not very high and that he might have to ask the prime minister to intervene. In the event, Pépin never did so, and as events later unfolded it became clear that such a request would have proven unproductive. As had been the case from the very beginning, again we were on our own.

A particular difficulty we faced was that the minister designated by the prime minister to have the lead responsibility for the federal government in Quebec, André Ouellet, had responded to the rising political pressure in the province by stating that he would vote against a system of payments to producers.[10] In doing so, he publicly contradicted the government's decision taken scarcely two months before to implement the Gilson report. It was neither the first nor the last time that the normal rules of Cabinet solidarity were left in abeyance when the Crow was in play.

Officials of the departments of Agriculture and Transport began working on ways of dealing with the Quebec situation, and Agriculture held meetings with the UPA and the Co-ops. One of our misfortunes during this period, however, was that Gaetan Lussier, the former deputy minister of Agriculture, had recently been promoted to a larger department. Lussier had been deputy minister of Agriculture in the Quebec government when he was still in his early thirties, before moving to Ottawa. He was energetic, articulate, had a good grasp of the issues, and was well known to the players in the province. As a former provincial deputy minister, he had credibility with Quebec farmers, which the rest of us lacked, and he could have been a highly effective exponent of the federal position. One of the "what ifs?" of this period is what difference it might have made if he had still been in his job in late 1982, and whether by intervening at an early stage he might have been able to prevent matters from spiralling out of control. In public policy, as elsewhere, individuals do make a difference.

At the end of November the Quebec government convened the agricultural summit that it had promised. On December 2 all parties in the Quebec National Assembly passed a resolution supporting the conclusions reached at the summit.[11] On December 22 came an announcement that a "Coalition for the survival of the agri-food industry in Quebec" was being formed to fight implementation of Gilson's recommendations. The leaders also announced that a series of public meetings would be held in rural centres across the province during January and February of 1983.

The first meeting was held in Sainte Hyacinthe, an agricultural centre east of Montreal, on January 17. Some five hundred local farmers attended, and the meeting went on for over three hours. At another of the rural meetings a group of burly farmers blocked the exit and refused to let their Liberal member of Parliament leave until he had promised to vote against implementation of Gilson. In late January an agriculture sub-committee of the Liberals' Quebec caucus sent a letter to Pépin in which they expressed "very serious reservations" and said that the measures in Gilson's report would have "negative and disastrous" effects on Quebec agriculture.[12]

The coalition grew rapidly as a sense of alarm swept the province. In addition to the UPA and the Co-ops, coalition members soon came to include the Grain Dealers' Association, the Quebec Millers, the Order of Agronomists, the Quebec Chamber of Commerce, and the Consumers' Association. The veterinarians joined because if the Quebec livestock industry were to be severely affected, as everyone was predicting, their livelihood would be in jeopardy.[13] The Quebec government departments of Transport and Agriculture became members. The provincial Liberal Party expressed its support, as did the Desjardins Credit Union.

The expressions of alarm in the province reached a sort of apogee with an article in Le Soleil of Quebec City, which speculated that implementation of the Gilson report could cause such a reduction in western grain shipments that the economics of the St. Lawrence Seaway would be seriously affected, which in turn could put at risk the distribution system for all commodities in Quebec.[14]

While the sovereignist Parti Quebecois government was only too happy to lead the attack on the federal initiative, the opposition in the province went far beyond party lines. The provincial Liberal party gave its full support to the coalition opposing Gilson's measures, and before long the federal Quebec Liberal caucus joined it.

Quebeckers have a term for the phenomenon that swept the province in late 1982 and early 1983: *une levée de boucliers*—a throwing up of shields. The expression has a more active connotation than the English equivalent, "circling the wagons." It derives from Quebeckers' sense of insecurity as a minority in Canada. When there is a threat to Quebec as a collective, there can be a sudden closing of ranks by all segments of society in the province. For example, the crisis over bilingual air traffic control that convulsed the province in 1976 was a precedent that came to the minds of some in the federal Department of Transport. In such cases, data and rational economic assessments are apt to be ineffective. Pépin's efforts to demonstrate that his measures would have little if any impact were angrily rejected by Quebec farmers and their organizations.

The near-panic in Quebec stood in sharp contrast to the reaction—or lack of it—in neighbouring Ontario. Because Ontario is geographically closer to the West, it was in principle more vulnerable than Quebec to competition from the western livestock industry. However, the manager of the Ontario Cattlemen's Association said that the Gilson measures would have a negligible effect in the province.[15] In the ensuing months, neither the Ontario Federation of Agriculture nor the provincial government came out against Pépin's proposals.

ANOTHER PROBLEM THAT we had to contend with during the series of Cabinet committee meetings in the fall of 1982 was an initiative taken by Senator Hazen Argue. Without consulting Pépin or the Department of Transport, he developed and put before ministers in early November what he called a "Third Option." Its principal elements were:

1. *The government's subsidy would be paid to the railways;*

Senator Hazen Argue.
SASKATCHEWAN NDP
PHOTO ARCHIVES

2. *The Crow rate would be doubled immediately, after which there would be further increases until the rate reached 50 per cent of actual costs in 1990;*
3. *Grain transportation costs should be capped at 8 per cent of the price of grain; and*
4. *The subsidized rate would be extended to all specialty crops and their products.*[16]

The key component of the senator's option was the first: eliminating the proposal for payments to producers. The premise of his option was that many in the West were more opposed to producer payments than they were to increased freight charges. Consequently, Argue was ready to offer a schedule of rate increases that would be more expensive to producers in the near term than what Pépin had proposed.

Had Senator Argue confined his proposal to the privacy of the Cabinet room, it would still have been unwelcome but at least it would have remained within the bounds that are supposed to govern discussions among ministers. In fact, however, a member of his staff confirmed to the media that he had shared it with the Pools, with the result that it soon became public.[17] In the end, the senator's option did not gain much traction with his Cabinet colleagues. It did, however, begin to generate a surge of support in the West.

On December 7 and again on December 14 the Committee on Priorities and Planning chaired by the prime minister reviewed and eventually approved what Pépin had proposed.

For our Crow group in the department it was an important milestone, but our response to it was more subdued than when we had opened a bottle of champagne a year before to mark the launch of the government's initiative. We knew that we were in rough water and that we would be for some time.

Even as the Cabinet was moving toward approval of Pépin's proposals, he and I began to develop second thoughts. We were becoming increasingly worried about the growing opposition in the West and in Quebec and concluded that we needed to back off from some elements in our package to increase its acceptability. On December 22 we returned to the Cabinet table with a request for some last-minute changes. In the document he circulated, the minister proposed:

> 1. An adjustment to the cost-sharing formula to reduce the potential burden on producers, by deleting their responsibility to pay half of any cost increases in excess of 6 per cent per year; and
> 2. To cap the share of the government's subsidy that would be paid to producers at 50 per cent rather than the 81 per cent that Gilson had recommended, in order to abate the opposition of Quebec and the Pools; and
> 3. To subject these provisions to a review in 1985–86, with legislation being required to change them.

Our document explained that, "matters have now reached a critical stage, and it is important to avoid an outburst of controversy..."[18]

We gained the assent of the Economic Development committee on December 22 and went before Priorities and Planning the next day. The committee eventually approved Pépin's proposal, but the prime minister expressed considerable skepticism, asking, "Aren't you just going to create a new Crow?" by which he apparently meant that in watering down our measures we would largely be perpetuating the status quo.

He was to be of a quite different mindset four months later.

‖‖‖‖‖‖‖‖‖‖‖‖‖

JANUARY 1983 WAS largely given over to preparations for the announcement of the government's decisions about modernizing the Crow.

The Cabinet mandate Pépin had obtained included drafting instructions for the Department of Justice concerning the preparation of the necessary legislation. On January 26 our Crow group, in order to get away from our offices, repaired to a VIP railway car owned by the Department of Transport that was parked near the Ottawa station. There we spent the entire day, with food being brought in periodically, working on the design and content of the bill that would eventually be presented to Parliament.

Repeating the process of twelve months before, Jim Roche and I took to the West the draft text of the policy statement that the government proposed to issue, although the list of those to be consulted was shorter this time because the Pools and some other organizations were now in open opposition to what the government intended to do. In Saskatchewan, even the Chamber of Commerce had come out in support of the Wheat Pool. Jim and I had meetings in Winnipeg with the Manitoba Farm Bureau, the Prairie Farm Commodity Coalition, the United Grain Growers, and Otto Lang. On a subsequent trip I briefed the Manitoba minister of Transport and the Manitoba Pool, which, as the smallest and most moderate of the three co-ops, was still open to discussions about what the government was contemplating.

A factor we had to contend with at this stage was that a number of agricultural organizations in the West, some in response to pressure from the Pools, had withdrawn their support from the Gilson report and had gone over to Senator Argue's "Third Option." Among them were the Federation of Agriculture in Saskatchewan, and Unifarm in Alberta. On January 21 the Western Agricultural Conference, which in 1980 had opened the way for change by announcing a willingness to negotiate the future of the Crow rate, endorsed the Argue option by a majority vote, with the Manitoba Farm Bureau and UGG dissenting.[19] During the same week the Pools sent a telex to the government urging that it either adopt Argue's option or simply begin transferring funds to the railways while resuming discussions about the future of the freight rate.

None of these organizations apparently saw any inconsistency between their endorsement of the Argue proposal, which called for an immediate doubling of the freight rate followed by a succession of further increases in subsequent years, and their claim that producers could not afford *any* increase in transportation costs. The appeal of the Argue formula apparently lay in the elimination of the proposal for payments to producers and the stipulation that transport costs would not be allowed to exceed 8 per cent of the price of grain in any year.

In Quebec, opposition continued to grow despite Pépin's energetic efforts, which included a letter to all producers in the province that set out the federal proposals and provided data to demonstrate that they posed no threat to the livestock industry in the province. He also had meetings with Ouellet and the Quebec caucus. There were few signs that his efforts were producing results.

At the end of January the stage was set for our second launch, but there was considerably more room for doubt about our prospects for success than a year before.

Lost Reforms

THE MINUTES OF THE CABINET meeting held on January 26, 1983, just before the government announced how it proposed to proceed with reform of the Crow rate, include the following passage: "The Minister of Transport was congratulated by his colleagues for bringing this very difficult issue to a successful conclusion."[1] Two days earlier, the new secretary to the Cabinet, Gordon Osbaldeston, concluded a letter to me with an expression of congratulations for the part I had played in the events of the past months.[2]

Gratifying as these messages were to both of us, Jean-Luc Pépin and I knew that they might well be premature. We were by this time under no illusions that we would soon be able to declare victory.

No single word in English is exactly equivalent to the French term, "*echec.*" The *Robert and Collins Dictionary* lists as its possible meanings, "setback," "defeat," and "failure." Whichever meaning one chooses, the term is a useful descriptor of our experience during the first part of 1983.

On February 1, 1983, the federal government released a comprehensive public statement setting out in specific terms how it intended to proceed on Crow reform. The document was the successor to the general policy framework it had issued a year before and set out the conclusions the government had drawn following the extensive consultations with western stakeholders. It was the product of many weeks' work by officials in Transport, Agriculture, Industry, and Finance. Once again, the site for the statement was Winnipeg.

In some eighty-four pages, it set out the government's policy objectives, announced a financial commitment of $3.7 billion for the next four years, described the formula for the sharing of costs with grain producers, and forecast the economic impact in western Canada. It attached exchanges of letters between the minister and the presidents of the railways, in which the railways detailed the billions in new investments they would make in return for being compensated for hauling grain. There were charts, tables, a capsule history of the Crow rate, and much else.

The events of the day in Winnipeg closely paralleled what had taken place at the launch announcement a year before: we had a meeting in advance of the announcement with farm leaders , which was followed by a press briefing. The Saskatchewan Wheat Pool, however, was not in attendance, having boycotted the entire event.

In his public statements in connection with the release, Pépin continued to emphasize his conciliatory approach: "our policy makes a great attempt to be non-confrontational. It is full of compromises and hybrid formulas and phase-ins and phase-outs."[3] And, he might have added, commitments to reviews in future years.

The reception by the media in the West was positive. The *Winnipeg Free Press* described it as "a brave attempt to find a path between economic common sense and political reality."[4] A columnist in the *Calgary Herald* remarked, "The amazing thing is that Pépin has had success so far in his Crow rate reform efforts...using his wit, charm, patience, iron will, and sound economic philosophy."[5] The *Saskatoon StarPhoenix* said, "There is something exhilarating in witnessing history in the making" but added that with this sense came a "wrenching realization" that a pillar of the West was to be relegated to obscurity.[6] In Ontario the *Cornwall Standard Freeholder* described Pépin as "one of the most effective Trudeau Ministers."[7]

Arthur Kroeger briefing the press in Winnipeg, February 1, 1983.

The reaction in the agricultural community, however, was markedly less favourable than it had been to our launch of the year before. Our last-minute scaling back of the cost-sharing formula and of the system of payments to producers had no effect on the opposition, nor did the announcement of the additional $400 million required to implement Gilson's recommendations. The Pools and other organizations that were now arrayed against the government issued critical statements that particularly focussed on the prospective increases in what producers would have to pay. Some media commentators remarked on signs that a consensus was forming against changing the Crow. The Canadian Federation of Agriculture, reflecting the shift in the positions of its member organizations, came out against the government's statement.[8]

Senator Olson must be given his due for the skepticism he had expressed in 1980 about the support for change in the West. The consensus in support of Crow change was neither as deep nor as durable as we had thought. But at this stage we had no choice but to press ahead.

Following the announcement in Winnipeg, we flew to Saskatoon to begin a media tour of the West. Upon arriving at the hotel where his press conference was to be held, Pépin encountered two hundred angry members of the National Farmers' Union, who blocked his way and hectored him for half an hour before allowing him to enter. The next day we flew to Regina. Reports of four hundred NFU members at the hotel led Pépin to move his press conference to the airport. We then flew on to Calgary, made a stop, and went on to Vancouver. In each city Pépin held meetings with the media and "opinion leaders." In Vancouver we also briefed Gary Duke, who was one of the principal organizers of the private sector group of shippers known as the Task Force on Canada's Crisis in Rail Transportation.

Edmonton was the next stop. While the minister was holding his press conference in the Hotel Macdonald, several hundred members of the NFU assembled outside the room. Profiting from our experiences in Saskatoon, we decided to call for an RCMP escort. When the minister's press conference ended, we formed up at the door behind the police. The officer in charge was very explicit in his instructions: "Stay tight behind us and don't stop, no matter what happens." The door was swung open and we swept out within the flying wedge of police, while the protestors angrily shouted abuse and waved placards as we headed out of the hotel and into our waiting cars.

Not everyone approved of the NFU's tactics. In the *Edmonton Journal* columnist Don Braid wrote, "Pépin has waded through crowds of angry farmers without once losing his dignity...[he] acts like a gentleman and makes his opponents look like bullies."[9] His views were echoed in a *Journal* editorial. When Pépin returned to

Ottawa, he found a letter from the mayor of Saskatoon apologizing for the way he had been treated in that city.

The reactions of the western provincial governments spanned the spectrum. British Columbia, which had nothing to lose and could only gain from the changes, was solidly in favour. In Alberta, Premier Lougheed's continuing anger at the federal government's National Energy Program initially kept the province on the sidelines, but as the pressure against Pépin mounted, his government came out in support of him in mid-March—too late to affect the debate. In Manitoba the legislature passed a resolution opposing the federal initiative, but the NDP government's approach was generally quite low-key.

We had taken it for granted that Saskatchewan would be opposed. What we had not foreseen was the erratic manner in which the Devine government would deal with us. Before entering politics, Grant Devine had been on the faculty of Agriculture at the University of Saskatchewan. He had been a public proponent of changing the Crow and had advocated paying government subsidies to producers.[10] His deputy premier and minister of Agriculture, Eric Berntson, was reputed to be a free market–oriented farmer. We knew that despite this history, we could hardly expect that the Saskatchewan government would openly support us, but we thought it might be possible to find some measures that would abate their opposition.

Berntson was highly likeable, and Pépin's meetings with him were invariably cordial. It turned out, however, that there was no relationship between what transpired with him in private and what he would subsequently say in public. On the day the government's statement was issued, Berntson released a telex he had sent to Pépin describing it as a "sledge hammer blow" to Saskatchewan. He also made a number of alarmist statements, including one in which he forecast that the federal government's measures would result in a 60 per cent decline in the province's net farm income over the next five years.[11] During the months that followed he kept up a verbal cannonade, interspersed with friendly private meetings.

The Saskatchewan government's approach touched bottom for us in late February, when Premier Devine said in a television interview that he would prefer the status quo, including *ad hoc* projects and continued financial losses by the railways, rather than see the federal government's legislation pass. When the startled interviewer, wishing to ensure that he had not misunderstood, asked the premier, "Let the Crow gap continue, the railways cutting back service, and so on?" To which Devine replied, "Yes."[12]

Devine could not have seriously believed in the approach he was advocating. He must have been aware of studies, such as one by the federal Department of Agriculture that had found that measures of the kind that Pépin had tabled could add $1 billion per year to the projected level of agricultural production in the West by 1990. The adverse consequences for the West if railway losses were allowed to continue were recognized even by Pépin's opponents. Consequently, the *Saskatoon StarPhoenix* had some company when it characterized the premier's statement as irresponsible.[13]

Nevertheless, the Saskatchewan government was a reality that we had to deal with, and at the end of February Pépin and I flew to Regina for a meeting with Devine and Berntson to see whether there was any scope for accommodation with them. They suggested that we provide a safety net for producers whereby future increases in transportation charges would not be allowed to exceed a specified percentage of the price of grain and that we extend the statutory rate to specialty crops to encourage crop diversification. We came away from the discussion with an impression that if these changes were made the Saskatchewan government would tone down its expressions of opposition. We were to learn later that this impression was mistaken.

‖‖‖‖‖‖‖‖‖‖‖‖‖‖

WHEN THE FEDERAL government announced in August 1982 that it intended to implement Gilson's proposal for payments to producers, and when the Pool presidents were unable to dissuade Pépin from this course of action when they saw him at the end of September, the Pool decided to add a new component to their strategy, or as one journalist put it, to play their trump card. They moved to form an alliance with Quebec. Vice-presidents of the Saskatchewan and Manitoba Pools, some of whom were strongly opposed to change, held meetings with representatives of the Quebec coalition and were quoted as saying that there were good prospects for finding common ground.

This strategy had the potential to greatly strengthen the Pools' position, but it came with a price. A column in the *Calgary Herald* on September 25 carried the headline, "Joining up with East could be considered traitorous,"[14] and went on to say: "If they do unite, the pools will kill a reform movement aimed at expanding and diversifying Prairie agriculture." Similar stories were carried in other western media. *Alberta Report* accused the Pools of "accepting forty [*sic*] pieces of silver."[15]

An embarrassed spokesman for the Alberta Wheat Pool said that his organization would have nothing to do with any alliance with the East. The Manitoba Pool professed itself hurt by accusations of "selling out to Quebec." Pool spokesmen initially sought to downplay what was happening with comments along the lines of, "we're just having a few conversations," but before long it was evident to all that a *de facto* alliance had been formed. On March 23 a Saskatchewan Wheat Pool broadcast reported that representatives from all three Pools were lobbying the Quebec Liberal caucus in Ottawa.

The Pools were supported in their efforts by the Devine government. The provincial minister of Finance described Ontario and Quebec as "the soft underbelly" of the federal government, in the sense that the provincial governments in those two provinces, particularly Quebec, had the political clout to block the federal initiative. He therefore promised that Saskatchewan would concert with those provinces to defeat Pépin's proposals.[16] In March the government made good on this announcement. Berntson travelled to Quebec for a meeting with Jean Garon, the minister of Agriculture. He then went on to a meeting of Maritime ministers of Agriculture, at which he successfully persuaded them to come out against the federal government's measures.

Berntson made several further trips to eastern Canada to stir up opposition. One of them happened to coincide with a visit to Moncton by Pépin, who was to make a speech to the Federation of Canadian Municipalities.

When I saw the minister the next morning, he remarked, "Eric was in Moncton while I was there." He added, "I gave him a lift back to Ottawa on my plane."

"You *what*?"

Pépin shrugged. "It seemed like the civil thing to do."

I shook my head. "Is there no limit to your civility?"

And evidently there was not.

There were also some lighter moments. While going through his daily pack of media clippings and transcripts one morning, Pépin came across a transcription of a French language report that made no sense. It recounted that "the eight chickens are angry at the government because...," "the eight chickens insist that...," "the eight chickens will not tolerate..." Eventually it dawned on him what he was reading. The French term for eight is *huit,* and the term for chickens is *poules.* The radio broadcast had been about "les Wheat Pools."

The minister's account of this incident to the department later in the day caused us considerable mirth. Eventually I responded with a memo proposing to him that for the coming months our slogan should be, *Les huit poules sont devenues les trois dindes* (the eight chickens have become the three turkeys).[17]

This was not the only case in which a phonetic transcription was to cause us some amusement. When the prime minister in a press conference affirmed that, if a consensus about the Crow were to emerge in the West, it would be "heeded," the transcript rendered the last word as "heated." To which we in the department, after months of experience with the fractious western stakeholders, could only say, "Indeed."

As the controversy over the government's statement mounted in the West, the dialogue became somewhat less civil. The presidents of the Alberta and Saskatchewan Pools speculated in the media that ministers had failed to accept the Pools' demands because officials in Ottawa were withholding information from them.[18] Accusations of this kind are often made when interest groups fail to get what they want at political level, but they are still offensive because accusations of withholding information from ministers amount to one of the most serious allegations of unprofessional conduct that can be levelled against officials.

There could be no doubt that the Pools were under serious pressure from their members. At a meeting in North Battleford, Saskatchewan, three hundred angry farmers verbally attacked Ted Turner for "selling out." The meeting rejected not only Gilson's but Argue's option, as well. A similar meeting was held in Swift Current. The Alberta Pool also encountered resistance, although opinion in the province was more divided; some meetings denounced the Pool for opposing payments to producers and for allying itself with Quebec.[19] From UGG we received a report that their members were increasingly moving toward the Pools' position. The western media reported a poll that had found a "startling shift" in sentiment against the government's measures, combined with expressions of fear about the consequences of changing the Crow.

THE STRATEGY OF THE Quebec coalition was to stir up as much alarm and opposition as possible, and by this means to bring onside the Liberal MPs who held seventy-four out of the seventy-five seats in the province. The strategy worked.

Pépin made strenuous efforts to reassure an increasingly nervous Quebec caucus and to contain the opposition in the province. On January 19, 1983, he had a meeting with the caucus; on January 22 he dispatched a lengthy letter to agricultural organizations in Quebec; and three days later he had another meeting with the caucus.

And so it went on. At one point I was dispatched to Montreal, accompanied by officials from Agriculture and Transport, to try to persuade the UPA and Coopératives fédérées that the federal measures posed no threat to Quebec agriculture. We got nowhere.

I also elected to accompany the minister to several of his meetings with the Quebec caucus. As a general rule, caucus is off-limits for officials. In particular, participating in discussions with the government caucus about how to deal with the opposition parties constitutes partisan activity and is quite improper. However, I had for some years operated on the principle that it was permissible for me to be at my minister's meetings with members of his own caucus if the purpose was to assist him in dealing with unrest among them, just as I did when the minister was meeting with disaffected groups from outside the government.

At one such meeting there was an unexpected development. Shortly after we had sat down and the minister was beginning to speak, a messenger came in with a note. Pépin read it, said he had to excuse himself, and hastily left the room. I thus found myself in company with Howard Migie, left to explain the intricacies of our proposed system of payments to producers, in French, for the next two hours. The discussion with the caucus was cordial, but I did not come away with the feeling that I had changed anyone's mind.

An intractable problem for the minister and the department was that the analysis on which the federal proposals were based did not lend itself to snappy formulations. The factors that determined feed grain prices in Quebec, the effects of the Crow on prices in the West, and the likely markets for increased livestock production on the prairies, took longer to explain than most people were prepared to listen. Another source of difficulty was the subsidy that would go to producers in the West without any matching subsidy for Quebec. When it was explained that the purpose of the subsidy was to offset increased transportation costs after the Crow was gone, the response was apt to be, "Well then, why not just pay the subsidy to the railways?" which required an explanation of distortions in the West. And so the argument went around and around.

A related problem that Pépin faced during the Cabinet debates was a question raised by his puzzled colleagues from different parts of the country: if, as he claimed, his proposal for payments to producers would be the best option for the West, why were the Pools against it? The answer was not easy for ministers unfamiliar with the prairies to grasp. They found it even more difficult to follow Pépin's arguments that the fears of the Quebec coalition were groundless. And arrayed against him in Cabinet were two native westerners, senators Olson and Argue, who insisted that the Pools were quite right, and André Ouellet, who had aligned himself with the anti-change coalition in Quebec.

One of the realities of Canadian politics is that the Quebec caucus of any party always receives attention of a kind that goes beyond what caucuses from other parts of the country normally experience. Individuals who served in Prime Minister Trudeau's office affirm that when a message was received that the chairman of the Quebec caucus had called, the call was returned very promptly. At one point during the protracted controversy over the Crow changes, Pépin remarked to me about the "childish fear" of the Quebec caucus displayed by usually tough-minded senior ministers from the province.

A factor in the minds of some was an episode that had taken place in 1976. In February of that year, in response to pressure from the Department of Finance and the Treasury Board, the government had increased the levies paid by dairy farmers under the national dairy program. The following November, when René Lévesque's Parti Quebecois came to power for the first time, many Quebec MPs and ministers of the day believed that the dairy farmers had taken their revenge on the federal government by voting for the sovereignist PQ. The memory of this episode increased the sensitivity of the Quebec caucus to the pressures from the coalition. It also made them wary of economic prescriptions advanced by officials.

As the political tug-of-war continued, I at one point offered an encouraging comment to Jean-Luc—as I had come to call him when we were alone. "If the worst comes to the worst, and we lose the fight over method of payment, what you are doing will still prove important. Once the Crow has been replaced, your successors as ministers of Transport will not be carrying eighty-six years of prairie history on their backs when they deal with grain transportation issues. They, and ministers of Agriculture, will be able to make decisions simply on the merits of whatever situations they face without constantly looking over their shoulders at the past." In the 1990s this would prove to be a more prescient observation than I realized at the time.

|||||||||||||||||||||

ACTING ON GILSON's recommendation, the government had agreed to establish a set of joint task forces to work out the specific measures required to implement his report. The task forces were chaired by federal officials but comprised lawyers and executives from western agriculture and the railways. The Pools, despite their opposition to the government's measures, chose to participate in the task forces on grounds that this enabled them to argue from time to time that, "If you've got to do X, Y, or Z, at least do it this way." We welcomed their participation and benefited from their advice.

One of the joint task forces, chaired by an official from the Canadian Transport Commission, had the task of working out the detailed rate structure that was to be the successor to the Crow. A second developed the specific functions of the Central Coordinating Agency that Gilson had recommended to oversee the workings of the post-Crow system. A third on the method of payment could not be established because of the deeply divided views about the subject in the West, so it was agreed that the Pools could submit a set of proposals of their own, while a group favouring producer payments would submit another.

The most unusual step the government took was to accept Gilson's recommendation for the creation of a fourth task force that would be responsible for preparing the legislation to implement the new system. Ordinarily, the drafting of legislation is kept strictly within the government, on the principle that Parliament should see a bill before anyone else. In the case of the Crow, however, representatives of all the principal stakeholders worked on the bill for many weeks with officials from the departments of Justice, Transport, and Agriculture. In late February 1983 I took over the chairmanship of this task force and saw its work through to completion.

During this period the government had the benefit of a lot of high-quality legal advice at no cost to itself. In addition to the lawyers from the grain companies, the railways, and other stakeholders, one member of the task force was Otto Lang, who had been Dean of Law at the University of Saskatchewan before going into politics and becoming a minister. Another member named Marshall Rothstein was a Winnipeg lawyer who had specialized in transportation and who in 2006 was appointed to the Supreme Court of Canada.

The unorthodox manner in which the Crow legislation was prepared would serve us in good stead when the bill went before Parliament and the legislative process got underway. During the committee hearings we were often able to explain in response to questions by the opposition parties that provisions in the bill were not simply the work of officials but reflected a consensus that had been arrived at in the legislative task force.

The task force included a clause that provided a small opening for the introduction of variable rates by the railways. The issue of variable rates had always been highly contentious for the Pools and some others in the West, who feared that allowing the railways to charge less for shipments on low-cost lines could pose a threat to inefficient branch lines and the communities located along them. To reassure those who entertained such fears, the government had included in its policy statement a commitment that rates for grain transportation would be "generally distance related." When I discussed this question with Nick Mulder and his Crow group, we concluded that the term "generally" allowed us some scope to depart from a rigid distance formula. Accordingly, we came up with a provision that in cases where a shipper and a railway were able to agree on a rate that was below the level prescribed in the rate schedule, the railway would be allowed to move the grain at this rate. We took care to draft the clause in such a way that the initiative for any rate reductions would have to come from shippers and not the railways. We also provided that any party affected by such an agreement could lodge a formal objection to the reduced charge, in which case the matter would be adjudicated by the Canadian Transport Commission. To make the provision still more palatable, we added a provision whereby in the first three years discounts would be allowed only for weekend loadings and shipments outside the peak season.

Our justification for including this provision lay in the fact that, in its seven principles of February 8, 1982, the government had called for measures to increase the efficiency of Canada's high-cost grain transport system. When Senator Argue learned of the clause that would permit producers to seek reductions in rates, he angrily declared it to be "sneaky." Nevertheless, the Cabinet gave its approval to the provision when the finished bill came before it for final vetting.

▓▓▓▓▓▓▓▓▓▓▓

As SPRING APPROACHED, whatever time was not taken up with work on our draft legislation was mostly given over to the continuing problem in Quebec. Pépin held further meetings with the Quebec caucus, and officials in Transport and Agriculture turned their hands to devising some "safety net" provisions for inclusion in the legislation that would protect Quebec producers if it should turn out that they were being adversely affected by western competition. By this time the Cabinet had also sought to abate the opposition in eastern Canada by authorizing the expenditure of $125 million on improvements to agricultural infrastructure in the East, of which $93 million was to be spent in Quebec.[20]

During this period there was also increasing discussion of the need for an advertising campaign, particularly in Quebec, to "get our message out"—a common reaction of ministers when a government faces public resistance. My own experience had been that advertising by governments to justify their actions almost never works, and I therefore expressed opposition to the idea of a campaign about the Crow. At one point during this period, I agreed to draw up a short, factual statement of the government's proposals that government spokespersons could draw upon in public discussions about the Crow. It was received with enthusiasm by political staffs when we met the next day, and someone said we should publish it. To illustrate my deep skepticism, I replied, "Minister, I personally wrote that document last night, and the contents are entirely accurate. But if you run it as a government advocacy ad, even I won't believe a word of it."

It was a losing battle. To counter the rising opposition in the West and Quebec, the government authorized a $350,000 campaign, including one advertisement with the boldface heading, "The Crow goes, without a flap." The campaign was received with derision by the public and the media, and earned the government a good deal of criticism in Parliament. The *Edmonton Journal* summed up the reaction of many when it rebuked the government for reducing complex issues to "slogans and rhetoric."[21]

The predictable failure of the advertising campaign left unanswered the question, which we never did resolve, of how a government *can* get public comprehension of controversial issues. The explanatory letters that Pépin periodically sent to grain producers in the West were apt to be returned to him with angry scrawls, "Stop sending me your propaganda!" His attempts to communicate with Quebec farmers met a comparable response. The government's case had solid analytical foundations but gained only limited acceptance. Although Pépin had the support of much of the western media, this, too, proved ineffective.

In April a delegation of 120 came to Ottawa from Saskatchewan. It had been organized by the Wheat Pool and comprised representatives of municipalities, business, and non-governmental organizations. They bore a petition with over 100,000 signatures that called upon the government to drop its Crow proposals.

The principal message in the petition was that producers could not afford to pay more for shipping their grain. When the group met with Pépin, he raised the question of how the Pool reconciled this assertion with their acceptance of Senator Argue's "Third Option," which called for an immediate doubling of grain freight rates, followed by further increases in the subsequent years. He did not find the response very convincing, and it seemed clear that acceptance of rate increases was being offered as a concession to stave off payments to producers.

The Pools' critics in the West accused them of simply behaving as grain companies that feared the impact that a system of producer payments could have in forcing a rationalization of their extensive network of country elevators.[22] The leadership of the Pools rejected such accusations. Ted Turner insisted that they at all times sought to act only in the interests of producers. This claim raised the issue of how to define "the interests of producers," but there was a good deal of evidence in support of the Pools' position.

The Pools' opposition reflected not only their own commercial interests but also the conservatism of their rural members. If the Pools had built and kept open too many country elevators, they did so in response to local pressures from their members. In his appearance before the Standing Committee on Transport in August 1983, Turner acknowledged, "This is one of the most difficult things we have to do—to go out and close an elevator."[23]

While the rationalization of the grain handling and transportation system under a system of payments to producers and variable rates would undoubtedly reduce the costs borne by producers, as the Hall Commission had acknowledged, there was always the possibility that these measures could also result in other changes that could have adverse effects. The most pervasive concern to producers was the negative impact that such measures could have on their communities, many of which had already begun to shrink in response to closures of elevators and railway branch lines. In the words of an analysis by the Ministry of State for Economic Development, "there is an inevitable resistance to change and a fear that removal of the Crow will loose uncontrolled forces disruptive of the organization of prairie life."[24]

A review of the prairie media during late 1983 and 1984 yields very little evidence that Pool members, particularly in Saskatchewan, wished their leadership to support a rationalization of the existing high-cost system. Indeed, the only major issue on which the leadership was pursuing a course that elicited criticism from a substantial body of their members was its agreement to treat the Crow rate as negotiable at all.

▉▉▉▉▉▉▉▉▉▉▉▉

ON APRIL 12 THE Committee on Priorities and Planning discussed the situation in Quebec, as did the Cabinet the following day. The minutes read, "The Prime Minister reported that there was a serious problem developing in the legislation on grain transportation. He said that the main issues included protection for livestock producers in Quebec..." At the end of a lengthy and diffuse discussion, the prime minister asked Pépin "to study the possibility of a change, but said that he would not countenance abandoning the entire initiative."[25]

Janet Smith, assistant secretary for Economic and Regional Development in the Privy Council Office prepared a long briefing note for the prime minister and sent it to me on for comments on Sunday, April 17. The note provided an extensive analysis of the issues in play and concluded, to my dismay, with a recommendation that the government drop the proposal for payments to producers. Her reasoning was that opposition had reached such a pitch that the government risked losing the whole initiative unless it backed off. In retrospect, her conclusion was probably quite justified.

Time was running short; our legislation was due to go into the House in a matter of days. On April 19 we had yet another meeting with the minister, and on April 20 the Cabinet with the prime minister in the chair discussed our Crow legislation in relation to Quebec. I was not present at the discussion, since officials other than those from the Department of Finance and the Privy Council Office are not normally allowed to attend meetings of the full Cabinet, but Pépin confirmed to me that discussion had not gone well.

The following day Pépin had a private meeting with the prime minister at which he raised the question of whether he could continue as minister of Transport if Cabinet rejected the existing draft of his legislation. The prime minister demurred and urged him to give up any thought of resigning.

On April 26 the Cabinet met again to discuss the Crow issue in relation to Quebec. I accompanied Pépin to the door of the Cabinet room and then sat down to wait in the anteroom. After perhaps an hour the minister emerged, looked across the room at me, and made a "thumbs down" gesture. The consensus of the prime minister and the Cabinet had gone against him. It was over. We had lost.

This outcome was a major setback from every point of view. Pépin found it especially painful that he would now have to let down people in the West, such as Lorne Parker of the Manitoba Farm Bureau, who had supported him throughout, some of them at considerable political risk. In economic terms, all of the analysis demonstrated that our proposal for payments to producers, which promised to stimulate crop diversification, agricultural processing, and livestock production would be far more beneficial to the West than subsidizing the railways to haul raw grain from the prairies to export points. And in political terms, the Cabinet's decision was going to cost us the support of our remaining allies among the agricultural organizations of the West.

For officials in the department, as much as for our minister, the Cabinet's reversal on producer payments came as a body blow. The qualities of objectivity and political neutrality that are mandatory for those who wish to serve as government officials should not be confused with an indifference to public policy outcomes. We were particularly dismayed because the fears felt by the farmers in Quebec, which had driven the Cabinet's decision, were clearly unfounded, as would be demonstrated in future years. So far as we were concerned, the Cabinet's decision was a clear case of politicians knowing the better and choosing the worse.

In recommending to the government that it implement Gilson's system of payments to the producers, the department and the minister had made a political judgement that the opposition of the Pools was not an insurmountable obstacle. I do not think we were wrong.

It is striking that when our legislation was before Parliament, the Progressive Conservative opposition in Parliament were sufficiently unconcerned about the Pools' position that in the fall of 1983 they sought to amend it to provide for their own version of payments to producers. Even in Saskatchewan, the government declined to come out in support of the Pools' position that the government's subsidy should be paid to the railways. The evidence suggests that we could have overcome the Pools' opposition had producer payments remained a purely western issue.

What proved decisive was the heavy intervention of Quebec. Unlike the West, Quebec was a political environment that Trudeau and many of his ministers understood, and the intense opposition of the seventy-four Liberal MPs from the province was more than the government could withstand.

The Cabinet's reversal lent credence to a view that had had some currency in the West for many years. When I was growing up in Alberta, I would periodically hear it said that not only was the West discriminated against in various fields, but if a situation should ever arise in which the West stood to gain an equal footing, the East (unspecified) would intervene to prevent this from happening. Even when I was living in Alberta these claims struck me as being far-fetched. During my years in government I was even more disposed to dismiss them. That said, what I witnessed in April of 1983 gave me pause. The stated objective of the Quebec coalition had been to prevent a reduction in the artificially high feed grain prices paid by livestock producers in the West. Many in the West took this as confirmation of what they had long believed about "the East." While the Pools came in for some of the blame for what had happened, there was also a view that the federal government had given in to Quebec's demands in order to keep the West at a disadvantage.

The day after the Cabinet's reversal, I had the grim task of chairing an interdepartmental meeting of officials on the amendments that would now have to be made to our legislation.

At the end of the day, shortly after I had arrived back at my office, Chris Mills of the Alberta Cattle Commission, Stan Price of the

Alberta Feed Grain Association, and Ivan McMillan, president of the Prairie Farm Commodity Coalition, turned up at my door.

All three had been among our strongest supporters during the battle over payments to producers. Now the battle had been lost, and we had been forced to go over to the other side.

They were carrying a bottle of whisky. Mills shook my hand and said, "This the last time we're meeting as friends. From now on, we're enemies." I got out some glasses, we opened the whisky, and sat down to hold a wake for lost reforms.

Democracy

ON MAY 6, 1983, A FRONT-PAGE story in the *Calgary Herald* described "a dejected Jean-Luc Pépin" who, under pressure from the Pools and Quebec, had been forced to redraft his legislation to provide that the government's subsidy for moving grain would be paid solely to the railways. The description of his state of mind was accurate.

"It's very sad. On this subject I was totally dedicated to the western interests," Pépin said. He went on to express the view that, despite his set-back, "a more valuable, labour intensive agricultural processing and livestock industry" would eventually "come to live in the West." He also observed that he had achieved a first in bringing matters to a point where Parliament would shortly be presented with legislation to modernize the 1897 Crow system; despite his setback he was determined to carry on.[1]

Following the Cabinet's adverse decision on April 26, events moved quickly. Within two days officials in the departments of Transport and Justice had prepared a document seeking Cabinet's authority for the specific amendments that would have to be made to our bill in the light of the decision to pay the entire federal subsidy to the railways. We also began work on the text of a statement that would formally announce what was already widely known in the West about the government's decision. Among those we briefed before the announcement were a number of prairie agricultural organizations, as well as Bruce Howe, the chief executive of BC Resources, and his vice-president, Gary Duke, who had been one of the organizers of the task force on rail capacity.

Cabinet approved the legislative amendments and the public statement on May 3. The minister held a press conference the next day. That evening he was scheduled to meet the presidents of the three Pools in Ottawa. I felt that I had nothing to contribute to this meeting and so left the minister to handle it while I went to Lisgar Collegiate's Music Night, in which my daughter's band was performing.

The government's decision to pay its subsidy only to the railways had the effect we had foreseen. The prairie livestock industry, agricultural processors, and others who had worked with us expressed bitter disappointment. They were joined by the Alberta government, notwithstanding that it had remained silent for months when the controversy had been escalating. In Saskatchewan the Devine government, which had given Pépin no support during the battle over payments to producers, now criticized the government's bill because it did not deal with the economic distortions caused by the Crow, and endorsed paying 50 per cent of the government's subsidy to producers by 1986, which was what Pépin had proposed.[2]

The Pools, having gained their principal objective, made it clear that they wanted other changes, as well. Their list was not short. They called for the government to prohibit variable rates, require stronger performance guarantees from the railways, reduce the share of future cost increases to be borne by producers, and eliminate the provision whereby the cost of grain shipments in excess of 30.4 million tonnes in any year would be borne by producers. They also expressed concern that the creation of the Central Coordinating Agency could impinge on the powers of the Canadian Wheat Board to allocate grain cars.

With the amendments to the legislation and the public announcement out of the way, the minister and the department began preparations for the introduction of the bill into Parliament. This was the moment of truth. Unless the legislation could make it through the House and Senate during the current session, all the effort of the past three years would go for naught.

A Canadian government that commands a majority in the House of Commons has, in theory, a virtually unlimited power to pass such legislation as it sees fit, subject only to legal and constitutional constraints. The reality is somewhat more complex. The principal weapon at the disposal of the opposition parties is delay, which can be brought about by a number of parliamentary tactics, such as the presentation of an endless number of petitions. The party that holds the status of official opposition derives an additional power from the convention that a vote cannot take place until the whips of the government and official opposition signify to the Speaker that they are ready. If the official opposition chooses not to so signify, no vote can take place and the bells summoning members to a vote continue to ring. In March 1982, in a major confrontation with the government over its legislation to implement the National Energy Program, the Conservatives repeatedly refused to turn up for votes, and the jangling of the bells continued for two weeks before an accommodation was reached between the Conservative opposition and the Liberal government.

If the principal constraint on a government is the risk of being seen as high-handed, the constraint on an opposition is the risk being seen as obstructive. When a contentious piece of legislation is in play, some subtle judgements have to be made by both sides, at times on an almost daily basis.

On Monday, May 9, following the daily question period, the minister tabled Bill C-155 in the House of Commons and moved that it be given first reading. Ordinarily this step is a formality and merely serves to place a bill before Parliament; it is at the second-reading stage that debate takes place. In this case, however, the NDP opposed first reading and demanded that a vote be taken. The Liberals were caught by surprise and found that they did not have enough members in the House to carry the vote. It was a Monday and a number of members were still on their way back to Ottawa from their constituencies. The Liberals had to delay the vote for seven hours by not having their whip signify that the party was ready for a vote. When they finally did so, however, the Conservatives elected to absent themselves, which had the effect of precluding a vote for the rest of the day. In so doing, the Conservatives, in effect, decided to repeat the tactics they had used the previous year against the National Energy Program.

On the day Pépin moved first reading, the bells rang until 10:40 PM, when the Speaker suspended the sitting. The next morning the bells began to ring again. Finally, after some twenty hours of delay, first reading was approved by a recorded vote. It was only the third time in fifteen years that a vote had been required on first reading. The episode was a harbinger of the battles that were to come. Both the NDP and the Conservatives were set on mounting an all-out opposition to the bill, although their respective motives were very different.

The NDP had a deep emotional commitment to the Crow rate. To them, it was essential for the survival of many grain producers and their communities on the prairies, as well as being a fundamental part of the West's history and a component of the Confederation bargain—in Carl Snavely's phrase, "a constitutional right." The party's declared policy was that the government should offset the CPR's losses from moving grain by making annual purchases of equity in the company. The policy did not address the question of what was to be done in the longer term. As Pépin put it in a speech to the Saskatchewan Association of Rural Municipalities, "one day, the taxpayers would end up with 100 per cent ownership of one of the finest money-losing enterprises in the country." In the same speech, Pépin went on to the role of the government's Crown corporation, "to say that the federal government should simply cover CN's costs is no answer. This assumes...that the Government of Canada has limitless amounts of money available. It doesn't."[3]

From the outset of the legislative process on C-155, the NDP openly stated that it would use every possible tactic to obstruct, delay, and, if at all possible, thwart the passage of the bill.

The Progressive Conservatives were in the last stages of a leadership contest at the time that C-155 came before Parliament. Their *de facto* leader for purposes of the bill was therefore Don Mazankowski of Alberta, who had been minister of Transport and who would in future years hold very senior ministerial posts, including Transport again in the period after the 1984 election.

The party's position on grain transportation was, on the face of it, not very different from that of the Liberals. In the election campaign of 1979, their platform had stated that the railways should be compensated, that the benefits of the statutory rate should be preserved, and that there should be extensive consultations with producers.[4] All of this sounded pretty much like what Pépin had been doing between 1980 and 1983, including the government's commitment to annual "Crow benefit" payments of $650 million per year. In 1979 Mazankowski had declared that the statutory rate should remain until there was a consensus for change—a formulation that would have been instantly recognizable to anyone who followed Prime Minister Trudeau's statements on the subject in the early 1980s. However, the Conservative Party's public position was sufficiently general that it still left plenty of room for criticism of anything the Liberals might propose.

A complicating factor for the party was that its MPs from the prairies were deeply split on the subject of the Crow. Members such as Bert Hargrave and Blaine Thacker from southern Alberta, where cattle-raising was a major industry, strongly supported Gilson's proposal for payments to producers. Manitoba members such as Jack Murta and Charles Mayer held a similar position. In British Columbia there was near-universal support for retiring the Crow by whatever means. On the other hand, the party's Saskatchewan contingent, led by such members as Bill McKnight and Len Gustafson, were against changing the Crow rate. The party therefore recognized that it was hopeless to try to establish a unified position and instead adopted a stance that called for its MPs simply to represent their constituents.[5] The result was what Mario Dumais of the *Union des producteurs agricoles* in Quebec once accurately termed, "one party with three policies."[6]

A further constraint on the party was that the government's decision to modernize the Crow had general support in the business community, with which the Conservative Party had long-standing links. The shippers of bulk commodities in major industries, such as coal and forest products, felt particularly strongly about the need for Pépin's legislation. The governments of BC and Alberta were also onside, as was—in a less explicit way—Ontario. For the Conservatives as a national party, these were not constituencies that could be ignored. On the other hand, there were many grain producers who were opposed to changing the Crow, and the Conservatives had to guard against being outflanked on the prairies by the NDP.

Whatever inhibitions the party might have felt in light of these factors were, however, overridden by one consideration. The government's defeat at the hands of the Pools and the Quebeckers had put blood in the water, and the Conservatives now saw the possibility of making a kill. They therefore opted to join the NDP in all-out opposition to the bill, in the hope of inflicting a major blow to the Trudeau government. This approach was, of course, very welcome to those members of the caucus who were in any case opposed to changing the Crow. For those Conservatives who favoured change—and other members of their caucus for whom western grain transportation was pretty much of a puzzle—the prospect of beating the Liberals took precedence over other considerations. A foreseeable consequence of this approach was that the Conservatives stood to inherit the Crow issue if they were to win the election that was expected in 1984. But this was a problem for another day.

A major task for the department in the first part of May was the preparation of the speech the minister would give to open debate on second reading. We put considerable effort into developing a comprehensive and articulate statement of the government's case, leaving it to the minister and his staff to add whatever partisan content they saw fit. The audience for the speech was nominally the opposition parties that would be voting on the bill, but this was only a theoretical consideration. The era in which parliamentary speeches persuaded anyone who was not a member of the speaker's party was long gone. The real audiences for the speech we working on were the media and the public outside Parliament and, within it, the minister's Cabinet colleagues and caucus whose support would become essential when the going got rough.

Following the vote on first reading, the government's House Leader, Yvon Pinard, who had responsibility for the management of the government's legislative program, set May 12 for the beginning of the debate. That day I went to the officials' gallery in the House and watched as the minister rose in his place and, with immense pride, moved second reading of Bill C-155, also to be known as the *Western Grain Transportation Act*.

The minister was followed by Mazankowski, who set out fourteen reasons why his party opposed the bill. He criticized the government for placing an excessive financial burden on grain producers, expressed opposition to variable rates, and advanced a "freedom of choice" proposal that would have allowed producers to choose between receiving the government's subsidy themselves or having it paid to the railways.

An interesting sideline to the second-reading debate was that, despite the intensity of the clash between the government and the opposition, the opposition parties went out of their way to depersonalize it. Charles Mayer of Manitoba began his speech by saying, "I believe, as do most members of the House, that [Jean-Luc Pépin] is a very honourable gentleman, well respected on both sides of the House." Les Benjamin of the NDP, too, declared that his criticisms should not be taken personally by the minister.

The debate continued for a second day and then, after the weekend, resumed on Monday, May 16. At that point the government made a major mistake, driven by its desire to have the bill become law before the summer parliamentary recess so that the new system could take effect on August 1, which was the beginning of the 1983–1984 crop year. The minister of Agriculture, Eugene Whelan, announced that, because the government had been unable to reach agreement with the opposition parties on the time to be allocated to the bill, it would move the following day that debate be limited. The House erupted, with opposition members expressing outrage at the announcement of time allocation after only three days of debate. In taking this step, the government played into the hands of the opposition parties by giving them a reason to delay the bill that had nothing to do with its merits. The issue now became the rights of Parliament rather than the Crow rate.

The following day a Conservative pro-change MP from Alberta, Blaine Thacker, moved the adjournment of the House. Under parliamentary rules, such a motion is not debatable, and the bells began to ring for a vote. The Conservatives declined to appear and the bells continued to ring until 6:00 PM, when the Speaker suspended the sitting. This was only the beginning. From that time on, whenever the bill was brought forward, the two opposition parties engaged in a variety of tactics that prevented debate from taking place. The Conservatives raised procedural issues, the NDP used up endless amounts of time by presenting one petition after another. On May 24, when the House Leader presented a motion to resume debate, the Conservatives again refused to appear for the vote and the bells rang for the rest of the day.

The opposition's tactics elicited some criticism in the West. The president of the Manitoba Pool described their actions as "childish," and there were reports that the provincial Conservative caucus in Alberta had tried to persuade its federal counterparts to desist, without success. The blockade went on.

The government was stymied. The House Leader took to calling other bills for debate in order to get on with legislation that the government had pending.

The Cabinet discussed the parliamentary situation at its weekly meetings, and Pépin reported that some ministers had begun to express doubts that the blockage could ever be overcome. The caucus was showing no stomach for a prolonged fight, and some members were restive at the amount of legislative time that was being burned up by a bill that was of little interest to them. We received reports from Privy Council Office officials that the prime minister appeared to be ambivalent.

The minister and I compared notes frequently about the outlook. On May 20, with his approval, I went to see Tom Burns, the president of the Canadian Exporters' Association, who had taken over the chairmanship of the private sector task force on rail capacity. The outcome of the meeting was a decision by Burns to organize a delegation of chief executive officers to come to Ottawa and press for passage of the legislation. The Pools had demonstrated their effectiveness in lobbying; now it would be the turn of other major industries, such as forest products and mining.

On May 25 the Cabinet authorized Pépin to announce two measures intended to soften resistance to the bill in the West: the government would amend the legislation to provide a "safety net" whereby rail transportation costs could not in future exceed 10 per cent of the price of grain and to make a number of specialty crops such as alfalfa and mustard seed eligible for the statutory rate.[7] As matters turned out, the tactic was unsuccessful: the 10 per cent level was widely criticized in the West as being too high, and the announcement about specialty crops merely elicited demands that still more products be added. It was neither the first nor the last time that government concessions made in the hope of garnering support instead simply gave rise to demands of one kind or another for "more."

Speaking to me after the May 25 meeting, the minister described with dismay the irresolution of his colleagues in relation to the impasse. Janet Smith of the Privy Council Office, who had been one of the recording secretaries at the meeting, shared my impression that the government was increasingly disposed to drop the whole project. Some ministers were recorded in the minutes as saying that "if the bill runs into further problems, the government will be able to say that it tried."[8] There was also some discussion of proroguing Parliament and beginning a new session, which effectively would have killed the bill.[9]

Media commentary was also turning against the bill. Representative of the trend was an editorial on May 25 in the *Saskatoon*

StarPhoenix, which in the past had given qualified support to Pépin's proposals for change. Under the heading, "Crow reform too divisive" it read: "Perhaps it's time the many antagonists in this mess collectively threw up their hands in recognition of the fact that the present initiative to kill the statute and rebuild the Western railway system simply will not work. That would mean abandoning for now the goal of a vastly improved transportation system. But the odds are growing that it is going to happen anyway."[10] The chairman of the CNR, former MP and minister Jack Horner, put the legislation's chances of passing at 30 per cent. A columnist in the *Calgary Herald*, Bob Parkin, wrote on May 30: "The momentum and confidence which once characterized the bid to rework the system are gone."[11]

On May 25, the private sector delegation on rail capacity organized by Tom Burns arrived in Ottawa. Their chairman was Bruce Howe, the chief executive officer of BC Resources. The thirteen other members included the CEOs of major corporations, some of whom had also been elected to speak on behalf of bodies such as the Canadian Manufacturers' Association and the Canadian Chamber of Commerce. I briefed them over breakfast the next morning, and they then began to make their rounds. Their first meeting was with Pépin and the minister of Finance, Marc Lalonde, at which I sat in. The prime minister joined the meeting after the first half hour.

I came away from the meeting uncertain about how to read the outcome. The prime minister had remained largely silent for the first part of the meeting, but toward the end he said the delegation represented a very important step and encouraged them to continue their activities. I was, however, left in doubt about how much support we could expect from him in the coming weeks.

The delegation then repaired to a meeting room to prepare for their discussions with the opposition parties. At noon they had a meeting with the NDP and then went on to a lunch discussion with the Conservatives.

Pépin and I remained pessimistic. On a trip to Quebec City the next day we discussed our Crow initiative, largely in the past tense. At one point the minister, referring to the personal role I had played

In the spring of 1983, it appeared that the Crow would once again triumph over its assailants. Cartoon by Phil Mallette.

in the past three years, used the phrase, "If you had been able to pull this off, ..."

Then reports began to come in that changed our perspective. When we returned from Quebec, Tom Burns and Gary Duke in separate calls told me that their meeting with the Conservatives had gone well. A large number of members turned out, and their leaders were well prepared. The key point that emerged in the discussion was that the Conservatives denied they were trying to stall the legislation—a claim that caused me to raise my eyebrows, but I let it pass. The Conservatives had stated that the key issue was the government's attempt to impose time limitation, and they implied that if this threat were removed they would end their blockade. They added, however, that since only a few weeks remained in the spring sitting, Parliament could not be expected to pass the bill before the summer recess. Burns thought that the size and composition of the delegation had probably made an impression on the Conservatives.

The next major development came at the weekly Cabinet meeting on June 1. Janet Smith called me to report that the prime minister had opened the discussion of the parliamentary situation with a combative statement: "We are not going to be defeated on this one."[12] No ground would be given. If the opposition maintained their blockade, the government would if necessary have the House sit through the summer. One way or another, the bill was going to pass. His fighting words rallied the Cabinet, and there was a burst of applause around the table.

It was a major turning point. During the preceding three years the prime minister's indifference to the Crow issue had caused us a number of problems, but he had now come through at the most critical juncture in the entire exercise.

More than two decades after the event, it is not possible to do more than speculate about what led the prime minister to become so steely. Given his past record, a strong interest in the contents of Pépin's legislation would be an improbable explanation; all past evidence suggested that, if anything, the subject of transportation bored him. Possibly Bruce Howe's delegation had made an impression on him by demonstrating that, while there was opposition on the part of many in the western farming community, there was broad support in the country for what the government was trying to do. The most plausible explanation, however, would probably be Trudeau's combative nature. All who knew him remarked that whenever he found himself in a confrontation, he pushed back aggressively. Whatever the explanation, the events of that week were a watershed.

The day after the Cabinet meeting, the minister had a meeting with Mazankowski, who identified parts of the bill that he would particularly like to see changed. He and Pépin also discussed the possibility of the House committee holding hearings on the bill during the summer months. The key subject, however, was the opposition's blockade, concerning which Mazankowski said that, in return for the government lifting its proposal for time allocation, the Conservatives would allow a vote on second reading "after another day or so of debate." This meeting cleared the way for the bill to be given second reading, even though it would be rather more than "another day or so" before the vote would take place.

During the week of June 6, the House Leader, perhaps wishing to allow the temperature to cool, scheduled debate on various other subjects. In any case, there was no longer any possibility that the bill could become law in time for the 1983–1984 crop year that would begin on August 1. After several days on other business, the House recessed for the Conservative leadership convention.

When the sitting resumed, Bill C-155 was brought forward for debate on June 16. The proceedings that followed bore a considerable resemblance to what had gone on in May, and the House began a series of sittings that went into the evenings. The NDP resumed its efforts to prevent debate by raising endless points of order and moving one amendment after another each day. In their manoeuvres they had at least the tacit support of the Conservatives, and on June 20 the Conservatives on their own initiative moved the adjournment of the House to tie up proceedings—all of which tended to confirm my skepticism about their protestations to Bruce Howe's delegation that stalling tactics were not part of their strategy. There was, however, an important difference this time. When it eventually came time for votes to be taken on the various delaying motions, the Conservatives showed up, and the votes were allowed to proceed. On June 21 the House sitting went on until nearly midnight. The next day the bill was finally given second reading. It had been six weeks since the minister had moved his motion.

#############################

DURING THE PROTRACTED period of parliamentary turmoil, there came a surprise development that affected me personally. On June 3 I had a call from the secretary to the Cabinet, Gordon Osbaldeston. He said he was going to have to make some changes of deputy ministers, and he wished me either to become deputy minister of Industry, or secretary of the Ministry of State for Economic and Regional Development (MSERD—the term "regional" and the accompanying responsibilities having been added in a government reorganization of 1982).

I remonstrated with him. "Gordon, this is crazy. You know that after three years of effort we've got legislation in the House to deal with the Crow rate. You can't move me now!"

His reaction was calm. "Take the Crow with you."

And so it turned out. My transfer was effective on July 1. From that day onward much of my time was given over to my new responsibilities, but whenever matters involving our Crow legislation came up they took precedence over current MSERD business, and Transport staff worked with me rather than my successor in Transport, General Ramsey Withers.

MSERD was what in government was known as a central agency, which meant that it was a member of the same family as the Treasury Board Secretariat, the Department of Finance, and the Privy Council Office. It had been created at the end of the 1970s, largely at Osbaldeston's instigation, and its functions were to co-ordinate the work of the dozen or so "line" departments in the government dealing with subjects like industry, fisheries, trade, communications, and, of course, transport. Osbaldeston had been the first secretary and had continued in that position until about a year before my appointment.

▟▟▟▟▟▟▟▟▟▟▟▟▟▟▟

FROM EARLY MAY onward, officials in the Department of Transport had been making extensive preparations for the parliamentary committee hearings that would follow second reading. The head of our legal services, Denis Lefebvre, and I examined various complex clauses in the bill to decide how they could best be explained to the committee. I wrote a "how it would work" paper, partly to clear my own mind, which explained how the producers' share of freight costs would be determined each year. From the Canadian Transport Commission, the regulatory agency that oversaw the railways, executive director John Heads came over to brief us on how the commission would calculate railway costs for purposes of rate setting. All of this activity resulted in our being very well prepared when the committee hearings got underway.

In parallel to this preparatory activity by officials, the minister had meetings with his parliamentary secretary and the chairman of the Standing Committee on Transport, which would have responsibility for our bill. During this period departmental officials provided a factual briefing to members of the Liberal caucus about the main elements of the bill. Under the rules that govern such activities, a briefing given to one party must be offered to all the others, which was done in this case, but none of them chose to accept, preferring to avoid being implicated in the government's initiative.

The legislative process in Canada calls for the second reading of a bill to be followed by the committee phase. This phase has two broad components: hearings about the general contents and effects of a bill, which usually involve the minister and officials from the sponsoring department, as well as interested parties from outside government, and then a detailed examination of the legislation, primarily with departmental officials, known as "clause-by-clause."

The standing committee held an organization meeting on June 28 and began to address the substance of the bill the following day.

The Conservatives fielded their "A" team. Their lead member was Don Mazankowski of Alberta. With him were Bill McKnight of Saskatchewan and Charles Mayer of Manitoba. They and one of their alternate members, Jack Murta of Manitoba, were all to hold ministerial posts in the future. Another alternate was Doug Neil of Saskatchewan, a very capable MP who was also highly knowledgeable about agriculture.

The NDP were entitled to only one seat on the committee, which at most of the sessions was filled by Les Benjamin. He was a former CPR station agent who harboured a deep populist dislike of the company. Throughout the many weeks of the committee's work, he continuously raised points of order, brought up procedural issues, and interjected comments into statements by others, all in pursuit of the NDP's declared objective of obstructing the bill to the maximum extent possible. In some of his statements he attempted a humorous tone, but I developed the feeling over time that he might have gained more support from other members of the committee, and thus been able to have some influence over the ultimate contents of the bill, if his interventions had been fewer in number and better considered. Some of his motions verged on being frivolous, and many were ruled out of order by the chairman.

The Liberals had five seats, which gave them a majority on the committee, reflecting their majority in the House of Commons. Their lead member was Pépin's parliamentary secretary, Jesse Flis. Although representing a Toronto riding, he was originally from Saskatchewan. His moderate and balanced personal style made him a good choice to lead the government side. Another Liberal member was Robert Bockstael from the urban riding of St. Boniface, Manitoba, who had been Jesse Flis's predecessor as Pépin's parliamentary secretary. He was also vice-chairman of the committee. The other three members of the committee were all from Quebec. They had only a limited interest in the substance of the bill, and their primary function was to make sure that some system of payments to producers did not get smuggled into the bill during the committee process by amendments, such as the "freedom of choice" measure that Mazankowski had proposed. Among the Liberals' alternate members was John Reid, member of Parliament for Rainy River—another future minister who proved to be a highly effective participant.

The chairman was Liberal Maurice Dionne from the Miramichi in New Brunswick. He was the ultimate plain Canadian in the best sense of the term: well endowed with common sense, entirely free of pretensions and ego, fair minded, and plain spoken. He was also very hard working and would keep the committee sitting until all the witnesses who wanted to be heard had had their say. The committee came to develop a high regard for him, and his rulings were invariably treated with respect, even on the rare occasions when a committee member chose to appeal one.

The minister appeared before the committee as the first witness when the hearings began, and then attended several of the subsequent sessions. Although he was the focus of the hearings, he also frequently turned questions over to his officials. No minister was ever more willing to share the spotlight with others. Pépin regularly spoke of himself as being only "the orchestra leader" and sometimes said—rather extravagantly—that he was surrounded by stars from the public service. Following his opening comments at the June 29 session, the committee gave me leave—over the first of many objections from Les Benjamin—to provide them with a half-hour overview briefing about the contents of the bill.

After these introductory sessions, the committee adjourned until July 26. Members of our Crow group thus gained several weeks of down time. In my own case, I spent much of the interval provided by the committee's recess in briefings about my new position in MSERD.

WHEN THE COMMITTEE resumed on July 26, the first witness was Clay Gilson. His statement was a model of moderation and balance. His calm manner, the plainness of his remarks, and his personal *gravitas* provided an insight into how he had managed to hold his disparate group together and produce a report that embodied agreement on a number of contentious issues. During the course of the meeting he remarked at one point that—as some of us in the department had suspected—those who had supported his recommendations and those who had opposed them had in both cases exaggerated the likely effect of implementing them.

Following Gilson's testimony, a succession of groups came before the committee: the Cattlemen's Association, the Trucking Association, the Canadian Manufacturers' Association, the Canadian Exporters' Association, and a group representing some 450 shippers known as the Canadian Industrial Traffic League. Their testimony was generally in support of the government's approach, although some criticized the bill for not going far enough. Those who were of the opposite persuasion would be extensively heard from when the committee began its hearings in the West.

The CPR and CNR also appeared before the committee. Predictably enough, they were subjected to abrasive comments by Les Benjamin, but other members of the committee were more restrained. Much of the questioning focussed on complex financial subjects, such as the cost of capital and the appropriate contribution for grain revenues to make toward meeting the railways' constant costs. Snavely had stated that a normal contribution would be 27.5 per cent to 35 per cent of variable costs. Gilson had eventually settled on a contribution of 20 per cent, which had been incorporated into the bill. Nevertheless, the general import of the opposition's comments was that the railways were being overpaid. It was easy for politicians to make this claim. The calculations involved were highly technical and involved a measure of subjective judgement, with the result that only a few specialists were in a position to challenge whatever assertions the opposition might make. In any case, no MP was much disposed to expend political credit defending the railways' revenues. When the minister sought to justify the bill's financial provisions by pointing out that they conformed to the established practices of the Canadian Transport Commission, he was dismissed by Mazankowski as a "bleeding heart for the railroads."[13]

The next phase of the committee's hearings took them out of Ottawa for two weeks. During the first two days in Edmonton the committee heard from twenty-five interveners, including the provincial minister of Agriculture, the Alberta Wheat Pool, the Chemical Producers' Association, and, among others, a delegation of thirteen from region seven of the National Farmers' Union. A woman from a rural community told the committee that she was not capable of using "eight cylinder words," but still wanted to be heard.

Many of the presentations set out the well-established positions of the various contending parties: the Alberta Wheat Pool opposed payments to producers, while spokesmen for the livestock industry supported them, as did the Alberta government. Symptomatic of our loss of supporters due to the government's reversal on this subject was a statement by the Alberta Cattle Commission that C-155 as presented would be harmful to the industry. The representative of the NFU, in company with others on the prairie left, rejected the data accumulated by Snavely and others, and flatly declared, "In my view, the railways have made money hauling grain."[14]

The next two days in Winnipeg were similar. The twenty-five interveners included the provincial government, the Winnipeg Labour Council, the United Grain Growers, the oilseed crushers, and the Diploma Agricultural Graduates' Association, together with the reeve of a small town and the president of a rural women's institute. In addition, thirty individual farmers from various parts Manitoba came to Winnipeg on the Saturday to express their opposition to the bill. A number of the presentations expressed deep concern that the new system would lead to the abandonment of railway branch lines and the destruction of small communities. At one hearing an official from the CPR observed a group of Hutterite women in a corner of the meeting room praying that the Crow rate would not be changed.

Most telling at the Winnipeg hearings was a thoughtful and carefully researched presentation by the president of the Manitoba Farm Bureau, Lorne Parker, who had been one of our strongest allies. He pointed out that the bill in its present form dealt only with the problem of railway capacity and left untouched the problem of economic distortions and the need for greater efficiency. He regretfully declared that, because of the changes requiring the payment of the entire government subsidy to the railways, he could no longer support the bill. At the end of his appearance, the chairman commented, "this is the most impressive session we have had from my point of view."[15]

The hearings in Saskatchewan took up four days and were the most intense. In all, the committee heard over one hundred presentations. Former Supreme Court Justice Emmett Hall, who had chaired a commission on grain transportation in 1977, appeared as the co-ordinator of the Crow Coalition. He declared that "all of Canada is at risk"[16] and that "nothing short of continuing either the Crow rate or a subsidy of equal value in perpetuity is necessary to sustain the industry."[17] He was convinced that if ever the Crow were allowed to become a matter of negotiation it would be only a matter of time until the entire benefit was lost. On behalf of the government of Saskatchewan, Deputy Premier Eric Berntson said, "This bill could have the most devastating and far reaching impact in the history of our province and perhaps of the country."[18] Ted Turner presented a comprehensive and well-prepared brief from the Saskatchewan Wheat Pool, which took a hard line. "No single agricultural policy issue has been as important to Saskatchewan farmers and the provincial economy as the statutory Crow's Nest Pass freight rate legislation...if our policy positions are not accepted, then the bill should not be proceeded with."[19]

Others heard from included rural municipalities, church groups, a variety of "Save the Crow" committees, the Swift Current Women's

Institute, eighteen separate locals of the NFU, fourteen locals of the Saskatchewan Wheat Pool, and thirty-nine individual farmers. One presentation was from the Family Farm Foundation founded by Gordon MacMurchy, who before his defeat in 1982 had been minister of Agriculture in the provincial NDP government. Many of the presentations in Regina were quite emotional, as had also been the case in Winnipeg.

A surprising number of the interveners during the prairie hearings believed that their grain freight rates were going to increase five-fold overnight, despite the efforts Pépin and the department had made to distribute accurate data to the public in the province. There was also a strong belief that the legislation would simply enrich the railways. During the Regina hearings, Liberal MP John Reid pointed out that in 1982 the CPR's return on equity had been 4.8 per cent as compared to 23.6 per cent for the Saskatchewan Wheat Pool, but this information had no evident effect on the hearings.

In this environment the Canadian Chamber of Commerce, which spoke in support of the bill, must have felt like a voice crying in the wilderness. The Prairie Farm Commodity Coalition and six of its member organizations, all former supporters, expressed deep disappointment at the turn of events that had forced a major change in the bill that the coalition had expected to support. The president, Ivan McMillan, said, "the government chose to base their legislation on politics rather than economics, and this is totally unacceptable."[20]

The great majority of the briefs heard by the committee during its tour of the prairies called upon the federal government to increase its expenditures in one way or another, in some cases by large amounts. Some proposals called for *all* crops grown on the prairies to be eligible for the Crow rate in the future. During the controversy Pépin at times tried to point out in public statements the need to maintain some kind of relationship between what the government did for the grain industry and what it did for other parts of the economy. On one occasion he expressed some frustration by remarking, "We're soon going to be spending $800 million a year. If it gets to be a billion, someone may notice."

The situation of prairie grain producers was that, although many of them were cash poor, they had on average considerably greater assets than the rest of the population. A survey by the Farm Credit Corporation in 1981 found that in terms of income, the farmers were fairly close to the rest of the population, with an average income of $16,676 versus $16,100 for an average Canadian family. The major difference lay in accumulated capital assets, which were $46,000 for an average family, as compared with $441,000 for a farm family. This disparity was a further constraint that the government had to take into account in assessing what scale of financial assistance it could provide to grain producers.

The one day that the committee spent in Vancouver was as dominated by briefs supporting the bill as the Regina hearings had been by briefs opposing it. The committee then went on to Quebec City for a final day. The principal intervenor was the coalition for the survival of Quebec's agri-food industry, which affirmed its opposition to any system involving payments of the federal subsidy to producers. The coalition also opposed the principle of using funds drawn from the entire country to support farmers in a particular region—apparently overlooking the federal government's dairy subsidy program, under which national funds provided a mainstay of farmers in Quebec and Ontario.

A low point of sorts was reached in the brief forwarded to the committee by the Parti Quebecois minister of Agriculture, Jean Garon. Earlier in the summer he had declared that a federal subsidy of $650 million for grain transportation in the West would be excessive and called for it to be reduced to $280 million. Now, in his August brief, he went further: "The method of subsidy to the railways, as proposed in Bill C-155, would have the same effects as the Gilson report and Mr. Pépin's proposal of February 1, 1983...We must return to the Crow's Nest Pass agreement of 1897."[21] Taken at face value, Garon's statement indicated that he wished to see the CPR and CNR's financial losses to continue, and to continue to increase, with consequences for the western railway system that were unmistakable. The minister's brief gave no indication that the adverse impact his proposal would have outside Quebec caused him any concern.

The coalition's position was marginally less severe than the minister's. They said that the bill would be acceptable if the final version incorporated the amendments they had called for, including a $20 per tonne subsidy for feed grains used in Quebec. If these amendments were not made, the coalition wished the status quo to continue.

Their absolutist position gave them something in common with a number of agricultural organizations in the West, each of which also insisted that the bill should not pass unless it was amended to incorporate all of the changes that the organization had called for— some of which were incompatible with the changes demanded by other organizations. Pépin accurately diagnosed the situation when he said that our problem was "too many 100 percenters."

During the course of its two weeks outside Ottawa, the committee had heard from 210 interveners and had received 245 briefs. No one who had asked to be heard was denied.

The committee was now ready to begin its clause-by-clause examination of the bill. Departmental officials in the Crow group—we had been preparing ourselves since late July—would move up to the firing line.

Where the Crow Lives

WHILE THE STANDING COMMITTEE on Transport was in Regina and Vancouver during the second week of August, I took a few days' leave. On Friday, August 12, Jean-Luc Pépin called me at home. He said that the prime minister had decided to carry out a major Cabinet shuffle and that he would be leaving Transport. He added, "Even more responsibility will rest on your shoulders now."

His new appointment was to be minister of state for External Relations. I had spent the first thirteen years of my government career in the Department of External Affairs (as it was called at the time) and knew what this meant. There were three ministerial posts: the minister of External Affairs, the minister of International Trade, and the minister of state for External Relations. The latter was the most junior position. Its incumbent's responsibilities included dealing with the francophone countries in Africa and filling in when the minister of External Affairs was not available for some task or other. It was the sort of post that might be given a bright young MP as a first exposure to being a minister.

I was incredulous. How could this possibly happen?

Pépin said that he and the prime minister had had several meetings in the past few days. The prime minister had asked him whether he intended to run again. Pépin replied that he probably would not, but he had not yet fully made up his mind. He then asked the same question of the prime minister.

The prime minister said that he was going to have to make his own decision before much longer. In the meantime, however, he had decided to make a number of Cabinet changes that would bring younger, energetic ministers to the fore and put a new face on his government. With regard to Transport, he wished to appoint Lloyd Axworthy as a westerner to take credit for the government's achievement—as it was now regarded—in modernizing the Crow system.

Why did Trudeau choose this course? Among officials who had worked closely with him during this period, the majority view is that he was intent on creating political conditions that would make it possible for him to seek a further term of office. In Pépin's conversation with me on August 12, he also said that he thought that the prime minister wanted to run again.

It was a quite plausible interpretation. The sweeping shuffle in which five ministers were dropped and nearly half of the Cabinet was affected in one way or another suggests that the prime minister's objective was not only to put a new face on his government but also to improve his own prospects for a further term in office. Otherwise, the normal course would have been for him to leave the renewal of his government to his successor. Some of his subsequent actions, such as the high-profile "peace initiative" that took him to a number of countries, also support the thesis that he was seeking to run again. Only in the late winter of 1984 when, as a former member of Trudeau's staff put it, "the numbers simply weren't there," did he take his famous walk in the snow and then announce that he would be leaving politics.

The Cabinet shuffle was announced shortly after Pépin's call to me on August 12. A few days later, I happened to encounter Gordon Robertson, who had retired in 1979 after a distinguished career in the public service that included eleven years as secretary to the Cabinet. He was puzzled by what had happened to Pépin and asked me about it. He listened as I recounted what the minister had told me, then he shook his head and said, "That must be the real explanation, all right. It's so shabby that no one would have made it up."

His reaction was echoed by many in the next few days, including the western media. Whatever views individual westerners might have held about the Crow, they respected Pépin and many liked him. Pépin received a large number of letters from the West praising his performance and expressing regret at his move. Among those he saved in his personal papers was one from Chris Mills of the Alberta Cattle Commission, who wrote, "The Crow reform process was a model of responsible democracy."[1] Members of the Liberal caucus also expressed their regard for him. In December 1983 the chairman of caucus wrote to the prime minister urging that Pépin be appointed Governor General.[2]

Officials in the Department of Transport were dismayed and some were angry at the way Pépin had been treated. The director general of Grain Transportation, Mike Farquhar, sent the minister a long-hand note expressing great respect for him and strong regret at his departure. Pépin saved this letter and pasted it in one of his scrapbooks, where I found it while working in the National Archives some twenty-two years later.

Transport officials were conscious of the fact that in 1980 and the first part of 1981, Axworthy had been among the ministers who opposed Pépin's proposals to modernize the Crow and thereby expand the western railway system to meet future capacity requirements. Instead, he had advocated the use of the $4 billion Western Development Fund to finance a number of politically attractive projects across the West, although by the time that Pépin was given leave to go ahead in the fall of 1981 Axworthy had become a supporter. He played an important role in his capacity as chairman of the Cabinet Consultative Committee on Western Affairs, and he also gave public support to Pépin's initiative. And he was a westerner. The political logic of his appointment was therefore clear.

For us in the department, however, there remained the reality that it had been Jean-Luc Pépin who had fought the lonely battle for nearly two years and had subsequently brought the initiative to the point where the government considered it a major success. Now he was being demoted. I observed to staff that there are not many fairy-tale endings in politics.

On August 15 the department held a farewell dinner for its departing minister in the same VIP railway car parked at the Ottawa station in which we had spent a full day in January working out the contents of our legislation to change the Crow. Many of us attended with decidedly mixed feelings. In his speech, the minister thanked us and included in his remarks some joking references to his particular quirks, such as phoning people late at night to ask what was meant by a particular passage in a document that we had sent him, his daily lists of "urgent" items, and his penchant for Sunday-night meetings in the basement study of his house. We had all become familiar with these and other happenings during the three-plus years that he had been our minister, but we were conscious of some other things as well. In my response, I quoted what Walter Gordon had said about Prime Minister Pearson: "He did all the important things well." It was an understatement.

FOLLOWING ITS TRAVELS in the West and Quebec, the standing committee returned to Ottawa and prepared to begin the phase of its work known as clause-by-clause. This process began on August 24, 1983.

I elected to become the principal witness for this phase, primarily because of the importance of the legislation, but also because I wanted to get some first-hand exposure to the legislative process, which had until then been lacking in my experience of government. I arranged for various officials to accompany me at particular meetings according to the subject scheduled for discussion that day. The one official who accompanied me to every session was Denis Lefebvre, whom the Department of Justice had assigned to be the head of Transport's legal services, and who with his staff had prepared our bill. His knowledge of transportation legislation, and his

Hon. Jean-Luc Pépin and Michael Farquhar,
sharing a laugh in the fall of 1983.
COURTESY OF MICHAEL FARQUHAR

interpretations of various clauses in our bill, were continuously drawn upon by the committee during the hearings. The two of us handled about one third of the sessions by ourselves.

Other frequent attendees were Mike Farquhar and two officials from the Canadian Transport Commission, John Heads and David Hackston, who brought to the table their considerable technical expertise in matters such as railway costing and rate setting. At some meetings we also drew in Howard Migie, a very knowledgeable director from the Department of Agriculture. In addition, Geoff Seaborn, an able young official whom we had seconded to Pépin, attended the meetings and provided a continuous link to Axworthy's office, as well as to Mazankowski's staff. Back in the

Department of Transport, support for our appearances was overseen by Nick Mulder, who by this time had been given responsibility for all surface transportation matters.

Following his appointment on August 12, Lloyd Axworthy had immediately flown to Quebec City, where the committee was holding hearings. When the committee returned to Ottawa he appeared before it at the first two sessions and again on September 7. In addition, departmental officials and I saw him periodically to report on how the hearings were going and to discuss possible amendments to the bill, but for the most part we functioned on our own during the detailed review of the various clauses. We had no difficulty arriving at a meeting of minds with him on specific issues, but the three months that I was reporting to him about the Crow were too brief a period for us to develop a full working relationship.

Second reading of a bill, which constitutes approval in principle of the contents, establishes the boundaries for a committee's examination. Members of the committee are free to propose amendments as the examination proceeds, but these must fall within the overall import of the bill that the House of Commons had approved. One of the principal tasks that fell to our chairman, Maurice Dionne, was to make rulings at virtually every session about whether proposed amendments met this requirement and to rule out of order those that he concluded did not.

A second constraint on the committee process is that any amendments to a bill cannot entail expenditures in excess of what the government had provided for when it submitted the legislation to Parliament—expenditures known as the "Royal recommendation," deriving from the historic concept of the monarch asking Parliament to vote funds. In some cases the analysis of whether a proposed amendment to C-155 would entail expenditures in excess of the Royal recommendation proved to be quite complex.

The hearings were held in the Railway Committee Room, which is the largest in the Parliament buildings—appropriately enough, given the historic fixation of Canadians with all matters related to transportation. It has a high ceiling, and the committee took up only about half of it, the rest being given over to public seating and, along the sides, the tables occupied by the media. The chairs around the committee table were all covered in what at the time was known as "government green" leatherette. The chairman and the clerk of the committee sat at one end of the rectangular table, with the opposition parties on their left and the Liberal members on their right. Officials sat opposite the chairman at the far end.

The first few meetings dealt with a detailed examination of Clause 2, which defined various terms in the bill, such as "system participant," "crop year," and "grain." This turned into several days of general discussion, which the chairman allowed in the interests of giving the committee an opportunity to become familiar with the workings of the proposed new system. These sessions also set the pattern for the weeks of meetings that were to follow, which for the most part were characterized by serious discussion and a generally collegial atmosphere. At the officials' end of the table, we made it a practice to give the committee as much assistance as possible and provided the members with briefing books and other material as issues arose. We also arranged for departmental staff to prepare papers for the committee on specific subjects that arose in the discussion, such as an analysis of a proposal from the Manitoba Farm Bureau about an alternative to Gilson's system of payments to producers.

From time to time there would be partisan exchanges, particularly at the opening sessions of the day. These clashes made me think of the dissonance of an orchestra tuning up before it turns to the score that it is to perform. As sometimes happens in parliamentary committees, once discussions of substance got underway the partisanship tended to subside as members of the committee collectively began to wrestle with what were often quite complex issues.

The NDP member, Les Benjamin, made a practice of moving a number of amendments every day, as part of his party's declared strategy of delaying and if possible permanently blocking the legislation. Most of his amendments were ruled out of order by the chairman after some discussion; the rest were more often than not "negatived" (as legislative parlance has it) by votes of 8 to 1, with the

Conservatives joining the Liberals in voting them down. His interventions alone probably extended the hearings by a week.

The Conservatives conducted their examination of the bill's provisions at a somewhat deliberate pace, and they frequently proposed amendments, but they usually did so in a serious way and with the intent of correcting what they regarded as deficiencies in the bill. The Liberals for their part also proposed some amendments, following Cabinet decisions, to give notice of the government's intention to propose others when the bill returned to the floor of the House.

There were frequent three-cornered dialogues between MPs from the government, the opposition parties, and departmental officials about possible amendments to particular clauses, and if so how such amendments might relate to other provisions. When the point was reached where an amendment was about to be moved we would quite often offer to put it into legal language. The following exchange is a representative example:

> *The Chairman: Mr McKnight has indicated that he has an*
> *amendment to move to Clause 2...*
> *Mr. McKnight: The amendment is very simple...it is adding as a*
> *definition the word "export" after line 24....*
> *Mr. Kroeger: Mr. Chairman, if the committee should arrive at a*
> *decision to adopt an amendment along these lines, perhaps we*
> *could be left an opportunity to develop exact wording which*
> *would pick this up. Mr. Lefebvre has pointed out there is*
> *something missing from the wording supplied by Mr. McKnight.*
> *We could I think easily remedy that if we had a few minutes...*

[And a short time later:]

> *Mr. Kroeger: I just wanted to state, Mr. Chairman, that Mr.*
> *Lefebvre has developed some wording on a definition of export*
> *that I think is agreeable to Mr. McKnight, if you would like me*
> *to read it to the committee.*

The Chairman: All right, let us deal with that now, since we are
still at line 24.
Mr. Kroeger: "export" means any shipment to a destination outside
Canada by any mode of transport.
The Chairman: Is that agreeable, Mr. McKnight?
Some hon. Members: Agreed....
Mr. McKnight: I so move.[3]

Exchanges of this character became an almost daily feature of our appearances before the committee. They found Denis's advice on a range of legal issues to be invaluable, and there were regular expressions of thanks for the kindness and expertise of our legal counsel.

A feature of the hearings that probably went unnoticed by most members of the committee was the way in which the parliamentary secretary, Jesse Flis, and I communicated with each other. When the Conservatives proposed an amendment about which Jesse was uncertain, he would give me an inquiring glance. I would do a quick assessment, perhaps have a word with Denis, then look up and give him a slight nod, meaning that from a functional point of view I saw no reason to oppose the amendment. Flis, as the leader for the government side, could then make his own assessment as to whether there were other grounds on which an objection might be called for.

At times the discussions became a bit speculative. On one occasion, Conservative MP Doug Neil of Moose Jaw asked me, "In retrospect, are there any other organizations or groups that you feel should have been part of the process and might have had input that would have assisted the committee in coming to conclusions?" In my reply, I said, "...if I had it to do over again...I would certainly have assessed the problem in eastern Canada, the kind of fears that exist in eastern Canada, differently"—a reference to the panic that our acceptance of Gilson had set off in Quebec.

The chairman's head snapped up: "Mr. Kroeger, will you give us your definition of 'eastern Canada'?"

Officials at a meeting of the Standing Committee on Transport. Left to right:
Mike Farquhar, Arthur Kroeger, Denis Lefebvre, John Heads, David Hackston.

Damn. I had put my foot in it. Maurice Dionne came from the Miramichi in New Brunswick, and a standing irritant to Atlantic Canadians was westerners' habit of referring to Ontario and Quebec as "the East." Then a moment of inspiration rescued me from my blunder. I replied, "Mr. Chairman, I come from Alberta, so eastern Canada starts at the Saskatchewan border."[4] The committee chuckled, and we went on to the next item.

An unusual feature of the hearings was the frequency with which officials explained a particular component of the bill by referring to the extensive consultations that had led up to it. The joint approach

Arthur Kroeger consulting the chairman, Maurice Dionne.

with western stakeholders that we had used in working out the specific elements of the system stood us in good stead. Following is a typical exchange which took place on September 8:

> Mr. Mazankowski: Mr. Chairman, in the document entitled *Central Coordinating Agency Task Force Report, November 1982, in appendix E where the question of car allocation is dealt with, it outlines a number of weaknesses and strengths of the present system...*
>
> Mr. Kroeger: *Mr. Mazankowski has put his finger on many of the more interesting debates we had in the legislative task force.*

The concept in the Central Coordinating Agency Task Force
Report *was that if there were an argument or a dispute about car
allocation you would appoint someone and he would deal with it
in 72 hours...the conclusion we arrived at in the legislative task
force was that it would not work...and instead...you should try to
get at the more systemic problems...*[5]

The MPS did not always take the conclusions of the task forces as the
last word, and they sometimes made up their own minds about particular clauses, but in doing so they knew that they were dealing with
something more than provisions developed by backroom officials in
Ottawa. We officials often explained why particular provisions were
in the bill not only in terms of substantive considerations, but also by
pointing out that knowledgeable stakeholders in the West had asked
for them to be included.

In political terms, an interesting feature of the hearings was
that the Conservative members of the committee, who had all been
elected in rural constituencies on the prairies, showed no hesitation
in advancing amendments disliked by the Pools. When the committee came to deal with the Senior Grain Transportation Committee
that was to oversee the workings of the new system, it approved a
Conservative amendment that cut Pool representation on the committee to one and then substituted a requirement for membership
by "representatives of producers," clearly implying that Pool nomi-
nees did not fall into this category. The Pools reacted angrily to these
changes, but without result.[6] The Conservative MPS all held safe seats
in the West, which gave them some latitude to vote their personal
preferences. In addition, most held wheat board permit books, from
which they derived a particular credibility because it meant that the
board had recognized them to be *bona fide* grain producers.

Of particular importance in the proceedings were two major
proposals by the Conservatives that would have opened the way
to paying the government's transportation subsidy to producers,
against which the Pools had waged an all-out campaign earlier in

the year. The fact that elected Conservative MPS from rural constituencies on the prairies were prepared to advance such amendments tended to confirm the judgement that Pépin and the department had previously made: the Pools' opposition to a system of payments to producers was not an insuperable political obstacle to implementing such a system. Further evidence for this belief was that the Devine government in Saskatchewan, while vehemently opposing the government's proposals to modernize the Crow, never endorsed the Saskatchewan Wheat Pool's demand that the government's subsidy be paid to the railways rather than to producers.

The first of these proposals, known as "freedom of choice," had been raised by Mazankowski in the second-reading debate, and he returned to it during the clause-by-clause examination. In essence, it would have enabled individual producers to choose whether to receive the subsidy themselves or to ask that it be paid to the railways. The other proposal, which he raised late in the committee process, addressed the period after the 1985–1986 review, and would have authorized the government to institute a system of payments to producers by administrative action without recourse to Parliament. The Quebec members of the committee were not slow to raise objections to these proposals, and both were voted down by the Liberals with the support of the NDP.

When the parties had agreed on the committee's work plan at the time of second reading in June, the bargain had been that the committee would be given leave to travel and in return would complete its hearings by September 12. As the hearings went on it became increasingly clear that the committee would be nowhere near completing its clause-by-clause review of the bill by that date, and the opposition members began to call for an extension. The committee also agreed to begin holding night sittings. A proposal by Jesse Flis for a limited extension to September 15 was met by a Conservative filibuster, and in the end the clause-by-clause hearings went on until September 22—a month less two days from the day they had begun. From the end of the first week of September on, the meetings regularly ran for seven to nine hours, and sometimes longer. I spent my fifty-first birthday in front of the committee at a session that began at 9:00 AM and ended, with breaks for meals, at 10:30 that evening.

In general I found the meetings stimulating, but also quite taxing: one had to be to be ready to answer a wide range of questions, some of which could be quite complex and technical, and to be continuously alert for unexpected developments. Federal deputy ministers typically work sixty-five to seventy hours per week, but at the end of a week in front of the Standing Committee on Transport during this period I felt as though I had done more than a normal week's work. And then on the weekends there were committee transcripts to be vetted for accuracy and briefs to prepare for the committee's meetings in the coming week. By the end of the committee's hearings I had accumulated a four-inch pile of documents including the texts of numerous amendments that had been proposed, a marked-up copy of the bill, explanatory briefing material that we had prepared for the committee, and notes I had prepared for myself on technical subjects, such as the cost of capital.

At the evening sitting on September 13 there was a major development. In a forty-minute speech, Mazankowski declared that producers had to be protected from open-ended cost escalation, that the government had an obligation to ensure the continuation of a low rate for moving grain, and that there should consequently be a three-year delay in implementing the rate increases provided for in the bill. Unless these changes were made, the bill would have a "devastating impact" on the prairies and could bring about the demise of 30–35,000 family farms.

If the amendment had been limited to these provisions, it would have been ruled out of order, because the government would have had to pick up the producers' share of cost increases in the first three years. Such additional expenditures would have breached the "Royal recommendation." The Conservatives got around this difficulty by also moving that the phased-in contribution to the railways' "constant costs" provided for in the bill be amended, and that the contribution begin only after the three-year freeze period. The estimated savings of $216 million would be approximately equal to the increased producer contribution that would be foregone during the three year freeze.

In political terms, it was an ingenious initiative. In essence, it involved shifting a financial burden from grain producers to the railways, which could scarcely fail to be popular with many in the rural West. Since the motion stayed within the limits of the Royal recommendation, it was not out of order and consequently would have to be voted on by the Liberals. Looking further ahead, in the event that the Conservatives won the election expected in 1984, they would be able to blame Liberal legislation for the increased costs to producers that would begin, without further recourse to Parliament, after the three-year freeze.

Ingenious as they were, the Conservatives' proposed amendments, which were widely reported in the media, had a mixed reception in the West. *The Western Producer,* which was owned by the Saskatchewan Wheat Pool, supported them, as did the Devine government. The *Brandon Sun,* on the other hand, acidly remarked that the Conservatives had arrived at their new position after "months of internal party squabbles and conflicting statements,"[7] while the *Winnipeg Free Press* called the motion "an opportunistic flip-flop."[8] The Manitoba Pool and the Manitoba Farm Bureau criticized the Conservatives for "political games," and the Alberta Wheat Pool also expressed reservations.[9] The railways for their part made it clear that they could not embark on major, multi-year capital projects if the Conservative amendments passed.

On behalf of the Liberals, Jesse Flis accused the Conservatives of a "major reversal" and of suddenly lining up with the National Farmers' Union and the NDP. The latter accusation tended to be borne out when Les Benjamin extended his congratulations to Mazankowski in a fifteen-minute statement. Following a lengthy and fractious debate, the proposed Conservative amendments were "negatived" by the Liberal majority in a series of 5 to 4 votes in which the NDP voted with the Conservatives.

During the eight days of sittings that remained, the committee worked its way through the rest of the bill. Somewhat to the surprise of officials, our variable rates clause was approved with little discussion and, perhaps because of inattention on the part of Les Benjamin, without a dissenting vote. Other matters that the committee dealt with included rate setting, the calculation of railway costs, grain shipments to the port of Churchill on Hudson Bay, railway joint line movements, and special financial provisions affecting Canadian National. The Conservatives put forward a number of amendments affecting the rate structure that were intended to give effect to their proposed three-year freeze, all of which were ruled out of order or voted down by the Liberal majority. As the end of the hearings neared, more of the Conservative amendments were proposed "for the record" rather than in the expectation that they would be approved, and there was accordingly less need for advice from Denis and myself.

After four weeks of clause-by-clause examination, the committee had approved eighty-nine amendments to the bill. Most of them were of limited import, such as the addition of the words, "for the purpose of maximising returns to producers" to a particular provision. Nevertheless, their acceptance contributed to the overall constructive atmosphere that characterized much of the hearings. Despite periodic partisan clashes, the discussions in the committee were generally characterized by a high degree of civility; a report in the *Winnipeg Free Press* spoke of a certain camaraderie having developed.[10] The committee also treated officials with respect throughout the hearings, and we were always given a hearing when we had something to say.

On the last day of its hearings, the committee came to Clause 66, which simply read: "Section 271 of the [Railway] Act is repealed." The historic juncture that had been reached was not lost on the committee:

Mr. Mazankowski: Mr. Chairman, just so we can be absolutely
clear of what we are doing here, by repealing Section 271 we

are now in effect repealing the statutory freight rate or the
Crow's Nest Pass Freight Rate Act...I wanted to have that
confirmed and articulated so that it could be properly
transcribed in the record, Mr. Chairman...I wanted Mr. Kroeger
to confirm that. He did it with a nod of his head, but I wanted
it to be recorded.

The Chairman: Mr. Kroeger.

Mr. Kroeger: Mr. Chairman, Section 271 of the Railway Act is
where the Crow lives.

Mr. Mazankowski: ...We are now being asked to vote for or against
Clause 66, and I am asking you so that I know how to cast my
vote. Does this clause, for all intents and purposes, repeal the
Crow's Nest Pass or statutory freight rate?

Mr. Kroeger: Yes, sir.[11]

A vote followed, and Clause 66 was approved by a 5 to 4 majority.
Appropriately enough, the vote ending the Crow—or formally, the
"statutory rate"—was the last major decision in the clause-by-clause
process.

The hearings ended with some exceptionally warm closing
remarks. Following are excerpts from the rather lengthy statements
that were made:

The Chairman: ...members of this committee...went through this
exercise with what I consider to be the most patience and the
most goodwill I have ever seen on a parliamentary
committee...I want to express to the members of the committee
my gratitude for their co-operation, their friendship, and
the thorough manner in which all members of this committee
attempted to do the job that was given to us.

Mr. Mazankowski: Mr. Chairman ...I think we have all marvelled at
your patience, your perseverance, your tolerance, and the cool
manner in which you have allowed yourself to preside over
this committee...I also want to echo and share the views you have
expressed about our witnesses...

> *Mr. Benjamin: Mr. Chairman, I want to echo the remarks you have made concerning all those who worked for and with the committee and appeared before it, and the witnesses. Of all the bills that I have been associated with in a total of five or six different standing committees since 1968...this has been the most thorough job I have ever seen done in the space of time we had.*[12]

I was sufficiently impressed by my own experiences that I decided to enter the concluding discussion:

> *Mr. Kroeger: Mr. Chairman, I hope I am not out of order in just asking if I can make one comment.*
>
> *The Chairman: I think after all the comments we have insisted you make, that would only be fair.*
>
> *Mr. Kroeger: Officials do not very often get an opportunity to participate in or contribute to, in a sustained way, the parliamentary process. It was four weeks ago today that we began clause-by-clause work and we began appearing in front of this group of members of Parliament. I think it has been a unique and valuable experience for all of us. You and your colleagues have commented on the way in which the committee has conducted its business. During some of the breaks...members of the committee remarked to me informally that it was a textbook of how a committee should work. I simply want to say that it has been a privilege for us, and I think we will all be better public servants in the future for the experience.*[13]

At 9:48 PM, the committee voted 5 to 4 to approve the bill and send it to the House of Commons.

When the committee rose, Jesse and I went back to his office in the Confederation Building. We opened a bottle of Scotch and sat until midnight reviewing past events and speculating about what might lie ahead.

That evening marked the end of my sustained involvement in the Crow. I attended a few meetings with Axworthy and a session

of the Cabinet Committee on Legislation and House Planning that
dealt with possible amendments to the bill that could be proposed
when the bill returned to the floor of the House. I also took it upon
myself to write some notes that Jean-Luc Pépin could use if he chose
to participate in the coming parliamentary debate—which he did
not. However, the completion of the Crow exercise was now largely
out of my hands, as the action shifted to the floor of the House. Only
when the bill went before a Senate committee did I again, for two
days, have to play an active role.

FOLLOWING A PARLIAMENTARY committee's hearings, the next phase
of the legislative process is "report stage," when a committee reports
back to the full House. The report sets out the position of the majority on the committee, and opposition parties can then state their
positions in minority reports. Each party can also propose amendments to the bill as it has emerged from the committee process.

Debate on the report stage of our bill began on September 29 and
immediately gave rise to the cacophony and acrimonious accusations that had characterized the spring debates. The contrast with
the serious discussions of issues, and the often collegial atmosphere
of the committee's clause-by-clause review of the bill, could scarcely
have been greater. A possible explanation was that the committee's
discussions had mostly taken place below the political radar, but
now that the legislation was back in the House members felt that
they had to start playing to the galleries again. Whatever the reason
for the abrupt change, as soon as the report-stage process began, the
Conservatives and the NDP adopted stances of all-out opposition.

During one of our meetings with Axworthy during the committee hearings in September, I had remarked on the rather civil and
collegial atmosphere that had come to prevail at our meetings. He
shrugged and replied, "That's all very well, but I just want to beat
these guys." Once the highly partisan debate on report stage was
underway, I found his combative approach to be fully justified.

At the end of September, Axworthy sought Cabinet approval to lower the "safety net"—the provision that freight charges could not exceed a specified percentage of the price of grain—from the announced level of 10 per cent to 8 per cent.[14] He did so in the hope of abating opposition to the bill in the West, but the Cabinet turned him down, and they were probably right to do so. Anti-change sentiment in some quarters in the West had reached the point where almost any concession would still have been rejected as inadequate. During the standing committee's tour of the West some had called for a limit as low as 5 per cent, which would have amounted to only a small advance from the existing Crow rate.

A number of commentators in the media and the opposition parties pointed out that, as a result of the Cabinet's reversal in April of its previous decision to pay the subsidy to producers, there was no longer a single agricultural organization in the West that supported the bill. They were quite correct. However, it was also the case that no one in the West or elsewhere had been able to come up with an alternative proposal that commanded widespread support either. And there was near-universal recognition that the status quo, with mounting financial losses by the railways, could not continue. As a result, the government had no real option but to push ahead with its legislation. As Axworthy put it, "We're just going to have to grind it through."[15]

Most of the adverse comments about the legislation centred on the extra financial burden it would impose on grain producers, but few of the critics chose to examine the relevant data. A Department of Transport analysis found that a producer with 700 acres (283 hectares) under cultivation, which might at the time have yielded annual cash receipts of $95,000, would pay an additional $800 in freight charges in each of the first three years of the new system. Mazankowski's proposal for a three-year freeze, according to the calculations he himself put forward, would have saved grain producers $212 million over a three-year period, which when spread across 140,000 grain producers would have translated into $500 per producer per year. It was not easy to discern how increased charges of this order could cause the 60 per cent reduction in farm income by 1990 that had been predicted by Eric Berntson, or wipe out one quarter of the grain producers on the prairies, as had been predicted by a group cited by Mazankowski during the committee hearings, or cause the $1.4–$1.9 billion annual loss to the Saskatchewan economy that MacMurchy had forecast.[16] According to the *Census of Agriculture,* in 1982 there had been a total of 410 farm bankruptcies in Canada, of which 327 were in provinces east of Manitoba.

But no matter. Hyperbole was the stock-in-trade of many who debated the Crow during this period.

The debate on the bill consumed most of the House legislative days in the month of October. Speaker Jeanne Sauvé expressed concern at the very large number of amendments that had been put forward: 120 by the NDP, seventy by the Conservatives, and five by the Liberals. She ruled ninety of them out of order and grouped a number of others to bring the total down to manageable dimensions. Nevertheless, as of October 20, only sixteen had been dealt with. On each amendment the NDP put forward ten to fifteen speakers. There were adjournment motions by the opposition accompanied by periods of bell ringing and a two-day procedural debate on the admissibility of amendments.

On October 25 the House Leader warned that the government was determined to see the bill through. The following day Axworthy moved time allocation, with two more days being given over to the report stage and then one day for third reading. The reaction by the opposition parties was predictably raucous. There were indignant claims that "the elected representatives of Western Canada are...being denied the opportunity to have their views debated," and that the bill was "being rammed through under double and triple closure."[17] Up to that point, nine days had been spent on second reading in the spring, the committee had met for thirty-one days during the summer, and seventeen days had been spent on the report-stage debate. The time elapsed since Pépin had moved first reading of the bill was over five months—by far the longest period spent on any bill at this session.

For the two days following Axworthy's motion for time allocation, the NDP tied up the House by presenting one petition after another. On October 31—Halloween night, appropriately enough—the House sat all night and adjourned only at 11:30 the next morning.

The *Globe and Mail* captured the views of many when it cried "enough" in an editorial of November 3: "Let it be finished. Let it become law."[18] That evening a series of votes brought report stage to a close.

The following day Axworthy opened the debate on third reading. He began with a generous tribute to Jean-Luc for his "perseverance, initiative, and intelligence," and pointed out that "the plan was based on the most extensive consultations ever undertaken on any piece of legislation." He also praised Maurice Dionne for his chairmanship, and members of the standing committee for their work during the long series of hearings. Then he went on to say, "A number of fine, highly qualified and dedicated public servants worked hundreds and thousands of hours...Those men and women are very much part of this historic moment."[19]

As he continued with his speech, he was increasingly interrupted by members of the opposition. The tone of the final day's debate was as fractious as that of the days that had preceded it.

By agreement with the opposition parties, the final vote was scheduled to take place following the House break, on November 14. The vote giving House of Commons approval to the legislation duly took place at 5:45 PM that day, and the bill then went on to the Senate.

The Senate had begun its examination of the bill in early October, in advance of the House giving its approval—a process known as "pre-study." Following the House vote on November 14, I spent November 15 and 16 before a Senate committee, following which the bill was voted through by the Liberal majority in the full Senate. When the legislation was given Royal Assent the following day in the Senate chamber, Bill C-155 became the *Western Grain Transportation Act*. As it happened, Pépin was acting prime minister that day and so represented the government at the ceremony.

Mike Farquhar, Arthur Kroeger, and Nick Mulder pointing at the clause in the copy of the final order-in-council that cancels the old Crow rate, December 1983.
COURTESY OF NICK MULDER

When the bill was finally passed, media comments in the West were predominantly favourable. An editorial in the *Edmonton Journal* concluded, "For this the Liberals deserve our thanks."[20]

On November 23 the bill was proclaimed into law, to come into force on January 1, 1984. At the end of the day Lloyd Axworthy held a reception in the Railway Committee Room of the House to mark the occasion.

Had Jean-Luc Pépin still been our minister, this event would very likely have been something in the nature of a family party, with some expressions of euphoria on the part of those of us who had worked together for so long. But Pépin had been moved out of the Department of Transport some three months before, and the memory of how he had been treated dampened our spirits. We were left mostly with a feeling of relief combined with a sense of exhaustion. It had all gone on for a very long time.

The Axworthy reception proved to be a quite political event designed to reap credit for the government for its accomplishment in ending the Crow. A number of displays had been prepared and deployed around the room, including photographs from past years and an enlarged colour print of the proclamation of the *Western Grain Transportation Act*. The media had been invited. Preparations were being made for a $1.5 million "Crow Sell" program in the West, involving promotional advertisements, the engagement of information consultants, displays, and ministerial speeches over the next four months—functions that I was glad to leave to my successor in Transport.

I was also conscious that the cast of characters had begun to change. I only half recognized a number of people at the reception. The world was moving on, and it was time for me to do the same.

I circulated around the room and inspected the displays with Nick Mulder and Mike Farquhar but was not disposed to linger. Shortly after the speeches I went home. The next day was my elder daughter's sixteenth birthday. As I had to be in Winnipeg that day with my new minister, I took her out for an advance birthday dinner.

Outcomes and Lessons

WHEN THE CONSERVATIVES WON the election of 1984, many in the West expected to see substantial amendments to the *Western Grain Transportation Act,* notably including some system of payments to producers such as the "freedom of choice" option that the Conservatives had proposed in the spring of 1983. They were to be disappointed. In 1985 the commission set up to review the WGTA recommended a variation on the system that Gilson had devised, but the government took no action. Some members of the Conservative caucus, during the life of the Mulroney government, say that on several occasions when the issue of payments to producers was brought up, the proponents were warned off by the party leadership, who did not want to stir up trouble with the farmers in Quebec. On the prairies today there are some who believe that the resulting disillusionment in some rural constituencies was one of a number of factors in the West's transfer of political allegiance from the Conservatives to the new Reform Party during much of the 1990s.

Don Mazankowski, who had returned to his previous post of Transport minister, legislated the third year of the three-year reduction in payments to the railways for their constant costs that he had called for in September 1983, and he applied the $72 million saving to the charges borne by grain producers. The government also intervened several times in subsequent years to abate the rate increases faced by producers, at a cost to it of $64 million in each case. But in 1987 John Crosbie, who had succeeded Mazankowski as minister of Transport, announced that no further amendments to the WGTA would be made during the balance of the government's mandate. The main elements of the WGTA were thus left untouched.

In the second Mulroney government that was elected in 1988, Mazankowski was minister of Finance. As part of an $8 billion set of expenditure cuts to reduce the government's budgetary deficit in December 1992, he ordered reductions in a number of subsidies, including two successive cuts of 10 per cent each in the WGTA subsidy over two years. When the Liberals replaced the Conservatives in office after the election of October 1993, they allowed these cuts to proceed.

By the early 1990s sentiment in Alberta had evolved to the point where Unifarm, with the acquiescence of the Alberta Wheat Pool, endorsed the implementation of a system of payments to producers in the province. In June 1993 Charles Mayer of Manitoba, who had become federal minister of Agriculture, tabled a paper announcing a decision by the government to implement payments to producers. He appointed Ed Tyrchniewicz, the former co-ordinator of analysis in the Gilson process, to head a committee that would work out an implementation plan. In the event, the Kim Campbell government was defeated in the October election, and when Ralph Goodale became the Liberal minister of Agriculture he left the system of payments to the railways untouched.

Former Alberta MP Jack Horner had predicted that once grain producers on the prairies had to pay more for shipping their grain, they would begin to look for ways of reducing costs in the system. In 1986, when rate discounting became broadly permissible under the WGTA, the CNR and a group of seven shippers developed an agreement for rate reductions on a set of shipments. As we had provided in the legislation, parties who considered that they would be adversely affected by rate reductions had the right to file objections with the Canadian Transport Commission (CTC), and twenty-seven did so. They included the Conservative government of Saskatchewan, the NDP government of Manitoba, the Saskatchewan Wheat Pool, the New Democratic Party of Saskatchewan, and the National Farmers' Union. The basis of their opposition was a fear that variable rates would set off an unduly rapid rationalization of the grain handling and transportation system and thus imperil many rural communities on the prairies.

After assessing the objections that had been filed, the Transport commission ruled that the rate reductions should be allowed to proceed. In subsequent years rate discounting grew steadily, and no further objections were filed. In 2000 rate discounts were applied to 49 per cent of grain traffic; by 2005 the figure had become 73 per cent.[1]

The railways achieved significant efficiency gains in the years after the WGTA came into force. In 1983–1984 the average cost of moving a tonne of grain from the prairies to a port was approximately $25.00. Fifteen years later, the cost was assessed by the CTC at $33.81, an increase of 35 per cent, or roughly 2 per cent per year, far below the cost increases for most agricultural inputs, such as fertilizer, during that period, which in some cases were as high as 10 per cent per year.[2] After the 1995 repeal of the WGTA and the loosening of some controls, particularly on branch line abandonment, the railways registered further reductions in their costs. The Grain Monitoring Agency reported that between 1999–2000 and 2003–2004 the average cost of moving wheat to export position increased by 1 per cent, as compared with a 37 per cent increase in the farm input index. After years of opposition by the Canadian Wheat Board, solid trains—trains entirely comprising grain cars—became common.

Once the WGTA was law, both the CNR and the CPR launched major capacity expansion projects. The largest single project was the CPR tunnel through Mount Macdonald in the Selkirk Range, which took nearly five years to complete and cost over $500 million. It was a

A CPR solid train of grain cars crossing a trestle in Alberta built as part
of the Crow's Nest Pass line.

CANADIAN PACIFIC RAILWAY, E7889

form of over-and-under double-tracking: the new tunnel was cut
through the mountain at a lower level than the existing one and had
a gradient of only 1 per cent. It was therefore used by heavily loaded
trains bound for the West Coast, while the existing tunnel with a
gradient of 2.2 per cent was used by trains hauling the empty cars
back to the prairies.

There was also extensive rationalization of the grain handling
system following the passage of the WGTA. The number of country
elevators peaked at 5,728 in 1933–1934. In 1980–1981, despite improvements in the prairie road system and the abandonment of some
branch lines, there were still some 3,000 in operation. In the years
following the passage of the WGTA, most were phased out, and by 2002

A modern high-capacity grain terminal.
CANADIAN PACIFIC RAILWAY, E8216-23

only 418 wooden primary elevators remained. In their place were very large, high-capacity, cement grain terminals that had been erected by the various grain companies. In 2005 the Saskatchewan Wheat Pool operated forty-seven terminals that were capable of handling as much grain as the five hundred primary elevators that it had had ten years before.[3]

One of the most striking developments on the prairies has been the changes in the producer-owned companies that had been created in the first part of the twentieth century. In the 1990s, high costs, low returns, and an increased need for capital had far-reaching consequences. In effect, the institution of "the caring Pool" increasingly had to adjust and seek cost reductions in response to commercial pressures. United Grain Growers altered its corporate structure to become a publicly held company, and then in 1997 sold a part-ownership to Archer-Daniels-Midland, a major American grain company. The Alberta and Manitoba Pools merged to form Agricore and in 2001 merged with UGG and became Agricore United. In parallel, the Saskatchewan Wheat Pool, after some ill-starred business ventures, also turned itself into a commercial grain company whose shares were traded on the Toronto Stock Exchange. Finally, in 2007, the Pool made a successful bid to take over Agricore United. Later the same year, it changed its name to Viterra.

The end result of these changes was that the producer-controlled companies became a thing of the past, as did the phenomenon of grain co-op democracy that had been a prominent feature of the rural West for many decades. There has been much discussion of the possible reasons for these transformations, particularly since co-ops in other sectors have continued to thrive in the West. In addition to financial pressures, some cite the coming of a new generation of farmers who were more business-oriented and less interested in co-op democracy. Whatever the explanation, the transformation left many producers in the West with a sense of loss.

There has also been considerable consolidation of farms on the prairies. In 1960 there were 224,000 registered grain producers. By the early 1980s the number had fallen to 140,000, and in 2006 it stood at 85,000. As this chronology indicates, this trend began while the Crow's Nest Pass rate was still in force and cannot be attributed to its demise.[4] Between 1961 and 1981, the farm population of Saskatchewan fell from 305,000 to 180,000. One factor, particularly in recent years, has been economic pressures. Large-scale subsidies to farmers in the United States and the European Union stimulated production in those countries and thus kept international prices depressed year after year. Farms on the Canadian prairies had to become larger in order to achieve the efficiencies that were essential if they were to earn any kind of return at all.

In the first five years of the twenty-first century there was no net return from market sales by the agricultural industry in Canada. In 2005, government subsidies accounted for 15 per cent of net farm cash receipts and virtually all net farm income. Agricultural economists in the West began to raise questions about the future viability of the grains and oilseeds sector and to assert that governments would need to face some basic decisions about the scale of support that it would be appropriate to provide in the future. More recently, the growth of ethanol production in Canada and the U.S. has brought about increases in grain prices, but the longer term future remains a matter of speculation.

░░░░░░░░░░░░░░░

WHEN THE LIBERALS returned to office in 1993, they were faced with a budgetary deficit that had reached $43 billion. In its budget of 1995 the government launched a sweeping program of expenditure reductions totalling $25 billion. Among them was the elimination over a three-year period of the annual subsidy paid under the *Western Grain Transportation Act*. To compensate for the reduction in land values that was expected to result (but did not, in the event), the government made a one-time payment of $1.6 billion, accompanied by a $300 million program of improvements to agricultural infrastructure in the West. The government ended the subsidy with considerable apprehension, and it is doubtful that they could have found it politically possible to do so had Pépin not broken the rigidity of the 1897 Crow rate through the process that he led in the early 1980s.

It was an unwelcome development for the West, but the reaction was fairly muted. A contributing factor was that grain prices in 1995 happened to be at exceptionally high levels. However, a more fundamental reason was that grain transportation issues in 1995 no longer carried the Crow overburden of prairie grievances. Populist legends about the land grants to the Canadian Pacific Railway had ceased to figure in the thinking of most producers. The "holy Crow" and the "Magna Carta of the West" belonged to history. In addition, the consolidation of the grain handling and transportation system, and its impact on communities that had generated so many fears in the 1980s, had largely run its course and so was no longer a matter of debate. The railways have not come to be loved on the prairies, but they are no longer demonized as the CPR was for much of the twentieth century.

What existed in 1995 was regarded by producers and the government alike as simply another subsidy. Its elimination increased financial pressures on producers, but it was only one element in the larger picture. The needs of the agricultural industry in the West were a subject that federal and provincial governments regularly had to wrestle with, and still do.

The repeal of the WGTA had the effect of eliminating the economic distortions in the West that had been caused by the system of payments to the railways. With full compensatory rates in effect, the prices for raw grain paid by agricultural processors and livestock growers on the prairies fell, while transportation costs borne by exporters of raw grain increased, resulting in a shift of agricultural production. This shift had been underway even before the repeal but was accelerated by it. Acreage planted to non-Crow specialty crops nearly doubled. Although the Wheat Board had set a target of increasing grain exports to 36 million tonnes by 1990, the opposite happened. As more grain was processed on the prairies or fed to livestock, shipments for export decreased from 30 million tonnes in 1983–1984 to 26.6 million in 2005–2006. The drop in barley exports was particularly marked. With increased livestock production, barley exports fell by 45 per cent, from 5.5 million tonnes to 3.5 million.[5] In the twelve years following the repeal of the WGTA, processed agricultural products displaced raw grain as Canada's leading agricultural export.

In brief, the changes that took place confirmed the calculations on which Pépin had based his advocacy of payments to producers as a means of diversifying and developing the western agricultural economy.

In Quebec, the UPA, the Coopératives fédérées, and their allies remained vigilant after their 1983 victory in forcing the government to pay its subsidy to the railways rather than to producers in the West.

During the review of the WGTA in 1985, they filed a brief reasserting their contention that a change to a system of payments to producers would result in an increase in western production that would saturate Canadian and U.S. livestock markets, with particularly detrimental effects on Quebec agriculture. They also intervened whenever the subject came up in subsequent years. When Charles Mayer tabled his paper on producer payments in June 1993, the Bloc Quebecois leader of the opposition, Lucien Bouchard, protested and called for a revival of the coalition that had fought and won the battle ten years before.

The primary objective of the Quebec interests was to ensure that livestock producers in the West would continue to function under the debility of artificially high livestock feed prices. After the announcement of the repeal of the WGTA, the Bloc Quebecois filed a dissenting brief to the report of the House Standing Committee on Agriculture of June 1995, stating that the result of the repeal would be to break the "competitive equilibrium" between producers in the East and the West. The West would thus gain a comparative advantage—or more accurately, would cease to be under a disadvantage—that would stimulate economic diversification in that part of the country.

One part of the Bloc's forecast was borne out in subsequent years: production of beef and pork in the West did increase substantially. On the other hand, its forecast about the impact of the change on Quebec agriculture was the opposite of what actually happened. Far from being the *coup mortel* that had been widely feared in the province, the increased western livestock production following the repeal of the WGTA went south to the United States and proved to have no discernible effects east of the Great Lakes. On the contrary, livestock production in Quebec increased substantially during the same period. Between the repeal of the WGTA in 1995 and 2002, hog marketings in Quebec increased by 44 per cent, while beef production went from $352 million to $456 million.[6]

All of this was just as the federal Department of Agriculture had predicted in the early 1980s, and as Jean-Luc Pépin had tried to persuade the Quebec caucus—without result in the face of the panic that swept the province. In politics, being right can take you only so far.

############

My experiences in dealing with the Crow issue led me to reflect on the different approaches that governments can adopt in dealing with particularly difficult issues.

The challenge that Pépin faced in dealing with the Crow was to find a way of doing so that would not pit the federal government against the West, particularly in view of the government's lack of elected members from that region. The approach that he and the department decided to pursue was to involve western stakeholders fully in the change process. Rather than developing a solution in Ottawa and then trying to impose it on the West, we elected to share the problem with leaders in the West and to enlist their help in devising solutions.

A comparison with the National Energy Program is instructive here. There were unquestionably important considerations that led Trudeau's government to bring forward the NEP, and the program elicited considerable support across the country. However, it was designed in secrecy by the federal government and then imposed on the West, where it inflicted psychic scars that have still not healed a full generation later. In the case of the Crow, we proceeded in a loose, open, collaborative manner. Everyone knew at every stage what we were doing, and many were given an opportunity to influence the specific measures, notably in the Gilson process and then in the joint task forces that were set up pursuant to Gilson's recommendations.

It is true that, in the end, the heated atmosphere that developed in 1983 left the government with no alternative but to force its legislation through despite objections by some in the West, but it did so only after compromise and accommodation had been pushed to the limit. As a result, the political impact of the Crow legislation was very different from that of the NEP.

The ultimate test of the two approaches came in the election of 1984. Within months of the change of government, the main elements of the National Energy Program were gone. The changes we had made to the historic Crow rate, on the other hand, were hardly an issue during the campaign, and during the ensuing nine years that the Conservatives were in power the changes they made to the *Western Grain Transportation Act* were relatively minor. This outcome suggests that we must have done something right.

A good deal of public and media commentary in the summer and fall of 1983 about "the government's battered bill" conveyed a sense that Parliament had gutted the government's legislation.[7] This was not true. Once the issue of producer payments had been settled by the Cabinet in late April there were no further major changes to the substance of the bill. The numerous amendments accepted by the government in committee during the summer were quite innocuous, and each attempt by the opposition parties to effect major changes was defeated by the government majority. The bill that was proclaimed into law on November 23 was in all important respects the one that the minister had introduced in Parliament in early May.

A further lesson of the Crow process was the importance of solid data and analysis. Nothing can so undermine a controversial government initiative than if its opponents are able to demonstrate that the government has its facts wrong. Whatever problems we encountered in dealing with the Crow, the factual and analytical case that we were able to assemble proved to be bulletproof. The government's reversal in April 1983 on the issue of payments to producers was the result of political pressures and not because of bad staff work by officials. In fact the Pools never seriously challenged the Department of Agriculture's analysis that payments to producers would be beneficial to the western economy.

A factor that contributed to the ultimate success of the Crow initiative was the diverse experience and expertise of the team that worked on the Crow within the government. Janet Smith in the Privy Council Office and I in the Department of Transport had grown up in two small towns within sixty miles (97 km) of each other in eastern Alberta and so had some knowledge of and "feel" for the West. Nick Mulder's six years as assistant deputy minister for Strategic Planning in the department had given him an comprehensive knowledge of transportation issues that stood us in good stead, and he was ably supported by the director general of Grain Transportation, Mike Farquhar. On the minister's political staff, Jim Roche had an excellent working relationship with the department and consistently provided good advice to Pépin. The legal skills that Denis Lefebvre brought to us from the Department of Justice proved invaluable in the legislative process. David Hackston and John Heads were able to draw upon the technical expertise of the Canadian Transport Commission in dealing with complex technical issues, such as rate setting.

Supplementing the expertise within the government were the analyses of railway costs that Carl Snavely produced during his succession of studies in the late 1970s and early 1980s, which effectively settled the debate in the West about whether the railways were losing money moving grain. Then, in the winter of 1983, the diverse knowledge brought to bear by the task forces of stakeholders and officials that Gilson had recommended ensured that our legislation was well drafted and free of errors.

#############

THE CENTRAL ISSUE in the lengthy Crow modernization process was the level at which the railways were to be compensated, but during much of the process, the main interaction was between the government and the western stakeholders, with the CNR and the CPR on the sidelines. They provided information in response to requests and made clear their positions on matters of substance as they arose. We in the department shared information with them in the same open manner that we did with other stakeholders. In general, however, both railways played a low-key role and had the maturity to avoid strident, accusatory language about the large financial losses they were incurring. In addition, the president of the CNR, Ron Lawless, and the president of the CPR, Bill Stinson, kept in regular communication with me and other officials to ensure that they did not miss important developments and also to ensure that they avoided taking actions or making statements that could inadvertently cause turbulence in our process.

CNR, on the one hand, being a Crown corporation, had the comfort of knowing that whatever the outcome of our process, the corporation would have to be financially back-stopped by the federal treasury. The CPR, on the other hand, was accountable to its shareholders and so felt considerably more exposed. Officials who dealt with the CPR throughout this period, myself included, regard their performance as a class act. They displayed a full recognition of the complexities that Pépin and the department were coping with and avoided putting forward simplistic proposals. Their performance when appearing before the parliamentary committee was solidly professional. When our legislation had finally passed, I sent personal notes to Bill Stinson and his chairman, Fred Burbidge, complimenting them on how they had conducted themselves through the long process and expressing appreciation in particular that at no time had they pressed me to make decisions that I would have regarded as bad public policy.

ONCE THE FACTUAL question of railway losses had to all intents and purposes been settled, primarily by Snavely's reports, the issue then became one of where the money was to come from. The answer from almost everyone in the West was, Ottawa. There were in fact quite a few, including the Hall Commission of 1977, who advocated that the federal government should add a number of products to the list of those carried at the 1897 rate and subsidize the transportation of them, as well.

This simple solution ran up against the reality of the fiscal pressures that the federal government was experiencing. It was running annual budgetary deficits of $15–20 billion, and in 1982 its revenues fell short of forecasts as the country sank into a severe recession. Many of the demands put forward by various groups in the West were simply beyond the fiscal reach of the government. The Cabinet minutes of the era record the contentious discussions among ministers as they struggled to find ways of reducing expenditures. It was only because of the additional revenues that flowed to Ottawa as a result of the National Energy Program that Jean-Luc Pépin was able to get the $1.35 billion he needed to begin subsidizing the railways as part of his Crow modernization program.

A more fundamental consideration was that there are limits to how much money a government can commit to a particular group. In 1980 all the forecasts indicated that, if no action was taken, the railways' losses would reach $1 billion or more per year by 1990. It was simply not in the realm of the politically possible for a national government to provide subsidies to western grain transportation on this scale, given the many other claims on the federal treasury. An analysis by the department showed that, with the passage of the WGTA and the payment of the $650 million "Crow benefit" to the railways, the grain industry would become the recipient of the largest subsidy paid by the department; in comparison, the subsidy to VIA rail was $500 million, while the government's contribution to the costs of operating the entire civil aviation system in Canada was just short of $400 million.[8]

Without questioning the sincerity of the NDP's emotional commitment to the Crow, even a government of that party would have found sooner or later that it had to take action along the lines of what Pépin did and begin requiring producers to start contributing more to the costs of moving their grain. Saskatchewan Premier Allan Blakeney acknowledged as much in January 1982, when he said, "Perhaps a revision of the deal makes sense...Now, I don't want to be quoted as saying that I'm happy to see the Crow increase...but I know that time goes on and costs go up and I think farmers are realistic enough to say that at some time they would look at increasing the Crow."[9]

Mr. Blakeney was quite right about the farmers. The major agricultural organizations in the West did recognize the realities that had come into play, which led them to offer to negotiate the sharing of future increases in the cost of shipping their grain by rail, which *de facto* meant the end of the 1897 Crow rate.

|||||||||||||||||||||||

THREE INDIVIDUALS PLAYED key roles in the Crow reform activities of 1980–1983.

The first individual who must be singled out is Ted Turner. He was the acknowledged leader of the three Pools and has been described as "the last of the Titans who led the Saskatchewan Wheat Pool."[10]

Nowhere in the West was opposition to change stronger than among the 70,000 members of SaskPool, and it was no small achievement on Turner's part that he was able to get from them even a limited mandate to participate in the negotiation of changes to the Crow. During the Crow process Turner continuously had to walk a tightrope and often took abuse from Pool members. He had to take a very hard line in representing his constituents on many issues while at the same time making accommodations that were dictated by the reality that change had to come. Had he taken the easy course and led his members in all-out opposition, Pépin would never have been able to persuade the Cabinet to let him proceed with Crow change. The result would have been a continued deterioration of the grain transportation system on which Turner's constituents depended. There was also a real prospect that, in the longer term, a government faced with railway traffic congestion would have had to take urgent action and impose drastic measures on the West. Turner recognized these future risks. His message to his members was, "We have to be involved with the talks or face the consequences." He was the type of leader who introduces his followers to the future.

After Turner ended his service as president of the Pool, the University of Saskatchewan recognized his stature in the province by electing him Chancellor in 1989.

The second key figure was Clay Gilson. I have already described his process and notably his success in forging a consensus, however fragile, among the very diverse groups that participated in his process. Had his consultations failed, and ended in recrimination, the already wary federal government might well have lost its nerve and elected to continue with expensive and ineffective *ad hoc* measures, such as branch line rehabilitation and hopper car purchases.

The third key figure was obviously Pépin. Whatever support we in the department may have been able to give him does not detract from his achievement. He was the minister and had to make the final decisions about the policy and procedural issues that frequently arose. To him also fell the task of persuading the Cabinet of the need for change and then of how it should be effected. He had the responsibility of representing the government in the West insofar as the Crow issue was concerned, and in this area his success was extraordinary. His sincerity, openness, and his patently honest approach disarmed his critics and won him widespread respect.

Striking evidence of the regard in which he came to be held was provided by statements by two Conservative MPs from Saskatchewan during a parliamentary debate in May 1984. Looking back to the Crow initiative, Len Gustafson from the rural constituency of Assiniboia—which had once been held by Hazen Argue—said that, "The former minister of Transport...has always occupied a sort of soft spot in the hearts of many farmers. That is particularly so...regarding the minister's work related to transportation."[11] His sentiments were echoed by Doug Neil of Moose Jaw: "I believe the minister has more credibility among the farming population in western Canada than any other member of the Cabinet. I am pleased that he is here today and is participating because he has an understanding. He gained that understanding when he was involved in the Crow bill."[12]

The Crow exercise was, in the Duke of Wellington's phrase about the battle of Waterloo, "a close run thing," and there is room for doubt that a lesser minister could have carried it off at the time that Jean-Luc Pépin did.

THERE IS AN INTERESTING, "What if?" that deserves to be addressed. Reflecting on his years in Transport, Pépin observed that his mistake had been to try to effect a transport revolution and an agricultural revolution on the prairies simultaneously.[13] In retrospect, would the wiser course for him have been to acquiesce in the Pools' demands rather than trying to implement Gilson's recommendations?

The answer must necessarily be speculative. When the minister and the department first set out to deal with the Crow, the stated intention in our Cabinet documents was to implement the quite conservative proposals emanating from the Western Agricultural Conference. It was the Gilson process that presented us with a more ambitious approach to Crow reform and one that all participants had at least agreed to discuss with their constituents. His report constituted the "made in the West" solution to the Crow issue that the government had declared to be its objective.

Had the government agreed to the Pools' demands, it would have had to put aside Gilson's report and substitute for it a "made by the Pools" approach to the Crow. The Pools unquestionably represented many in the West, but they did not have a monopoly. A substantial minority of western grain producers favoured Gilson's proposal for payments to producers. There were also others in the West, such as the cattlemen and the oilseed crushers, who favoured Gilson's report and were entitled to have their interests taken into account. Gilson had pointed out that livestock and livestock products accounted for $2 billion in 1981, while the value added from the processing of agricultural products came to $1.2 billion, for a total of $3.2 billion as compared with $6.4 billion in prairie crop sales. These were not components of the western economy that could simply be dismissed by the government.

In 1982 journalist Philip Mathias observed that, "The Canadian grain industry is an unlikely partnership of warring ideologies cemented by self-interest."[14] The co-op ethos that had dominated the prairies from the early twentieth century on had been broken in the 1970s by the emergence of groups such as the Prairie Farm Commodity Coalition. Members of these groups believed that western agriculture would benefit from a less regulated system that gave more play to market forces. At the other end of the spectrum, the Pools feared that a too rapid rationalization of the system could put at risk their large investments in country elevators and have an adverse impact on the rural communities where Pool members lived.

Gilson managed to bridge the divisions in the West during his consultations, but his fragile consensus did not last and the Crow process became increasingly divisive. Opinion in the West was split within communities and among grain producers. Internal disagreements tore apart a number of agricultural organizations and brought an end to the Western Agricultural Conference. The governments of Alberta and BC supported the changes, while Manitoba and Saskatchewan opposed them. It follows that any approach, including doing nothing, was bound to be controversial.

There was another development that probably made it inevitable that the legislation dealing with the Crow would meet strong resistance. As the possibility of a change in the Crow began to emerge as a reality in late 1982 and on into 1983, there was a surge of fear among grain producers about the increased transportation costs they would have bear in future years, particularly in the medium term. Thus, at a meeting in mid-February 1983, delegates of the Saskatchewan Wheat Pool voted unanimously to reject the plan that Pépin had proposed *"in its entirety"*[15] [emphasis added], which presumably included a rejection of the requirement for producers to bear part of increased costs in future years. This amounted to a "keep the Crow" position. To some extent, the leadership of the Pools and UGG lost control of their members during this period, just as they had feared might happen during the earlier years, and much as Senator Olson had foreseen when he questioned the strength of the consensus in the West on the subject of changing the Crow.

In retrospect, it is remarkable how difficult changing the Crow proved to be. Throughout the process, the government was supported by most of the urban dailies and other media in the West. The future of the western railway system was at stake. Representatives of major industries across the country, such as mining, forest products, and manufacturing, as well as business associations, such as the Canadian Chamber of Commerce and the Manufacturers' Association, regarded the passage of Pépin's legislation as urgent. The Conservative Party, which constituted the official opposition in Parliament, was hopelessly divided on the substance of the issue. Of the 6 million residents of the West in the early 1980s, only 140,000 were grain producers, and even among them a succession of polls reported that something over 40 per cent favoured change, as did—at least initially—the organizations that represented them. And yet the whole enterprise took three and a half years and was almost lost in the spring of 1983.

Possible explanations for the difficulties we encountered might include the political power that agriculture has in many western democracies, including Canada, and public sympathy in urban areas for the prairie communities that were undergoing far-reaching changes. No doubt there are many other possibilities. But to describe and analyze them all would require another book.

Finally, Jean-Luc Pépin's legislation accomplished 100 per cent of what he had first set out to do in the fall of 1980: it ended the mounting losses incurred by the railways; it gave them the financial capacity to effect essential expansions to their systems; and it thus ensured that the West, including grain producers, would have an adequate transportation system. Most important of all, it brought to an end the historic Crow rate in a way that did not do lasting damage to relations between the West and the federal government.

TOWARD THE END OF 1983 and into 1984, members of the Trudeau Cabinet and individuals in the Prime Minister's Office came to the view that the government would be remembered for three major accomplishments: the patriation of the Constitution (including the establishment of the Charter of Rights and Freedoms), the National Energy Program, and the reform of the Crow.[16] Given that the National Energy Program did not survive the change of government, the list could be shortened to two. It was a surprising outcome for everyone. In particular, the prime minister, who sent Pépin to Transport in part to keep him away from the Constitution, could never have imagined at the time what this appointment would lead to.

In the spring of 1984, Jean-Luc Pépin confirmed his earlier inclination not to seek re-election. In June he entered hospital and underwent heart bypass surgery. When he recovered, he accepted an invitation from the University of Ottawa to resume teaching and began giving courses in politics. He also did work for the Institute for Research in Public Policy and accepted frequent invitations to give speeches on current subjects. During the public debate over the Meech Lake agreement on constitutional change between 1987 and 1990 he spoke in favour of the agreement.

During the same period, Prime Minister Mulroney arranged for the Governor General to confer upon some individuals the honorific title of "Member of the Queen's Privy Council for Canada." Mulroney also raised some existing members to bear the designation of "Right Honourable," which is normally reserved for the Governors General, present and former prime ministers, and chief justices of the Supreme Court. Among those designated to bear this title was Jean-Luc Pépin.

Some years later, Tom Axworthy, who had served in Trudeau's office during the Crow saga, wrote an article for the *National Post* setting out what he thought would be an "all-star Cabinet" comprising the best ministers to occupy various posts since Confederation. His nominee for the post of minister of Transport was Jean-Luc Pépin.

Jean-Luc and I saw one another only infrequently after he left office. From time to time, however, my phone at home would ring, usually at about 10:00 in the evening, and a familiar voice would say something like, "Arthur, I have to give a lecture to my students tomorrow on the subject of relations between ministers and senior officials, and I was wondering whether you would agree with my view that…" The ensuing conversation would then go on for up to an hour, moving from some of the nuances of political science to a discussion of the current state of governance in Canada and then on to other matters.

In early September 1995 I was driving in southern Manitoba and listening to the news on the CBC. Partway through the newscast there came a jarring item: "A former minister from the Pearson and Trudeau eras has died. Jean-Luc Pépin was..."

It had been his heart. Bypass operations are generally reputed to be effective for only about ten years, and this may have been the explanation in Jean-Luc's case. Some speculated, as well, that a contributing factor had been the stress he felt with the approach of the Quebec referendum on sovereignty that was scheduled for the end of October. Important as his achievements in Transport had been, the Constitution and national unity were always subjects that preoccupied him. From time to time when he was my minister in the Department of Transport he would casually ask me questions like, "What did you think of Claude Ryan's *Beige Paper* on the Constitution?" In response I would have to mumble something intended to conceal the fact that I had not read it.

On the day of his funeral I flew back to Ottawa and landed at noon. The flag at the airport in Ottawa caught my eye. It was at half-mast, notwithstanding the fact that it was over twelve years since Pépin had been minister of Transport, and notwithstanding the rule that the death of former ministers and other members of the Privy Council would normally be marked only by lowering the flag on the Peace Tower to half-mast.

In 2001 the University of Ottawa decided to create the Jean-Luc Pépin Chair in Politics. One of the university's active collaborators was Mauril Belanger, who had been a bushy-tailed young assistant in Pépin's office during the early 1980s. He later became a member of Parliament and then a minister. As part of their fundraising campaign, the university and Belanger decided to approach the two railways for donations.

It was a reasonable enough step. While Pépin's efforts to end the Crow rate between 1980 and 1983 had been driven by considerations of public policy, the two railways were unquestionably the major beneficiaries. Had Pépin failed, their very large financial losses, amounting to hundreds of millions of dollars every year, would have continued until some indeterminate point in the future. There is no room for doubt that the balance sheets of both railways were very substantially affected for the better by the eventual success of Pépin's initiative.

To the considerable surprise of the university, together with Mauril Belanger and the rest of us who had become involved in the fund raising, the Canadian Pacific Railway refused to make any donation at all to the Pépin Chair. The CNR for its part for its part agreed to donate $10,000, which eventually led the CPR to offer a matching contribution. Subsequent discussions with the CNR led the railway to increase its donation to $300,000 over three years. When the CPR was then approached about the possibility of increasing its donation, the company refused, despite representations from a number of quarters.

The negative decision had not been made somewhere in the middle ranks of the CPR bureaucracy. The letter conveying the company's final refusal was signed by the chief executive officer, Rob Ritchie, who stated that it was the outcome of a discussion in the company's executive committee.

Following Pépin's death, Nick Mulder, who by this time had returned to the Department of Transport as deputy minister, invited me to write a retrospective piece. In response, I did the following article for TC *Express*, the department's house organ:

> I am grateful to Nick Mulder for inviting me to write an
> appreciation of Jean-Luc Pépin for TC Express. We both served
> under Mr. Pépin from March 1980 until the summer of 1983, and
> I know he shares the sentiments I want to express.
>   Ministers are entitled to the loyal service of their officials as a
> matter of right. Some also win great respect for their conduct in office.
> Jean-Luc Pépin did so, and something more, as well: he generated
> strong affection on the part of those privileged to work with him.

He was conscientious to a fault, and would spend hours studying a subject that the rest of us were ready to deal with summarily; when he did render a decision, however, the judgement he displayed was impeccable. He refused to engage in the artifices of politics and thereby earned a widespread reputation for genuineness and integrity. He was dedicated to the principle that good government is good politics, and his record in office demonstrated the many ways in which this principle can be put into practice by a committed minister.

Nowhere was this more true than in the contentious case of the Crow's Nest Pass rates, on which he and Nick and I spent so much of our time in the early 1980s. On the face of the matter, nothing was more improbable than that a former professor from the University of Ottawa, a native of Drummondville, Quebec, could persuade the West that the 1897 freight rate that many regarded as their birthright had outlived its purpose.

More than one minister of Transport with strong western roots had tried only to discover what a tough bird the Crow was. Undaunted by this knowledge, Mr. Pépin elected to deal with what was by then the most pressing transportation problem in the country. He brought to the task a combination of diligence, candour, and a willingness to listen that he displayed at countless meetings with people in the West. Even those who strongly opposed what he was proposing found it impossible to dislike him, much less to question his honesty of purpose. After more than three years of effort he was rewarded with success.

Jean-Luc Pépin had a special affection for the West. In some of our more relaxed moments, he often used to say that he would like to run for election there someday, and he believed that he could win. I think he was right.[17]

Afterword

John M. Fraser

AFTER THE TRIUMPHANT CONCLUSION to his four years as deputy minister of Transport, Arthur Kroeger went on to fill a succession of senior positions in the public service and weather a change of government. He became known as the "Dean of Deputy Ministers" or "the wisest of the old mandarins," and was held in the greatest respect by ministers and public servants alike.

That is not to say that he was simply a good, or even the best, grey public servant. He could—and did—stand up to his minister when he thought it necessary to do so. His testimony before parliamentary committees on the Canada–U.S. Free Trade Agreement has been described as "absolutely masterful. He managed not to say a word that would undermine the position of the government, but leaving no doubt to anybody who could read between the lines that he didn't really like the agreement."[1] He was particularly uneasy about its provisions on energy (then being deputy minister in the Department of Energy, Mines and Resources), and remarked rather sourly to friends that the government was not content with dutiful public servants who would carry out government policy; they wanted cheerleaders.

In 1988 he moved to the Department of Employment and Immigration as deputy minister. In that capacity he testified in 1991 before a parliamentary committee on the allegedly hasty admission to Canada of Saddam Hussein's ambassador in Washington (the so-called "Al-Mashat Affair"). Arthur readily agreed that deputy ministers were responsible for everything that went on in their department. "As," he added, "are ministers." The controversy about Al-Mashat arose not only because he had been admitted to Canada in the first place—and with what seemed like remarkable speed—but because no minister had been advised of the decision.

In fact, the speed was fortuitous. He was first considered as a possible defector, and the routine hurdles—medical examination, checking of police records, etc., had been more or less completed by the time that the Defectors Committee determined that he could not be considered a defector. His application was then considered under the "retiree" category and did indeed go forward with great speed, the preliminary spadework having already been done. The late Anthony Vincent, then director of the Security Division in the Department of External Affairs, was anxious that if Al-Mashat was to be admitted to Canada the decision be taken quickly. A decision on the application of another Iraqi ambassador seeking refuge (not in Canada) after having been ordered to return to Baghdad was still pending when his dead body was found on a Mediterranean beach.

Arthur's reference to the responsibility of ministers reflected a deeply held belief in their role. This was spelled out in a speech to the Empire Club of Canada in February 1990, for which he chose the title "In Praise of Politicians." He deplored the common tendency to denigrate politicians:

Politicians are important people with important responsibilities. What they do every day is too well known and too little understood. There is inadequate public comprehension of the constraints within which our politicians must function and the complexities that are the common fare of public life. In addition, elected people

in government and opposition alike are regularly maligned with
regard to their lifestyles and remuneration. Often, sadly, public and
private commentary alike conveys an impression that politicians are
simply freeloaders on the public purse whose primary interest is ego
gratification.[2]

He went on to say that he had "developed a respect for the seriousness of purpose that all but a handful consistently display, an
admiration for their willingness to make sacrifices in their personal
lives, and a certain wonderment that they put up with some of the
things they do."

He also insisted that "being a senior official does not tempt one
to think that government by technocrats would be a great idea. On
the contrary, the experience tends to reinforce one's democratic
instincts....The public may have reservations about its politicians,
but officials are not magicians either, and we know it."

It was his respect for elected politicians that lay behind his
concern about some of the recommendations by Mr. Justice Gomery
in his report on the so-called Sponsorship Scandal, which would
give unelected public servants a constitutional identity independent
of ministers and even allow the former to prevail in cases of tensions
in the management and administration of government programs.
Arthur Kroeger was one of the sixty notable figures in public life
who signed a letter to the prime minister in March 2004 with their
comments on the Gomery Report. Kroeger, who had participated in
round tables organized by the Gomery inquiry, believed that "the
core problem of the Report is that he was working with a subject that
I don't think he really understood."[3]

From January to March 1992 he organized a series of what
seemed to be highly successful public constitutional conferences
on the Charlottetown Accord. As it turned out, they were successful
in the same sense as "the operation was successful but the patient
died," since the Accord was rejected by all parts of Canada in the
subsequent referendum.

In 1992 Arthur Kroeger retired after thirty-four years in the public service of Canada. "Retired" is not exactly the right word. Shortly after his retirement, he took the chair of the Public Policy Forum, which he held until 1994. For the rest of his life he held a variety of high-level academic and non-governmental positions.

His counsel had frequently been sought when he was a senior official. Prime Minister Mulroney, for instance, had him look into the highly controversial subject of Canadian participation in the Strategic Defence Initiative (a.k.a. "Star Wars") being pursued by Washington. Those who supported a role for Canada argued that it was unbecoming for an ally of the United States to turn down a request—particularly one that asked so little of us. Those opposed, probably a majority and certainly more vocal, objected that for us to take part in what they considered a dubious and obnoxious plan flew in the face of our long-standing opposition to the militarization of space. There were also those who worried that American reactions to a refusal would be damaging. The level-headed conclusion of Arthur Kroeger's June 1985 report was that there was no need and little advantage for the Canadian government to become directly involved but that we should not discourage Canadian firms from seeking contracts in the project.

Nor did his retirement put an end to requests for his advice. When the Liberals came to power in 1993, according to the *Globe and Mail*, Paul Martin (whom Arthur had known since the days when he was deputy minister of Transport and Martin was head of Canada Steamship Lines) was anxious to join the Cabinet, preferably as minister of Industry. "A big mistake," Mr. Kroeger told him, and urged him instead to become the Finance minister, because that was "where the power lies."[4] Twelve years later, in November 2005, the minister of Industry, David L. Emerson, announced that Industry Canada had "engaged the services of Arthur Kroeger to advise on the design of the new Transformative Technologies Program." He would "provide independent advice to Industry Canada's senior management on the overall transparency, governance and accountability of the new program, as well as its terms and conditions, due diligence and the selection process for projects."[5]

It was clearly not his technological expertise that was being called upon. While he had become perfectly competent in the use of a computer, he had little enthusiasm for the galaxy of high-tech gadgets that seem to have taken over the world. Indeed, he prided himself on still using a wet-nibbed pen. When his daughters, one in India and one in Bosnia, persuaded him that he would really have to upgrade his computer equipment to be able to communicate with them, he gave the old set to Rockcliffe Park Public School. The principal sent him an appreciative letter of thanks, noting that his gift was already in use—in the kindergarten.

His comments were also frequently sought by journalists, with whom he had always enjoyed a cordial relationship. When a member of the Parliamentary Press Gallery, who was also a friend, apologized for presuming upon the friendship by taking up the time of a busy deputy minister with questions, Arthur replied simply that he had always considered responding to questions from the press as part of his job.

In 1989 he received the Public Service Outstanding Achievement Award and was appointed an Officer of the Order of Canada, becoming a Companion of the Order in 2000.

Also in 2000, he was elected an honourary Fellow of Pembroke College, Oxford, and also received the Distinguished Alumnus Award from the University of Alberta.

He served as Chancellor of Carleton University from 1993 to 2002, and subsequently as Chancellor Emeritus. As might be expected, he chose an active, not just a ceremonial role. A woman who served as a representative of the Carleton staff on the board of governors wrote in a letter to the student newspaper that Arthur, as Chancellor, was extremely supportive of the rights of students and women and liked to see them excel.

For part of the time he was Chancellor at Carleton, he was also a visiting professor at the University of Toronto and a visiting Fellow at Queen's University. In 1999 Carleton named its new faculty for the study of public affairs "The Kroeger College of Public Affairs." A university colleague who was present when the proposal was made said that it was the only time he had ever seen Arthur embarrassed. He was totally unpretentious, and, characteristically, took a close interest in the college. As one recent graduate wrote not long after Arthur's death,

> Arthur Kroeger gave more than his name to the college of public affairs and policy management at Carleton University. Insisting that the students call him Arthur, he was present each September to meet first-year entrants to the College. He also attended each convocation ceremony to applaud jubilant graduates and found ample opportunity to support and engage with individual students....Despite his absence in this [2008] spring's convocation, AKC students will continue to be eminently proud that their diplomas pay tribute to a wonderfully kind and fiercely intelligent Canadian icon.[6]

He clearly had great skill in management, but, unlike some other senior managers in the public service, did not see "management" as an end in itself. Nor was he ever heard to indulge in the jargon of "management-speak." He had, after all, taught English at a private boys' boarding school after graduating from the University of Alberta, and even though he abandoned his degree course in English in favour of Philosophy, Politics and Economics shortly after he got to Oxford and discovered that the Oxford English curriculum was designed to produce academics in the subject, he retained a healthy respect for the language.

Although many things about the English irritated him, Arthur always retained his affection for Oxford and for Pembroke College and was active in the Canadian Association of Rhodes Scholars until his death. He was instrumental, as president of the association, in designing a program in Ottawa for Scholars-elect on the eve of their departure for Oxford. Previously, Canadian Scholars-elect had joined their American colleagues for pre-departure festivities in New York. At his insistence, the Canadian "pre-sailing dinner," as it is anachronistically known, ended with a glass of port to introduce them to an Oxford custom. As president and subsequently as a member of the executive of the association, he was anxious to encourage women Scholars and those of more recent vintage to be active in the association and to assume positions of responsibility.

This concern mirrored his efforts to encourage and advance women in the public service, reflected in a book published by the Canadian Centre for Management Development under the title *Now Comes the Turn of Women*. Perhaps because his wife, Gabrielle (Gay) Sellers, had had to resign from the foreign service when she married Arthur, he was always conscious of the failure of government to take full advantage of the talents and potential of its female employees. One woman working in a department of which he was deputy minister had just returned to work after the death of her husband. She had two small children. Arthur took her out to lunch and told her that he understood what she was going through (Gay died in 1979, leaving Arthur with two small girls to look after) and was sure that she would be able to cope.

Not the least of Arthur's accomplishments was bringing up two impressive daughters and giving them encouragement and support while holding a series of demanding high-level positions in the public service. He had always been something of a workaholic, and clearly became, of necessity, highly skilled in managing his time, even going so far as to take a course in speed-reading. He always had time for his family and his friends, who will remember him as unfailingly kind, helpful, and generous, with a quiet but engaging sense of humour. His life was also enriched by the companionship of Huguette Labelle, who, like Arthur, had held a series of senior positions in the public service. These included under-secretary of state in the Department of the Secretary of State (1980–1985), chairman of the Public Service Commission of Canada (1985–1990) and deputy minister of Transport (1990–1993), and president of the Canadian International Development Agency (1993–1999). In 1994 she was appointed Chancellor of the University of Ottawa. She is clearly just as much of a workaholic as Arthur was.

Lest he succumb to idleness, he was chairman of the Canadian Policy Research Network and the National Statistics Council up to the time of his death. He also took pleasure in participating in the CBC's federal budget "lock-up" and broadcast every year after he left the public service—even in 2008, when he had to find a place to lie down for naps and was exhausted for a day or two afterwards.

An outline of his distinguished career gives a slightly misleading impression. He was rarely solemn and never pompous. As someone who worked in the Department of Employment and Immigration when he was deputy minister put it, "He was fun to be with."

Notes

2 Hallowed Arrangements

1. Howard Palmer, with Tamara Palmer, *Alberta: A New History* (Edmonton: Hurtig Publishers, 1990), 59.
2. Library and Archives Canada (LAC), RG 6, vol. 107, file 5471. See also the brief submitted by the Manitoba government to the Standing Committee on Transport, Winnipeg, 4 August 1983.
3. LAC, RG 6, vol. 107, file 796.
4. Barry Wilson, *Beyond the Harvest* (Saskatoon: Western Producer Prairie Books, 1981), 171.
5. Board of Transport Commissioners for Canada, *Royal Commission on Transportation Hearings*, vol. 1, by M.A. MacPherson (Ottawa: Board of Transport Commissioners for Canada, 1959–61), Preface. LAC, file CAZI.1959.3.
6. LAC, RG 12, vol. 1350, file 3916.13.
7. J.M. Gibbon, *Steel of Empire: The Romantic History of the Canadian Pacific, the Northwest Passage of Today* (Toronto: McClelland & Stewart, c.1935).
8. Board of Transport Commissioners, *Royal Commission on Transportation Hearings*, vol. 2, 76, table 2.
9. Paul D. Earl, *Mac Runciman: A Life in the Grain Trade* (Winnipeg: University of Manitoba Press, 2000), 177.

10. Interview with Otto Lang.
11. *Western Producer*, 5 November 1974; 28 November 1974; 5 December 1974.
12. G.E. Britnell, and V.C. Fowke, *Canadian Agriculture in War and Peace, 1935–50* (Stanford: Stanford University Press, 1962), 55.
13. LAC, MG 26 019, vol. 34, file 3.
14. The Canadian Press, 24 February 1982.
15. *Regina Leader-Post*, 4 February 1982.

3 The Art of the Possible

1. *Toronto Star*, 9 December 1980.
2. Arthur Kroeger Personal Archive, draft memorandum to Cabinet from the minister of Transport, 25 November 1981.
3. G. Fairbairn, *From Prairie Roots* (Saskatoon: Western Producer Prairie Books, 1984), 165, 208.
4. Privately commissioned poll by Earnscliffe Strategy Group, Ottawa, December 1999.
5. Privately commissioned poll by Earnscliffe Strategy Group, Ottawa, December 1999.
6. Fairbairn, *From Prairie Roots*, 120.
7. Arthur Kroeger Personal Archive, notes of telephone conversation with Allan Blakeney, June 2005. Found in author's notebook after his death.
8. *Western Producer*, 10 December 1981.
9. *Western Producer*, 12 February 1979.
10. *Western Producer*, 12 July 1980.

4 The Shoals of History

1. Cabinet documents 710–74 RD, 710–74 RD (1) (c), 710–74 RD (1975) 230–81 RDC.
2. Liberal Party Resolution, Winnipeg, July 1980. The resolution called for judicial inquiry into CP.
3. Board of Transport Commissioners, *Royal Commission on Transportation Hearings*, vol. 2, 72–76.
4. Cabinet document 65–80 CBM, 19 June 1980.
5. Arthur Kroeger Personal Archive.
6. Arthur Kroeger Personal Archive, paper on transportation initiatives in western Canada, prepared by Transport Canada in response to a request from the Ministry of State for Economic Development, 24 June 1982.

7. Arthur Kroeger Personal Archive, Policy Proposal Designed to Retain the Benefits and Minimize the Negative Impact of Statutory Grain Freight Rates, Western Agricultural Conference, August 1980.
8. Cabinet document 70–80 CBM, 24 July 1980.
9. Arthur Kroeger Personal Archive, notes from meeting, 9 September 1980.
10. Cabinet document 8–80 MAHWA, 7 October 1980.
11. Arthur Kroeger Personal Archive, draft Cabinet document, 31 October 1980.
12. Arthur Kroeger Personal Archive.
13. Arthur Kroeger Personal Archive, Cabinet memorandum of 12 January 1981.
14. Cabinet document 5–81 CBM, 12 February 1981.
15. Arthur Kroeger Personal Archive, transcript of press conference by Prime Minister Pierre Trudeau, National Press Theatre, Ottawa, 12 February 1987.
16. *House of Commons Debates* (13 February 1982) at 7212 (Hon. Pierre Trudeau).
17. *Montreal Gazette*, 10 February 1981.

5 On Hold

1. Arthur Kroeger Personal Archive, memo from Bill Haney to Michael Kirby, 12 February 1981.
2. Communiqué from four western provinces following meeting of First Ministers on the Constitution, 16 April 1981.
3. "Dead Crow," *Financial Post*, 16 February 1981.
4. *Western Producer*, 26 February 1981.
5. Arthur Kroeger Personal Archive, notes. See also *Regina Leader-Post*, 16 December 1981.
6. See the analysis in the minister of Transport's memorandum to Cabinet, 25 November 1981.
7. Cabinet document 430–81 RD.
8. Cabinet document 431–81 CBM, meeting of 6 September 1981.
9. *Saskatoon StarPhoenix*, 30 November 1981.
10. Arthur Kroeger Personal Archive, draft Cabinet memorandum of 29 October 1981, recommendation 11.
11. *Regina Leader-Post*, 21 January 1982.
12. Bob Beaty, "Argue Rails Against Demands for Crow Rate Increase," *Calgary Herald*, 28 November 1981, p. 1.

13. *Brandon Sun*, 3 November 1981.
14. Arthur Kroeger Personal Archive.
15. Arthur Kroeger Personal Archive, letter of 7 December 1981.
16. Arthur Kroeger Personal Archive, letter of 7 December 1981.
17. *Regina Leader-Post*, 13 December 1981.

6 At Centre Ice

1. Arthur Kroeger Personal Archive, departmental briefing note of 1 February 1983. See also David R. Harvey, *Christmas Turkey or Prairie Vulture?* (Montreal: Institute for Research on Public Policy, 1980), 1.
2. *Saskatoon StarPhoenix*, 11 February 1982.
3. Quoted in *Transport Canada*, 15 February 1982, p. 75.
4. *Edmonton Journal*, 9 February 1982.
5. Jack Francis, "Most Farm Groups Applaud Crow Move," *Winnipeg Free Press*, 9 February 1982.
6. Mark Wilson, "Pépin's Grain Rate Stance Furthers his Gutsy Image," *Vancouver Province*, 10 February 1982.
7. Bob Beaty, "West Farm Leaders Happy with Gilson," *Calgary Herald*, 9 February 1982.
8. "Crow Future Still in Question," *Saskatoon StarPhoenix*, 11 February 1982.
9. "Liberals' Gain, Farmers' Loss," *Swift Current Sun*, 11 February 1982.
10. "Announcement a Beginning," *Melfort Journal*, 10 February 1982.
11. "Cold Reality," *Manitoba Co-operator*, 11 February 1982.
12. *Alberta Report*, 19 April 1982.
13. Taking Aim at the Crow," *Montreal Gazette*, 11 February 1982.
14. Arthur Kroeger Personal Archive, activity report from Henry Ropertz, 15 March 1982.
15. *Globe and Mail*, 9 February 1982, column by James Rusk.
16. Bob Hainstock, "Early Innings in the Crow Game," *Manitoba Co-operator*, 11 March 1982.
17. *Regina Leader-Post*, 26 February 1982.
18. *House of Commons Debates* (9 February 1982) at 14804; *Saskatoon StarPhoenix*, 9 February 1982.
19. *Assiniboia Times*, 10 February 1982.
20. *House of Commons Debates* (26 February 1982) at 15434 (Don Mazankowski).
21. Arthur Kroeger Personal Archive, copy of letter from Ted Turner to Prime Minister Pierre Trudeau, 2 April 1982.

7 Cobbling Together a Consensus

1. J.C. Gilson, *Western Grain Transportation: Report on Consultations and Recommendations* (Ottawa: Ministry of Supply and Services, 1982), Section 1-1.
2. Gilson, *Western Grain Transportation*, Section 1-1.
3. Alan Daniels, "Dead Crow Casts Shadow over Railways," *Vancouver Sun*, 9 February 1982.
4. Arthur Kroeger Personal Archive, briefing memos of 28 February 1982 and 15 December 1982.
5. Grain Handling and Transportation Commission. *Grain and Rail in Western Canada: The Report of the Grain Handling and Transportation Commission*, by Emmett Hall (Ottawa, Minister of Supply and Services Canada, 1977) 143.
6. Arthur Kroeger Personal Archive, memos from Carl Snavely to Mike Farquhar, 12 October and 17 October 1982.
7. *Western Producer*, 29 June 1978.
8. See also the submission of the Saskatchewan Wheat Pool to the Standing Committee on Transport, Regina, 9 August 1983.
9. Farm Report, radio station CKCK Regina, 15 September 1982.
10. Grain Handling and Transportation Commission. *Grain and rail in Western Canada*, Vol. 1, 70.
11. *Western Producer*, 25 February 1982; Toronto *Globe and Mail*, 15 February 1982.
12. *Regina Leader-Post*, 16 February 1981.
13. *Regina Leader-Post*, 22 January 1982.
14. The Canadian Press, 12 March 1982.
15. SaskPool *Report*, March 1982.
16. *Alberta Report*, 5 April 1982.
17. Clay Gilson, *Western Grain Transportation*, Section 1-2.
18. Western Grain Transportation Office, news release no. 6, 16 April 1982, Winnipeg.
19. Gilson, *Western Grain Transportation*, Section 11-2, para. 4.
20. Gilson, *Western Grain Transportation*, Section vi-7. Sent to Jean-Luc Pépin, 15 June 1982.
21. Gilson, *Western Grain Transportation*, Section iv-4.
22. Gilson, *Western Grain Transportation*, Section v-37.
23. Gilson, *Western Grain Transportation*, Section v-37.
24. Gilson, *Western Grain Transportation*, Section vi-10-i.
25. Gilson, *Western Grain Transportation*, Section v-37.

26. Gilson, *Western Grain Transportation*, Section IV-5.
27. Cabinet document 166–82 MC (R), 9 July 1982.
28. *Saskatoon StarPhoenix*, 24 July 1982; Toronto *Globe and Mail*, 29 July 1982.
29. *Western Producer*, 7 October 1982.
30. *Calgary Herald*, 7 July 1982; see also CNR release, 29 June 1982.

8 The Centre Cannot Hold

1. Barry Wilson, "Crow Landscape More Complicated all the Time," *The Western Producer*, 14 October 1982.
2. *Winnipeg Free Press*, 18 January 1983.
3. *Winnipeg Free Press*, 11 September 1983.
4. *Le Devoir*, 18 February 1983.
5. Arthur Kroeger Personal Archive, memorandum to Cabinet: Western Railway Transportation—Proposals for Implementation of a Comprehensive Solution, 12 January 1982. Presented by Jean-Luc Pépin, minister of Transport, Section 7.0, Federal-Provincial Relations Considerations.
6. *Manitoba Co-operator*, 3 November 1982.
7. *Le Devoir* and *Le Droit*, 3 September 1982.
8. *La Presse*, 27 September 1982; Radio-Canada, 6 October 1982.
9. Radio-Canada, 26 September 1982.
10. *Le Droit*, 12 December 1982.
11. *Le Devoir*, 18 January 1983.
12. LAC, MG 32 B56, Vol. 104–27, letter from Jean-Guy Dubois, chairman, sub-committee of the Quebec Caucus on the Gilson Report, to Jean-Luc Pépin, 25 January 1983.
13. *Le Soleil*, 24 November 1982.
14. *Manitoba Co-operator*, 24 March 1983. See also letter from Premier Davis, 16 January 1984, LAC, MG 26 019, file 32.18.
15. *Saskatoon StarPhoenix*, 20 December 1982.
16. Arthur Kroeger Personal Archive, document entitled "A Third Payment Option," presented by the minister of state for the Canadian Wheat Board, 8 November 1982.
17. *Western Producer*, 21 January 1983.
18. Cabinet document 599–82CR(1)/624–82CR(1)/631–82CR91), Report of Committee Decision: Western Transportation Initiative, 22 December 1982.

9 Lost Reforms

1. Cabinet document 2–83 CBM.
2. Arthur Kroeger Personal Archive, letter from Gordon Osbaldeston to Arthur Kroeger, 24 January 1983.
3. Mark Wilson, "Crow Plan Final, Says Pépin," *Vancouver Province*, 4 February 1983.
4. "Crow Rate Compromise," *Winnipeg Free Press*, 2 February 1983.
5. "Pépin Christens New Era in Western Agriculture," *Calgary Herald*, 1 February 1983.
6. "Trauma in Crow Demise," *Saskatoon StarPhoenix*, 2 February 1983.
7. "Time Crow was Killed," *Cornwall Standard Freeholder*, 5 February 1983, p. 4.
8. The Canadian Press, 10 February 1983.
9. Don Braid, "Pépin Shows Grace that Trudeau Lacks," *Edmonton Journal*, 4 February 1983, A10.
10. *Regina Leader-Post*, 20 February 1982.
11. *Western Producer*, 19 March 1983.
12. Interview with Barry Wilson on CTV, 24 February 1983.
13. *Saskatoon StarPhoenix*, 26 February 1983.
14. Bob Beaty, "Joining up with East could be Considered Traitorous," *Calgary Herald*, 25 September 1982.
15. Link Byfield, "The Crow Will Tell us what really Matters to Ottawa," *Alberta Report*, 1 November 1982.
16. The Canadian Press, 18 April 1983.
17. Arthur Kroeger Personal Archive, "Happy New Year 1982–83," memo to Jean-Luc Pépin, 1 September 1982.
18. *Grainews*, February 1983; *Regina Leader-Post*, 28 January 1983.
19. *Regina Leader-Post*, 2 February 1983.
20. Cabinet document 125–83 RD, 30 March 1983.
21. The Canadian Press, 15 April 1983; *Winnipeg Free Press*, 16 April and 18 April 1983.
22. *Saskatoon StarPhoenix*, 6 October 1983; CBC, 6 October 1983; *Western Producer*, 7 October 1983.
23. House of Commons, Minutes of Proceedings and Evidence of the Standing Committee on Transport, Respecting Bill C-155, *An Act to Facilitate the Transportation, Shipping and Handling of Western Grain and to Amend Certain Acts in Consequence.* Issue no. 114, Regina, 9 August 1983, p. 134.
24. Cabinet document 11–83 CBM, April 13, 1983.

25. Minutes of Committee on Priorities and Planning meeting,
    12 April 1983.

10 Democracy

1. Bob Beaty, "Pépin's 'Heart Crying' over Final Crow Bill," *Calgary Herald*,
    6 May 1983.
2. *Regina Leader-Post*, 24 February 1983.
3. Arthur Kroeger Personal Archive, speech by Jean-Luc Pépin to the
    Saskatchewan Association of Rural Municipalities, Regina,
    12 March 1982.
4. The Canadian Press, 7 May 1983; Toronto *Globe and Mail*, 11 May 1983.
    See also LAC, MG 26 019, Vol. 33, file 33–2, memo of 9 May from David
    Miller to the minister.
5. Carrol Jacques, *Unifarm: A Story of Conflict and Change* (Calgary:
    University of Calgary Press, 2001), 240.
6. Mario Numais, "Les conservateurs et le nid-de-corbeau: Un parti, trois
    politiques," personal archive, undated, untitled newspaper cutting.
7. Cabinet document 17–83 CBM, 25 May 1983.
8. Cabinet document 17–83 CBM, p. 7, under the heading "Business
    of the House."
9. *Western Producer*, 3 June 1983; *Saskatoon StarPhoenix*,
    20 December 1982.
10. "Crow Reform Too Divisive," *Saskatoon StarPhoenix*, 25 May 1983.
11. *Calgary Herald*, 30 May 1983.
12. Cabinet document 19–83 CBM, 1 June 1983.
13. Minutes of Proceedings and Evidence of the Standing Committee on
    Transport, Issue no. 109, Edmonton, p. 43.
14. Minutes of Proceedings and Evidence of the Standing Committee on
    Transport, Issue no. 107, Ottawa, 28 July 1983, p. 17.
15. Minutes of Proceedings and Evidence of the Standing Committee on
    Transport, Issue no. 110, Winnipeg, 4 August 1983, p. 84.
16. Minutes of Proceedings and Evidence of the Standing Committee on
    Transport, Issue no. 114, Regina, 9 August 1983, p. 10.
17. Minutes of Proceedings and Evidence of the Standing Committee on
    Transport, Issue no. 114, Regina, 9 August 1983, p. 8.
18. Minutes of Proceedings and Evidence of the Standing Committee on
    Transport, Issue no. 115, Regina, 10 August 1983, p. 86.
19. Minutes of Proceedings and Evidence of the Standing Committee on
    Transport, Issue no. 114, Regina, 9 August 1983, p. 111.

20. Minutes of Proceedings and Evidence of the Standing Committee on Transport, Issue no. 115, Regina, 10 August 1983, p. 9.

21. Minutes of Proceedings and Evidence of the Standing Committee on Transport, Issue no. 118, Quebec City, 16 August 1983, p. 80.

11 *Where the Crow Lives*

1. LAC, MG 32 B56, Vol. 38, letter from Chris Mills to Jean-Luc Pépin, 15 August 1983

2. LAC, MG 32 B56, Vol. 38.

3. Minutes of Proceedings and Evidence of the Standing Committee on Transport, Issue no. 123, Ottawa, 30 August 1983, p. 100.

4. Minutes of Proceedings and Evidence of the Standing Committee on Transport, Issue no. 122, Ottawa, 25 August 1983, pp. 97–98.

5. Minutes of Proceedings and Evidence of the Standing Committee on Transport, Issue no. 128, Ottawa, 8 September 1983, p. 16.

6. *Edmonton Journal*, 2 September 1983.

7. Alex Binkley, "Axworthy Fuming at Crow Flip-flop," *Brandon Sun*, 14 September 1983.

8. "Scuttling Crow Reform," *Winnipeg Free Press*, 15 September 1983.

9. *Calgary Herald*, 15 September 1983; *Winnipeg Free Press*, 15 September 1983.

10. *Winnipeg Free Press*, 20 September 1983.

11. Minutes of Proceedings and Evidence of the Standing Committee on Transport, Issue no. 142, Ottawa, 21 September 1983, p. 19.

12. Minutes of Proceedings and Evidence of the Standing Committee on Transport, Issue no. 143, Ottawa, 21 September 1983, p. 56–62.

13. Minutes of Proceedings and Evidence of the Standing Committee on Transport, Issue no. 143, Ottawa, 21 September 1983, p. 56–62.

14. Cabinet document 505–83 MC (BILL), 22 September 1983.

15. CBC *Sunday Morning*, 2 October 1983.

16. Statement issued by MacMurchy, 8 March 1982; and *Western Producer*, 19 March 1983.

17. *House of Commons Debates* (4 November 1983) at 28800 (Don Mazankowski).

18. "One Crow, to Go," *Globe and Mail*, 3 November 1983.

19. *House of Commons Debates* (4 November 1983) at 28790–28791 (Lloyd Axworthy).

20. "Credit to the Liberals for Killing Crow," *Edmonton Journal*, 16 November 1983.

12 Outcomes and Lessons

1. *Western Producer*, 9 June 2005.
2. Library of Parliament, Table 7; and *Western Producer*, 9 June 2005.
3. Library of Parliament, *Grain Transportation in Canada*.
4. *Globe and Mail, Report on Business*, May 2005; and *Canadian Business*, 20 June 2005.
5. *Western Producer*, 9 June 2005; 20 October 2005; and 1 December 2005.
6. Library of Parliament, Table 5b; and Kurt Klein, "Agricultural Production and Value-Added Activities: The Crops Sector," in Chorney, *The Agricultural Industry after Western Grain Transportation Reform*, 63–77.
7. Edward W. Tyrchniewicz, "Agricultural Production and Value-Added Activities: The Pork Sector," in Chorney, *The Agricultural Industry after Western Grain Transportation Reform*, 78; and Janet Honey, "Agricultural Production and Value-Added Activities: The Beef Sector," in Chorney, *The Agricultural Industry after Western Grain Transportation Reform*, 86.
8. *Calgary Herald*, 15 September 1983; *Alberta Report*, 26 September 1983.
9. CBC Farm Show, 10 January 1982.
10. *Western Producer*, 6 October 2005.
11. *House of Commons Debates* (25 May 1984) at 4054 (Len Gustafson).
12. *House of Commons Debates* (25 May 1984) at 40060 (Doug Neil).
13. *Montreal Gazette*, 22 August 1983.
14. *Saturday Night*, July 1982.
15. Arthur Kroeger Personal Archive, summary of the Saskatchewan Wheat Pool Special Delegates' Meeting, 17 February 1983. Typed summary prepared for the Department of Transport.
16. See for example a speech by John Fraser, MP, to the Vancouver Rotary Club, 4 October 1983.
17. Arthur Kroeger, "In Appreciation of Jean-Luc Pépin," *TC Express* 1440, no. 167 (September/October 1995): 1.

Afterword

1. Gordon Ritchie, quoted in *Ottawa Citizen*, 11 May 2008.
2. Speech to the Empire Club of Canada, 8 February 1990, http://speeches.empireclub.org/.
3. *Toronto Star*, 7 March 2006.
4. *Globe and Mail*, 12 May 2008.
5. Industry Canada press release, 21 November 2005.
6. Nora Adario Draper, "I Remember...," *Globe and Mail*, 13 May 2008.

Bibliography

Board of Transport Commissioners for Canada, *Royal Commission on Transportation Hearings*, by M.A. MacPherson. Ottawa: Board of Transport Commissioners for Canada, 1959–61.

Britnell, G.E. and V.C. Fowke. *Canadian Agriculture in War and Peace, 1935–50*. Stanford: Stanford University Press, 1962.

Canada. Royal Commission on the Shipment and Transportation of Grain. *Return to an Order of the House of Commons, dated March 19, 1900, for a copy of the Report and Evidence of the Royal Commission on the Shipment and Transportation of Grain*. Sessional Paper no. 81a, 63. Victoria, 1900.

Canada Grains Council. Grain Handling and Transportation Committee. *Grain Handling and Transportation: State of the Industry: A Special Committee Report*. Winnipeg: Canada Grains Council, 1973.

Chorney, Brenda, ed. *Proceedings of the Conference on The Agricultural Industry after Western Grain Transportation Reform: The Good, the Bad and the Unexpected*. Winnipeg: University of Manitoba, Department of Agribusiness and Agricultural Economics, October 23–24, 2003.

Christopher, John. *The Crow's Nest Pass Freight Rates*. Ottawa: Library of Parliament Research Branch, February 5, 1982.

Cruise, David and Alison Griffiths. *Lords of the Line*. Toronto: Penguin Books Canada, 1988.

Earl, Paul D. *Mac Runciman: A Life in the Grain Trade*. Winnipeg: University of Manitoba Press, 2000.

241

Fairbairn, G. *From Prairie Roots*. Saskatoon: Western Producer Prairie
    Books, 1984.
Gibbon, J.M. *The Romantic History of the Canadian Pacific*. Toronto:
    McClelland & Stewart, 1935.
Gilson, J.C. *Western Grain Transportation: Report on Consultations and
    Recommendations*. Ottawa: Supply and Services Canada, 1982.
Grain Handling and Transportation Commission. *Grain and Rail in
    Western Canada: The Report of the Grain Handling and Transportation
    Commission*, by Emmett Hall. Ottawa: Minister of Supply and Services
    Canada, 1977.
Grain Transportation Authority, Transport Canada. *Costs and Revenues
    Incurred by the Railways in the Transportation of Grain under the Statutory
    Rates*. Washington, DC: Snavely, King and Associates, 1981.
Harvey, David R. *Christmas Turkey or Prairie Vulture?* Montreal: Institute
    for Research on Public Policy, 1980.
Heads, John, ed. *Proceedings of a Conference, January, 1989, Occasional Paper
    No. 7*. Winnipeg: University of Manitoba Transport Institute, 1989.
Innis, H.A. *A History of the Canadian Pacific Railway*. 1923. Toronto:
    University of Toronto Press, 1971.
Jacques, Carrol. *Unifarm: A Story of Conflict and Change*. Calgary: University
    of Calgary Press, 2001.
MacEwan, Grant. *Illustrated History of Western Canadian Agriculture*.
    Saskatoon: Western Producer Prairie Books, 1980.
Murta, Jack. *Final Report of the Emergency Grain Movement Task Force*.
    Ottawa: Library of Parliament, October 30, 1979.
Palmer, Howard with Tamara Palmer. *Alberta: A New History*. Edmonton:
    Hurtig Publishers, 1990.
Rea, J.T. *T.A. Crerar: A Political Life*. Montreal and Kingston: McGill-Queen's
    University Press, 1997.
Wardhaugh, R.A. *Mackenzie King and the Prairie West*. Toronto: University
    of Toronto Press, 2000.
Wilson, Barry. *Beyond the Harvest*. Saskatoon: Western Producer Prairie
    Books, 1981.
———. *Farming the System*. Western Producer Prairie Books, 1990.

Index

Blakeney, Allan, 27, 47, 54, 84, 103, 109, 212

Bloc Quebecois, 207

Board of Railway Commissioners, 10

Bockstael, Robert, 93, 166–7

Borden, Robert, 12

Bouchard, Lucien, 207

Braid, Don, 47, 134

branch lines: Bill C-155 and, 169–70; deterioration of, 14; freight rates and, 143; government control over abandonment of, 13, 36, 83, 98, 201; and prairie settlements, 82–3; rehabilitation of, 16, 41, 61, 66, 96; subsidies, 63; and urban migration, 36

Brandon Sun, 189

British Columbia: and Bill C-155, 156, 172; and changes to Crow, 30, 66, 135; coal production, 7–8; Liberal representation in federal government, 34; PC MPs from, 155

Broadbent, Ed, 34, 92

Burbidge, Fred, 211

Burns, Tom, 60, 159, 160, 162

Cabinet: Argue and, 68; and CPR, 39–40; and Crow modernization, 53; expenditure cuts, 116; Legislation and House Planning committee, 193; memoranda, 69, 71; Pépin and, 47–8, 103; Priorities and Planning committee, 4–5, 50–1, 62–4, 72, 76, 80, 126, 127, 147; and producer payments, 148; and proposals for Crow

modernization, 69–74, 75–6; and Quebec, 147, 148; task force on future rail capacity and, 65; and transportation issues, 47–8; WAC and, 51

Cabinet Committee on Economic Development: and consultative process, 73; and Crow modernization proposals, 31, 43, 44, 45, 50, 69, 80, 127; and Gilson recommendations, 112; oral presentations and, 71; and systems approach, 73

Cabinet Committee on Western Affairs: Axworthy as chair of, 37–8, 46, 177; creation of, 37–8; and Crow modernization proposals, 41, 43–4, 45, 80, 112; and inquiry into CPR, 40, 43–4; meeting in Winnipeg, 93; and Western consensus, 69; and Western Development Fund, 49

Calgary Herald, 132, 137, 151, 160

Campbell, Doug, 81

Campbell, Kim, 200

Canada Grains Council, 29

Canada West Foundation, 56

Canadian Association of Rhodes Scholars, 228–9

Canadian Cattlemen's Association, 79

Canadian Chamber of Commerce, 79, 160, 171, 217

Canadian Co-operative Federation (CCF), 25, 46

Canadian Exporters' Association, 60, 159, 168

Canadian Federation of Agriculture, 18, 42, 50, 51, 86, 133–4

cost sharing, 107–8, 117–18; federal government and, 117–18; and grain producers, 110–11, 117–18; and grain transportation costs, 117; on hybrid subsidy system, 108, 118–19; and joint task forces, 108, 208; as "made in the West" solution, 109, 215; Ontario and, 125; Prairie Farm Commodity Coalition and, 111; and Quebec, 120, 121–2, 123, 124, 172; and railways, 111–12, 168; release of, 109; and Saskatchewan government, 109–10; and WGTA, 199; and Wheat Pools, 110, 111

Globe and Mail, 81, 196

Gomery report, 225

Goodale, Ralph, 84, 92, 200

Gordon, Walter, 178

grain: agricultural processing industry and cost of, 99–100; exports, 17, 58, 119, 206; prices, 8–9, 15, 120–2, 140, 159, 194, 205, 206; WGTA and rationalization of handling system, 202–3

Grain Monitoring Agency, 201

grain producers: Bill C-155 and, 194–5; and change to Crow rate, 45; compensation for, 15; and compensation for railways, 105; cost increases for, 18, 44, 105, 107–8, 112, 117–18, 121–2, 145–6, 216; costs for transportation, storage, and handling, 15–16, 24–5; and Crow gap, 72; division on subject of Crow, 102–3; equalization of costs by SaskPool, 101–2;

federal government subsidy and, 97; freight rates and, 8; and Gilson consultations, 103–4; Gilson report and, 110–11; impact of Crow change on, 89; and impact of Crow changes on local communities, 146; income and assets of, 172; letter from Pépin to, 88; numbers of, 204, 217; PCS and payments to, 199; percentage of cost of grain transportation, 95, 96; on Senior Grain Transportation Committee, 186; size of farms, 204; and variable rates, 94; Wheat Pools and, 146; Wheat Pools and payments to, 111

grain terminals, 98, 203

grain transportation: distances of, 10; efficiency of system, 96, 97–8, 144; federal government spending on, 23, 24; railways' losses in, 13; Royal Commissions and inquiries, 11–12. *See also* railways

grain transportation costs, 126; in Canada *vs.* U.S., 98; and federal government, 96; federal government subsidies for, 105, 108, 112–13, 122, 125, 127, 140, 186–7; increases in, 48, 107–8, 117–18, 216; paid by producers *vs.* railways, 189; for producers, 15–16, 95; by rail, 15–16, 98, 159, 201; sharing of (*see* cost sharing)

Grain Transportation Division, 59, 63

Gustafson, Len, 155, 214

Hackston, David, 179, *184*, 210
Hall, Emmett, 65–6, 170
Hall Commission, 98, 102, 146, 211
Hamilton, Alvin, 92
Hargrave, Bert, 92, 155
Hartman, John, 3
Heads, John, 165, 179, *184*, 210
Horner, Jack, 160, 200
House Standing Committee on
    Agriculture, 207
Howe, Bruce, 152, 160, 163–4

Ignatieff, George, 37
Industry Canada, 226
Interstate Commerce Commission,
    73

King, Mackenzie, 10, 12–13
Kroeger, Arthur, 29, *133*, *184*, *185*,
    197; agricultural organizations
    and, 149–50; appointed deputy
    minister of Transport, 2; and
    Axworthy, 193, 197–8; and
    Burns, 159; and Canadian Policy
    Research Network, 230; career
    of, 2, 223–4; as Chancellor of
    Carleton University, 227–8;
    and Charlottetown Accord, 225;
    charts of, 71–2, 80, 85, 110;
    and clause-by-clause phase of
    Bill C-155, 178–9, 182–6, 188,
    192; and committee phase of
    Bill C-155, 167; and consultative
    process, 80–1; daughters of,
    1, 31, 198, 229; in Department
    of External Affairs, 175; early
    life in West, 3, 209–10; end of
    involvement in Crow, 192–3;
    and Gomery report, 225; and
    high technology, 227; honours

received by, 227; and Kroeger
College of Public Affairs, 228;
and Martin, 226; media and, *133*,
227; with mserd, 164–5, 167; and
National Statistics Council, 230;
Now Comes the Turn of Women,
229; and Oxford University,
227, 228–9; and Pépin, 1–2,
22, 141–2, 218–19; personality,
230; and policy statement for
Cabinet, 79–80; on politicians,
224–5; and Priorities and
Planning Committee, 50–1; at
Public Policy Forum, 226; in
Quebec, 139–40, 140, 160, 162;
and Queen's University, 228;
on responsibility of ministers,
224–5; retirement, 226;
retrospective on Pépin for *tc
Express*, 220–1; and Strategic
Defence Initiative, 226; as
teacher, 228; and Transformative
Technologies Program, 226–7;
and University of Toronto, 227;
in West, 24–5, 28–31, 42–3,
48–9, 78–9, 84–5, 110–11,
132–6; Western trips with Pépin,
24–5, 28–31, 48–9, 110–11,
134–6; on women in public
service, 229; writing speeches
for Pépin, 67, 156–7
Kroeger College of Public Affairs,
228

Labelle, Huguette, 229–30
Lalonde, Marc, 116, 160
Lang, Otto: agricultural
    organizations and, 28; bold
    approach to Crow change, 15;
    and Canadian Wheat Board, 15;

on freight charges for producers, 194–5; as Transport minister, 2, 19, 199–200

McCarthy, Leighton, 11

McKnight, Bill, 92, 155, 166

McMillan, Ivan, 60, 150, 171

media: and Bill C-155, 159–60, 189, 197; and Crow modernization, 85–6, 132, 139, 145, 217; and Kroeger, *133*, 227; on Pépin, 86, 132, 134–5, 145, 151, 177; and Quebec objections to Crow change, 122

Melfort Journal, 86

Migie, Howard, 105, 140, 179

Mills, Chris, 106, 149–50, 177

ministers. *See* Cabinet

Ministry of State for Economic and Regional Development (mserd), 164–5

Ministry of State for Economic Development (msed), 37, 38, 146

Montreal Gazette, 86

Mulder, Nick, *61, 197*; at Axworthy reception, 198; as Coordinator, Crow Task Force, 59; as deputy minister of Transport, 59; and Gilson consultations, 105, 106; and Gilson implementation committee, 109; and questions raised by ministers, 73; responsibility for all surface transportation, 180; and retrospective piece on Pépin, 220; and Ropertz as speaker, 88; value to team, 210; and variable rates, 143

Mulroney, Brian, 198, 200, 226

Murta, Jack, 18–19, 92, 155, 166

National Energy Program (nep): and Alberta, 47, 135; *Financial Post* on, 57; as legislated in Ottawa, 77, 117; Progressive Conservatives and, 153, 154, 218; secrecy of, 47; and subsidies to railways, 212; Trudeau and, 33–4; vote on legislation, 153, 154; and Western Development Fund, 38, 63; wgta compared to, 208–9

National Farmers' Union (nfu): activism of, 27; and committee phase of Bill C-155, 169; and Crow modernization, 31; demonstration in Ottawa, 58; and free market orientation of groups, 28; and Gilson consultations, 104, 109; hostility to cpr, 35; and Pépin's visits to Saskatchewan, 89, 134–5; Progressive Conservatives compared with, 189; and rate reductions, 201; and wac, 52

National Transportation Act, 14, 16

national unity: and Liberal representation in West, 53–4; Pépin and, 4, 219; task force on, 4

Neil, Doug, 166, 183, 214

New Democratic Party (ndp): amendments to Bill C-155, 181–2, 195, 196; Argue and, 46; and Bill C-155, 154; and clause-by-clause phase of Bill C-155, 181–2, 187, 189; coalition with Liberals, 34; commitment to Crow rate, 25; and committee phase of Bill C-155, 166; and Crow, 154, 212; and delegation on rail capacity, 160; and first reading of Bill C-155, 153; hostility to CPR, 35; Liberal Party and, 37; and Mazankowski's "freedom of choice," 187; PC Party and, 156; reaction to government announcement, 91–2; and report stage of Bill C-155, 193; and second reading of Bill C-155, 158, 163

Now Comes the Turn of Women (Kroeger), 229

Olson, Bud: attitudes, 46; background of, 46; and changes to Crow, 51, 134; on consensus in West, 216; and CPR, 39–40, 46; letter to Trudeau, 49–50; meetings with, 31, 80; as minister of State for Economic Development, 34; on mountain railway tour, 41; and Pépin, 141; and railways, 60, 73; and Western Development Fund, 49, 60–1

Ontario: and Bill C-155, 156; dairy farming in, 172; federal government and, 137; and Gilson report, 125; livestock industry in, 125

Ontario Cattlemen's Association, 125

Ontario Federation of Labour, 125

Osbaldeston, Gordon, 131, 164, 165

Ouellet, André, 123, 129, 141

Oxford University, 227, 228–9

Page, Garnet, 60, 65

Palliser Wheat Growers, 27, 42, 44

Parker, Lorne, 148, 170

Parkin, Bob, 160

Parti Quebecois, 4, 124, 141, 172

Pawley, Howard, 66

Pearson, Lester, 4, 14, 23, 178

Pépin, Jean-Luc, *29, 61, 75, 179*; achievement of, 214, 217; AK's retrospective piece for TC *Express* on, 220–1; and Anti-Inflation Board, 4; and appointments to Crown corporations, 90–1; Axworthy and, 177, 196; and Berntson, 135, 138; and Bill C-155, 156–7, 167, 171, 193, 196; and Cabinet, 47–8, 103; and Cabinet committees, 75–6, 77; career, 3–5, 218; on CNR, 154; and Constitution, 37, 218, 219; death of, 219; and Delisle Meeting, 89; early life, 3; and Gilson, 85; Gustafson on, 214; heart problems, 219; honours, 218; and Kroeger, 1–2, 141–2, 218–19; and Mazankowski, 22–3, 163, 169; media and, 86, 132, 134–5, 145, 151, 177; and Meech Lake, 218; meeting with Pool presidents, 119; as minister of Industry, Trade, and Commerce, 4; as minister of state for External Relations, 175–6; as minister of Transport, 1–2, 5, 21, 22–3, 44, 147–8, 176–8; in Moncton, 138; on mountain railway tour, 41; and national unity, 4, 219; Neil on, 214; and NFU protests, 134–5; office staff, 22; personality, 22–3, 90, 132, 167, 178; and policy *vs.* operational issues, 22–3; and Priorities and Planning Committee, 50–1; and

Rothstein, Marshall, 143
Runciman, Mac, 18, 78, 80–1

Saskatchewan: Chamber of
Commerce, 128; co-operative
traditions in, 25; and committee
phase of Bill C-155, 170–1; Crow
Coalition, 170; and Crow rate,
25, 30, 43, 66, 102–3, 135–6;
farm population in, 204; grain
production in, 25; Liberal Party,
84, 93; Liberal representation in
federal government, 34; PC MPS
from, 155; Trudeau in, 93–4; and
WAC position, 43
Saskatchewan Association of Rural
Municipalities, 119
Saskatchewan Federation of
Agriculture, 18, 26, 56, 79, 119,
128
Saskatchewan government: and
changes to Crow, 54, 92, 103;
and Gilson report, 109–10; and
railways, 56; and rate reductions,
201; and Saskatchewan Wheat
Pool, 103, 187; and subsidy to
railways vs. producers, 152, 187;
and Wheat Pools, 149
Saskatchewan Wheat Pool, 26–7;
accusation of information
withheld from ministers, 139;
and Agricore United, 204;
annual meetings, 48–9, 67–8;
and anti-change sentiment in
province, 103; Argue's speech
at, 67–8; boycott of federal
government public statement
in Winnipeg, 132; Chamber
of Commerce and, 128; as
commercial grain company, 204;

and committee phase of Bill
C-155, 170; delegation to Ottawa,
145; and federal government
communications effort, 88;
grain terminals operated by,
203; and increased costs for
producers, 216; Kroeger's visit
to, 42; and Lang's suggestions,
15; payment to producers by,
101–2; Pépin's speech to, 67, 68;
politics of members, 25; poll of
producers, 102–3; and Quebec,
137; rate of return on equity, 171;
Saskatchewan government and,
187; and Task Force on Canada's
Crisis in Railway Transportation,
60; Turner and, 213; and
variable rates, 201; and WAC, 45,
48–9, 51, 65, 68; and Western
Agricultural Conference (WAC),
55–6
Saskatoon StarPhoenix, 85, 86, 132,
136, 159–60
Sauvé, Jeanne, 195
Schreyer, Ed, 37
Seaborn, Geoff, 179
Sellers, Gabrielle (Gay), 229
Senior Grain Transportation
Committee, 186
Smith, Janet, 51, 147, 159, 162,
209–10
Snavely, Carl: on contribution from
grain revenues to railway costs,
168; on cost of moving grain, 23,
98; on Crow "as constitutional
right," 154; and effect of Crow
on railways, 16–17; Gilson
consultations and, 105; NFU and,
169; on railway costing, 92, 210,

transportation: Cabinet and, 47–8; Canadians' beliefs regarding, 22; capacity, 62–3; exports and costs of, 58; federal government initiatives, 38–9; and grain exports, 17; importance in Canada, 10; modernization of, 62–3, 64; NEP revenues and, 63; 1960s rationalization of, 98; "A Strategy for the West" and, 66; Trudeau and, 47–8; and West, 10–12, 38–9, 62, 66; Western Development Fund and, 49, 62. *See also* grain transportation

Trucking Association, 168

Trudeau, Pierre Elliott: and 1979 election, 18; and 1980 election, 2, 19; appointment of Cabinet, 4–5; and appointments to Crown corporations, 90–1; and Bill C-155, 160, 162–3; Cabinet shuffle, 175, 176; and Constitution, 33, 34, 47, 57; and Crow rate, 15, 34, 49–50, 52–3, 55, 63–4, 127, 162–3; decision on own future, 176; and Lalonde, 116; and Lang's proposals, 15; meeting with chairman of CPR, 61; meeting with WAC, 51–3; NFU and, 58; "peace initiative," 176; and Pépin, 1, 4–5, 76, 81, 94, 127, 147–8, 175, 218; proposal for coalition with NDP, 34; and provincial governments, 57; and Quebec, 141, 147, 149; in Saskatchewan, 93–4; and task force on Canadian unity, 4; and transportation issues, 47–8; Turner and, 94; and West, 34, 53, 76

Turner, Ted, 26–7; attacked by Pool members, 102, 139; on changes to Crow, 48; and committee phase of Bill C-155, 170; contribution to Crow process, 213; and draft policy statement, 78; on elevators, 146; and Gilson consultations, 106; and interests of producers, 146; and Lang's proposals, 15; meeting of Pool delegates, 102; meeting with provincial government, 103; and payments to producers, 101, 111; and Task Force on Canada's Crisis in Railway Transportation, 60; and Trudeau, 94; and WAC position, 45, 48, 49, 65, 68

Tyrchniewicz, Ed, 106, 200

Unifarm, 18, 26, 78–9, 92, 119, 128, 200

Union des producteurs agricoles (UPA), 120–1, 122, 123, 124, 140, 206–7

United Farmers of Alberta (UFA), 12

United Grain Growers (UGG), 12; and Agricore, 204; and Archer-Daniels-Midland, 204; and Argue's Third Option, 128; change to publicly owned company, 203–4; and committee phase of Bill C-155, 169; and Crow modernization, 28, 139; and Gilson consultations, 106; and Gilson proposals, 119; meetings with, 79, 128; Runciman of, 18, 81; SaskPool and, 48; size of, 26; and WAC, 18, 28, 48

under, 205; PCS and, 209; and
producer-owned companies,
203–4; Quebec and, 207; rate
discounting under, 200–1;
rationalization of grain handling
system after, 202–3; reductions
in subsidies under, 200; repeal
of, 201
The Western Producer, 86, 115, 189
Western Transportation Advisory
    Council (WESTAC), 3, 30, 56, 71
wheat. *See* grain
Wheat Pools, 12; acquiescence
    to demands of, 215–16;
    alliance with Quebec, 136–7;
    amendments to legislation, 152;
    and Argue's Third Option, 126,
    128–9; and compensation for
    railways, 107, 112–13; delegation
    to Ottawa, 59; and Gilson
    consultations, 104, 106; Gilson
    report and, 110–11; and interests

of producers, 146; on joint task
forces, 142; meetings with, 31,
78, 79, 110–11; and payments
to producers, 109, 111, 118–19,
148–9, 186–7; and Quebec,
141; and Runciman, 81; size of,
26; and subsidies to railways
vs. producers, 105; uneconomic
decisions by, 100–1; and variable
rates, 143; and WAC, 18, 26, 28;
WGTA and, 203–4. See also *names
of individual pools*
Whelan, Eugene, 41, 67, 157–8
Wilkins, Jaffray, 67
Winnipeg Board of Trade, 9
Winnipeg Free Press, 85, 132, 189,
    190
Winnipeg Labour Council, 169
Withers, Ramsey, 164
World War I, 12
World War II, 13